Combat Infantry

A Soldier's Story

Pearl Harbor • Guadalcanal • Luzon
35th Regiment
25th Infantry Division
1940-1945

Donald E. Anderson
and D.E. Anderson Jr.

Combat Infantry

Combat Infantry

A Soldier's Story

Donald E. Anderson
and D.E. Anderson Jr.

1663 Liberty Drive Suite 200
Bloomington, IN 47403

Order this book online at www.trafford.com
or email orders@trafford.com

Most Trafford titles are also available at major online book retailers.

Combat Infantry Badge illustrations by D. E. Anderson Jr.

Printed in the United States of America.

ISBN: 978-1-4269-6877-8 (sc)
ISBN: 978-1-4269-6876-1 (hc)
ISBN: 978-1-4269-6878-5 (e)

Library of Congress Control Number: 2011909113

Trafford rev. 05/31/2011

 www.trafford.com

North America & international
toll-free: 1 888 232 4444 (USA & Canada)
phone: 250 383 6864 ♦ fax: 812 355 4082

For

General James L. "Dusty" Dalton

"…always lead from the front…"

Killed in Action

May 16, 1945

Balete Pass, Luzon
Philippine Islands

When they were got together in one place,
shield clashed with shield, and spear with spear,
in the conflict of mail-clad men.
Mighty was the din as the bossed shields
pressed hard on one another –
death cry and shout of triumph of slain and slayers,
and the earth ran red with blood.

Homer – *The Iliad*

CONTENTS

FOREWORD

Growing up, we rarely heard my father speak about his service in World War II. Whenever I would ask questions, he would avoid an answer and refer to that time as "old history." He had related only a few incidents to my mother, who, when asked about them, would reply, "Your father will talk when he's ready."

On the eve of my reporting for induction into the Army after enlisting on my eighteenth birthday in May 1969, he told me that as a seventeen-year-old recruit in 1940, he had envisioned serving his country as a noble and exciting endeavor. He was silent for a few moments. As he squeezed my shoulders, obvious pain shone in his eyes as he said, "Combat is the worst thing you could ever experience. I pray to God you never have to—"

In January of 1997, we sat quietly at his kitchen table holding our favorite mugs of steaming tea; ready nearby were a neat stack of newly purchased yellow writing pads and several beat-up pens—next to a plate of butter cookies. A tape recorder lay poised between us. He looked at the recorder, exhaled and folded his hands. Steam began to fog his glasses; now he was ready to talk—and to write.

Two years later, he handed me a box containing the bones for this book: his dog-eared, laboriously hand-written notes, microcassettes of our taped interviews, fading "old history" photographs, his Decorations and discharge papers.

He smiled and said, "Not much, is it?"

What he was compelled to share was more than I could ever imagine.

In January 2007, I sat next to him as he lay sleeping in a hospital bed; the only sounds were gently beeping monitors and the soft flow of oxygen.

My mother was at the nurses' desk to get a cup of ice chips for him. As I held his hand, he opened his eyes, smiled and said, "They're all waiting for me," and closed his eyes again.

Shortly thereafter, he lost his long battle with Parkinson's disease; he was finally at peace.

A quiet man, my father simply hoped to honor the stories of ultimate sacrifice made by the men with whom he served.

His story is one shared not by a few—rather—many, many veterans and families.

D. E. Anderson Jr.

PREFACE

1997

This a personal story of my experiences with the 35th Infantry Regiment, 25th "Tropic Lightning" Division in the Pacific Theater in World War II. I have reached back over five decades to recall names, dates and places as accurately as I could. Many small combat actions and the tiny barrios where they took place on the island of Luzon in the Philippines are blurred or have run together over time. From January until May 1945, we were moving and fighting around the clock for weeks on end. Most of the time, we had no idea of the "big picture." Our world was confined to muddy foxholes, a dust-clouded stretch of mined road or a rocky, fog-shrouded mountain ridge. Five months of constant combat, confusion, fear and fatigue took its toll. Thus, many details are irretrievable.

I have endeavored to give the reader a general idea of the combat we fought through. Unless someone has experienced war, it is impossible to understand the utter despair, unbearable pain, futility and sheer madness of it. Therefore, many things I have omitted because most were simply too horrendous to recount. Neither could I find the words. I have tried, unsuccessfully every day for more than half-a-century to forget them.

Most of the men with whom I had the privilege to serve from our arrival in Hawaii in 1940 were killed in action on far-off islands with strange-sounding names: Guadalcanal, Vella Lavella and Luzon. To those of us who fought beside them, they are not simply engraved names on cold granite monuments. They are familiar faces and voices, laughter and suffering, smiles and sorrow, bravery and devotion. Each of us owes them a debt of gratitude, and, collectively, we should always remember what they helped to achieve with their selfless sacrifices.

In 1973, I traveled to Hawaii with my wife, June. As we approached the airport for a landing, I peered through the window for a glimpse of paradise as I remembered it from those days long past, when I had first set foot on the shores of the beautiful island in 1940. I was dismayed to see the toll that over thirty years of development had taken.

We spent many days traveling among the islands, visiting the many tourist sites and strolling along tranquil beaches. But I couldn't bring myself to relax. I had returned for a meeting I needed to keep with Oahu and Pearl Harbor.

As June and I stood on the Memorial of the *Arizona*, I was lost in thought. I could still see the mighty ship as she was back in November of 1941, gleaming in the bright sun, when our outfit was invited aboard to celebrate Thanksgiving.

My wife by my side gently held my trembling hands and I quietly prayed for the men who had died on that terrible Sunday, December 7, 1941.

The following day we traveled to the Punch Bowl, the crater of an extinct volcano, where an enormous cemetery had been created to be the final resting place for many of the thousands of men and women killed in the Pacific Theater in World War II. For me this was an impressive sight mixed with a heart-rending memory.

As we approached the giant battle maps detailing the actions fought by the United States and her allies during the war, June asked me if I could show her where I had fought during my five years overseas. She had heard me recount bits and pieces about my combat experiences and helped me through difficult years of horror-filled nightmares and relapses of malaria. But now we were at the very place where it had all begun. I didn't really know what I could tell her or where I should start.

She asked me when I first learned that war was coming.

And everything came flooding back as if it had just happened.

ACKNOWLEDGMENTS

I would like to thank my beloved wife, June Swindell Anderson. Her understanding and encouragement has sustained me since I first read her letters as I crouched alone, near-despair in a mud-filled foxhole on Luzon, the Philippines in 1945. I could not have told this story without her. Whenever the pain of releasing the horrors back into the light seemed overwhelming, her love and support always reminded me of why it was being written.

My deep appreciation goes to my son, Donald, for pulling together my handwritten notes and photographs, recording my memories, creating, typing and proofing the numerous drafts and helping me find the words.

Special thanks to Christine Anderson for her tireless and invaluable assistance in reading, editing and proofing the manuscript and offering her professional suggestions as it took shape. My thanks to Peter Coppola for his editorial suggestions.

Oahu, Hawaiian Islands

1941

CHAPTER 1

Rising Sun

She emerged from the cloud layer and swept past us and over the lagoon, a magnificent white flying boat. Banking slightly, her engines changed pitch as the pilots brought her in for a landing on the blue-grey water.

We anxiously waited; the only sounds were the idling engines, the lapping of waves against the low concrete seawall and the scuffing of the watchers' shoes as they snuffed out cigarettes that joined a carpet of others. The sense of foreboding was as thick as the clouds blanketing the island's rim and the surrounding ocean.

We impatiently crowded the dock, as fledgling chicks might await their mother, clamoring to receive the first morsels, snapping them up with expectation of more. Our waiting band of soldiers and sailors sought valuable global news. On this day, there was none.

The *Philippine Clipper* was one of three flying boats with passenger routes between the West Coast of the United States and the Pacific Islands: Pearl Harbor in Oahu, Hawaii, Wake Island to the west of the Hawaiian Islands and on to the Philippines.

In July 1941, we had been training and preparing for a possible conflict with Japan, but when and where? There was never enough news or information to be had. Of course, everyone had an opinion or knew the latest "straight dope" from on high. Rife with rumor and wild speculation, these tidbits were mostly guesswork pieced together from other speculation, embellished as it made the rounds.

Our outfit, the 25th Infantry Division, stationed at Schofield Barracks outside Honolulu would be facing the Japanese somewhere in the vast Pacific.

As a driver for my company commander, I had embarked on an extensive survey of our fighting positions with Captain James Dalton. We sat eating lunch in silence, high on a ridge, overlooking Honolulu and the naval base at Pearl Harbor. I asked him the question that had been gnawing at me for months.

"Sir, are we going to war with Japan?"

He looked me in the eye and nodded, sadness clouding his face.

"Yes, there's no way around it."

"When, do you think?" I asked, dreading an answer.

"By Christmas. Intelligence reports that Germany is trying twenty-four hours a day to convince Japan to enter the war. The War Department wants to reinforce all our positions in the Pacific but the people in Congress don't want to offend the Japanese."

He turned away and gazed out over the vast, bustling expanse of Pearl Harbor.

We had no way of knowing that the plans for the destruction of our fleet at Pearl Harbor were already under way by the Japanese. They knew the only way to possibly have a chance of winning the coming conflict was to cripple our fleet before it sailed out to meet their invasion forces in the Pacific. A simultaneous strike on the Philippines, Guam, Wake and Hawaii would not only divide our forces, but without a fleet to escort troop convoys, reinforcement would not be possible.

The first week of August, we went on full alert, assigned to roving patrols with half-ton Chevy pick-up trucks. There was a driver and non-com in front, and four armed men in the back with a pedestal-mounted 30 caliber machine gun. Everyone carried live rounds. We drove four hours on, four hours off, around the clock, usually out in the boonies.

We stopped and checked every bridge and culvert. At night, we used paver lanterns to check the superstructures for explosives and communication junction boxes in remote areas. To prevent any observers from plotting our movements, we constantly changed our patrol patterns. This lasted for twelve weeks.

In November, we were suddenly taken off alert status and our weapons and ammunition were locked up. Everything reverted back to normal.

Two weeks later we had a full dress parade for the Japanese Emissary, Saburo Kurusu. He was on his way to Washington to confer with our government concerning the growing tensions between the United States and Japan. Stopping off at Hawaii, he was given a first-hand look at our troops and weapons. Perhaps our leaders considered this a show of strength to impress Japan with a parade of power. With war rumors thicker than ever, this show didn't go over very well with the troops: a violation of the old street fighter's adage; never lead with your chin.

Following the parade, I was given two weeks leave to go to the big island of Hawaii, where Kilowea military rest camp was located. It was great to get a real break from the grinding rotation on Oahu.

The camp was built on the slopes of the Mauna Loa Mountains. We visited the observatory and were shown the seismograph that measured tremors inside the volcano. We hiked over the mountains and visited the town of Hilo, looking much like an old western frontier town. When the weather was overcast and drizzling, we went to a café and enjoyed hot buttered rum with cinnamon sticks, and just sat around shooting the breeze. There really wasn't much else to do. I guess that's why it was called a "rest camp."

It seemed as if I'd only been there a few days when it was already time to return to Schofield Barracks, just in time for Thanksgiving dinner. That Sunday, November 30, our outfit was invited to have lunch aboard the battleship *Arizona* at Pearl Harbor. As an inter-service exchange program, some of her sailors visited Schofield Barracks at the same time.

The *Arizona's* sailors gave us a guided tour of the entire ship. We walked for what seemed like miles through hatches, down corridors, up and down ladders, in and out of the massive gun turrets—everything sparkling, gleaming, polished and spotless. It was a magnificent ship and they loved her. After she was lost in the attack, I often thought about all the men who had treated us so warmly. In a few days most of them would be killed and entombed forever when the ship was hit and sunk in the attack.

The following week was a normal routine: no alerts or motorized patrols. We felt that we should at least be on alert status: have our weapons and ammunition available, not locked up. If anything happened, how would we get the keys to the Arms Room? The supply sergeant didn't live at the barracks, nor did our colonel. The Officer of the Day was supposed to be available at all times, but each day he went home and let the Sergeant of the Guard take over the responsibilities. We were to find one man on the Post and convince him to give us the keys to the Arms Room? It was ludicrous.

On December 5, I received a bomb from home, a "Dear Don" letter from my girlfriend. She was getting married at one o'clock on December 7, 1941. My buddy from Maine also received one from his girlfriend. We both went off base together and drowned our sorrows. Somewhere in the mix, we each got a tattoo, a large American eagle with *Hawaii, 1941* in red, white and blue scrollwork grasped in its claws. In a few days, I wouldn't need a tattoo to remind me.

Saturday, December 6, dawned bright and clear. Details were finished up, equipment squared away and plans made for our day off: Sunday, December 7. My buddies and I had a pass to go into town, no details. We could kick back and enjoy another beautiful day in the Islands. Most of our discussions centered on what we would be doing the following day. I had only six more months to go before I could go home.

December 7, 1941

7:00 am—I was out of my bunk and ready to wash and shave. The sun was shining; it was a beautiful day, and I had a pass to go to town. I returned to the squad room and dressed in my "civvies." I was one happy dogface. No duty, no driving, just a day off to relax and have a good time. My two buddies and I walked down to the mess hall. I picked up my dishes and silverware. Moving along the line, I asked the server for eggs over-light, bacon and toast, then picked up a bottle of cold milk. We walked over to a table and sat down together; it was going to be great, all right. One whole day on the town and no duty. As we turned our attention to our bacon and eggs, I said, "Yeah, just watch some sonofabitch screw it up."

7:50 am—Suddenly the scream of a diving plane shattered the quiet morning, getting louder and louder. Thinking it was one of our planes from Wheeler Field in trouble, I said, "Oh, Christ! He's going to crash!"

We jumped up and ran to the door.

Just as we stepped out, there was a tremendous explosion. Glancing up, we saw a plane fly over us, large red meatball markings on the wings. I smelled the sharp, biting stink of explosives from the bomb he had just dropped.

The screeching sound of diving planes was joined by the heavy stutter of 20mm cannon shells. Chunks of cement flew from the barracks walls as the shells impacted in vicious, sparking lines around the quadrangle. Men ran to break into the locked supply room to grab weapons and ammunition.

My buddies and I decided to try and get to the motor pool to disperse our vehicles. Like sitting ducks, perfectly lined up next to each other. Running across the open ground, I heard planes diving on us for another attack. We kept running as fast as we could, intent on reaching the vehicles before they were destroyed. We needed every vehicle to repulse an invasion on the beaches.

The low flying enemy planes curved in and started strafing before we could reach the motor pool. We threw ourselves down on the ground as shells from their machine guns and cannon ripped into the neatly manicured lawn all around us as chunks of dirt, grass and shrapnel flew in all directions. But we weren't hit.

As soon as the planes swept by, we jumped up and ran like the devil himself was after us—which he was. We made it to the cabinet where all the keys were kept for the vehicles. I thanked God—it was unlocked.

I grabbed my keys and ran like hell for my truck. I saw a plane firing at me, so I swerved and dove headlong into a drainage ditch, tumbling heavily into the bottom. Hugging the side towards the strafing plane, I felt the jarring impact of 20mm cannon shells striking the other side of the ditch.

As he flashed by, I saw the pilot looking down at me. I jumped up, trying to reach my truck again, when another plane angled in towards me—hanging a bomb and heading straight for the lines of nearby vehicles. I hit the dirt and flattened out, waiting for the explosion that would send me to oblivion—

Praying as loudly as I could, I watched the plane scream in. I heard a loud *"click"* as the bomb dropped free of its shackles. Time crawled as the ugly black shape of the bomb fell towards me. The banking plane passed just overhead, its huge wing markings obscenely brilliant. The bomb exploded nearby on the other side of the motor pool with a tremendous earth-shaking blast, vomiting dirt and grass skywards.

An instant before the pilot dropped his bomb he banked sharply to avoid a tall tree directly in his path. The violent movement threw off the trajectory of the bomb, causing it to miss. The Japanese pilot was concentrating on watching *me*. At the last possible moment he threw his plane to the right, barely missing the tree. Fortunately, he also missed our vehicles.

Jumping up again, I dashed to my truck, jammed the key in the ignition and started the engine. I looked up, hearing the sound of another plane cruising in. The enemy fighter was gliding over at about fifty feet, as if he was at an air show. As unconcerned as if he was over his own airfield, he grinned at me like we were old buddies. He wore a tight-fitting leather flying helmet and goggles with a long, pure white scarf streaming back along his open canopy. I wasn't as mad at him, as much as I was at the incompetence of the turkeys who had taken us off alert status and disarmed us.

As the enemy planes flew off, I drove my truck into a field and ran back to the barracks as quickly as I could. Just then, one of our planes flew over. It was a P-40 that must have been at one of the auxiliary airfields on the other side of the island. Guys had started firing at him, so he kept banking to show everybody his markings. I could see the white stars on his fuselage as he flashed past. They looked mighty good to me. So far, all we had seen were Japanese.

I was still in my "civvies," so I ran up to the squad room, quickly changed into my uniform and grabbed all my equipment. An officer told me to get three trucks and report to the base hospital. We ran to our vehicles, threw all our equipment in the back and raced off to the hospital. The attendants tied large Red Cross flags over our trucks' grills and told us to go to Diamond Head to pick up medical supplies and head back as quickly as possible.

While the enemy planes were hitting us, their second strike formations had been attacking the naval base and the surrounding airfields at Wheeler, Hickam, Bellows, Ewa and Kaneohe. The B-17s, fighters, observation planes, and flying boats were hit and burning before anyone could react.

Bombs, bullets and cannon shells made short work of the hangers, vehicles and runways. Clouds of thick, black smoke rose everywhere from the blasted ruins. Only a few of our aircraft managed to get airborne from small satellite fields. The devastation was complete. Rows of planes, parked closely together, were destroyed. Burning fuel set them on fire, and one after another they blew up, throwing debris hundreds of feet in the air.

High numbers of casualties at the airfields were due to so many new men arriving from the States, they had to be quartered in the hangers because the barracks were overcrowded. Some of the Japanese planes flew straight down the runways at a height of fifty feet or less, firing into the hangers as men struggled to escape the infernos around them. The mess halls were also full when they received bomb hits.

The Air Corps had just completed building revetments around the airfields to protect the planes from just such an attack, but every Saturday the planes were arranged in nice, even lines for inspection. Why weren't they moved into the revetments after the inspection?

Since the attack, the most prevalent explanation was that the planes were lined up close together to keep them safe from sabotage, as Japanese spies roamed the island, bent on destroying every plane before they took off. There was only one real spy arrested after the attack.

All the rest were phantoms.

We drove past our barracks as our outfit loaded on vehicles and prepared to move out. As we sped past, everyone held up two fingers, flashing the "V for victory" sign. Pulling onto the road, we were sickened by the stench of burning flesh, mixed with smoke and cordite from exploding munitions—still over a mile away from the airfield where the slaughter was taking place,

Racing by Wheeler Field, we were shocked by the terrible scene. Mutilated bodies were strewn about on the runways amid scattered debris from shattered buildings. Flames leaped from the wreckage of the riddled aircraft, easy targets. Men were dragging the wounded away from exploding planes and vehicles, trying to save as many as they could before the Japanese planes returned for another sweep.

The first strike, consisting of fighters, dive-bombers, torpedo planes and high level bombers, hit Pearl from the west and south. The second wave struck from the east, north and northeast. Sweeping in on our ships, they blasted them one after another. Caught in the anchorage, the battleships, cruisers, and destroyers were unable to escape because most of them didn't have their boilers on line, ready to steam. Sporadic firing from the ships couldn't stop the torrent of explosives from the wave-hugging Japanese aircraft.

Using specially designed, shallow-running torpedoes, they decimated the heavy ships, exploding and settling where they were docked. Burning oil spread over the surface of the water, killing men who had either been blown overboard or jumped to escape the flames from bomb explosions.

Thousands of soldiers, sailors and marines died trying to stop the savage attack. Civilians killed in the indiscriminate strafing of vehicles, schools and houses by marauding aircraft, lay scattered about in bullet-riddled cars, yards, stores, and streets.

Our tiny convoy raced toward Honolulu as fast as the vehicles would go. Miles before we arrived we could see the enormous, billowing black clouds from Pearl Harbor, tinged with dark red and yellow. We drove past at 40 miles-per-hour and then slowed to 20 in the city itself, through thick, choking smoke from Hickam Field and the burning oil and exploding ammunition from the blasted ships in the harbor. Pearl looked like an exploding volcano, spewing flames and burning debris.

I couldn't believe the terrible carnage before my eyes. I didn't want to believe it. Beautiful Honolulu was blanketed with smoke, blotting out the sun. The gentle tropical breezes had been replaced by the stench of burning oil and death.

From Honolulu, we drove up to Diamond Head. Our trucks were loaded with supplies without leaving our vehicles or even shutting down the engines. Retracing our route at the same speeds, we made two round trips on our mercy missions, and returned to Schofield to hook up our anti-tank guns.

Reporting to the company CP (command post), located near Waianae, we were told to go up on the ridges overlooking the area and watch for Japanese paratroopers. If we saw any, we were supposed to fire three warning shots in the air. We were ready to fire a hell of a lot more than three.

Patrolling high above the lower bivouac area, where we could see for miles. A huge pall of oily, black smoke shrouded Pearl. It appeared to be an enormous funeral pyre. Explosions continued to tear apart the ships from oil-fed fires and burning ammunition. As night approached, everyone's nerves tightened in anticipation of another attack. There was no way to tell if an invasion was approaching or not. The whole island had become one raw, exposed nerve.

Soon, it was pitch black, as if we had been placed inside a sealed room. There wasn't a light anywhere. We checked and re-checked our ammunition and weapons. We had no radio, food or water—we were on our own.

Later that night, searchlights came on, and anti-aircraft guns began firing at our own planes arriving from one of our carriers offshore. Even later, they fired on some of our own bombers that had flown in from the States.

We heard scattered shots all night long. Men were challenging cows and then riddling them with bullets. Wild boars also became casualties of taut nerves. It became very dangerous to move around. Every sound was a Japanese paratrooper to the trigger-happy, taut-nerved sentries. Many were shooting first and challenging later. Simply knowing the password wouldn't guarantee safe passage at night.

We were relieved about nine o'clock the next morning, and had a chance to eat a meal at noon. Our outfit dug individual foxholes and covered them with pup tents. Two blankets were laid inside to sleep on as scorpions, centipedes and large spiders crawled in with us to stay warm.

That night, Anson, one of the men in my squad, was scheduled to relieve a sentry. As he passed by me, I noticed he had a blanket over his shoulders. I asked him why he was carrying it and he said he felt lousy, had a headache and felt chilly. I told him to go back to his hole and I would pull his duty. He replied that it was his job and he would do it. In the meantime, it had gotten fairly cool and was pitch dark. I climbed back into my hole and dozed off.

About three hours later, the Sergeant of the Guard woke me from a fitful sleep and told me to report to the Officer of the Day. I grabbed my gear and weapon and found the OD, a first lieutenant and West Pointer… all Brass.

"Get your ass over to Post Number Three and stay there until you're relieved!" he yelled at the top of his lungs. I asked him who I was relieving but he wouldn't say. I cautiously walked down to Post Three and tried to find the sentry. It was really hairy out there, absolutely pitch black, and I couldn't see a damned thing. The sentries were carrying live ammunition and wouldn't hesitate to use it.

"Sentry, relief!"

"Sentry, relief!"

I kept whispering.

I didn't want a jittery soldier to shoot me while I was trying to find him. When there was no answer, I began worrying that something had happened to him. Normally, either the Corporal or Sergeant of the Guard was supposed to escort you to the sentry and relieve him. Not this time. *Somebody* was screwing up by the numbers.

When in doubt, you were supposed to fire one round and yell, "Corporal of the Guard! Post Number Three!" But when you did, all hell broke loose. The Brass showed up, ready to relieve all their pent-up anger. I didn't fire the shot, but hollered as loudly as I could…

"Corporal of the Guard! Man down!"

Well, enough people arrived to have a luau. A sergeant asked me what the hell I was hollering for. I told him I was supposed to relieve the sentry on that post but the man was missing. The sergeant turned to the lieutenant and asked if he had briefed me on the situation. The lieutenant replied that he didn't think that it was any of my business. The sergeant respectfully disagreed with him and said that he intended to pursue the matter further with the CO at the earliest possible moment. He then proceeded to brief me by the book.

"Soldier, the previous sentry on this post was observed sleeping by Captain Dalton and was placed under arrest. The reason you weren't escorted to this post was because of this unfortunate episode. The OD should have made you aware of that."

I found out that it had been my friend that earlier had told me that he didn't feel well and wouldn't let me take his place. I thought for sure that he would get sentenced to a firing squad. Sleeping on guard in wartime was one of the most serious offenses you could possibly commit.

The following morning, I went to see Captain Dalton and explained how Anson insisted on pulling his duty, even though he was sick and close to keeling over. The Captain thanked me and I was dismissed. Before I left, I requested to be a defense witness. We were all worried sick. He was an excellent soldier and a good friend.

The day of the court martial, I was sent on some fuzzy detail to the other side of the island. I was mightily pissed off. When I returned, I went straight to Captain Dalton. He could see that I was upset. Before I could say a word, he looked me in the eye and told me not to sweat it, Anson was only going to get thirty days in the brig and then be returned to active duty. I should have known he would be more than fair.

Our defense area was roughly from Ewa to Kaena Point. It covered about twenty miles of shore-line called Waianae. The area also included the Navy's massive ammunition dumps, protected by Marines, tough and highly trained. The sprawling oil tank farm at Pearl had survived the attack, as well as the submarine base, and most of the ammunition dumps.

I would learn later that it had been a disastrous error for the enemy to leave the adjacent facilities at the base intact. On his return to the attack force, the leader of the Japanese air squadrons went to Admiral Nagumo and requested a second strike to destroy the fuel, submarines and ammunition that remained virtually untouched. Evidently, fearing retaliation, Nagumo refused and set a course for Japan while his luck still held. He missed a golden opportunity to wipe out our only remaining strike forces. Unrestricted use of our subs after the attack would have been impossible if the oil supplies had been destroyed.

The Japanese had attacked Pearl and crippled the fleet as planned, with one important exception. The American aircraft carriers were not in port at the time. They were at sea and survived with their aircraft and supporting ships. They were virtually the only vital surface ships left to carry the war to the enemy. That was the only bright spot.

We had to prepare for the expected invasion of our cruelly-ravaged Paradise.

The first priority: string three parallel barbed wire barriers, twelve feet high, along the stretches of beach with coiled concertina wire thrown up over each row. One crew drove the metal posts into the ground, followed by a second crew, wearing heavy gloves stringing out the wire strands and a third crew attached the strands to the posts, creating large coils. The coils were then expanded like a giant Slinky to be thrown up over the top of the parallel strands, landing in between the rows. The Brass claimed that thousands of miles of wire were used on the island. I believed it.

Our next job was to cut down thousands of trees to clear firing lanes for our weapons. For months, the surrounding area rang with the crisp, biting sounds of axes and the crashing of splintered timber.

On January 27, 1942, a month and a half after the attack on Pearl, we began working with the Engineers, installing heavy beach defenses and explosives. Everyone was still running on full adrenaline and shattered nerves, working feverishly to prepare for an invasion, which everybody expected was just around the corner. All our people were required to learn new skills as quickly as possible.

We assisted the Engineers constructing a new road to connect our battalions to the Regimental Headquarters. Clearing the area for the road crews with demolitions, we were shown how to properly drill the holes, safely plant the explosives, and then wire them up to detonators. In the middle of this work, I was pulled off the detail and sent to pick up a load of steel pipe. The lengths were much longer than the truck and obviously too heavy a load, but it was no time to argue.

I headed back to the construction site trying to take it easy. As I neared the road we had been working on, I stopped to look for someone to ask if I could continue. An officer drove up and berated me for apparently goofing off. I told him the road was scheduled to be blasted soon. Red faced, he yelled that the Engineers would have left a flag man if they were ready to blow the road. Seeing as there wasn't a man there, I should get *my sorry ass* moving. I was holding up everyone at Battalion. I snapped him a fast salute. If he had looked closely, it would have looked more like a thumbed nose. Satisfied, he was soon gone.

I drove over the rough, deeply rutted road as quickly as I could under the conditions. Just as I came to the last bend, the entire section erupted in a series of volcanic blasts, lifting the rear of my over-loaded truck clear off the ground. As it crashed back onto the road, dirt and stones from the explosions rained down all around me. I sat there in the cab, choking on the thick, swirling dust—and shook.

As the last of the debris settled around my vehicle, several men in another truck flew around the sharp curve in the road just ahead of me and almost crashed into my front end. They were just as amazed as I was to meet another truck coming out of the explosive-induced haze, where there shouldn't have been any. The Engineers had done everything by the book *except* post a flag man to warn traffic to hold up until after the detonation of the planted explosives.

I finally arrived at the Third Battalion CP situated on the side of a hill and backed my truck up to unload the dust-covered pipes.

As I was climbing back into my vehicle, someone in the showers next to the delivery point hollered up the hill, "Hey, you numbskull! You just ran over my tent pegs!" I had been going for over eighteen hours without a break and had only one cold meal on the run. I was dead tired and the episode on the road had really rattled my nerves. The only retort I could think of was, "Blow it out your *ASS* buddy!"

I jammed the truck in gear and drove off.

At the edge of the CP area, a speeding jeep cut me off and I skidded to a stop. A highly exasperated GI jumped out of the jeep and ran over to me, demanding my name, rank, serial number and unit. I was ordered to be on my way, with the fuming soldier still standing in the middle of the road behind me.

Driving into my own CP, I would have thought that I was an important dignitary. My grinning buddies were lined up along the road, at attention, saluting me. What the hell was *that* all about? I pulled in near the CP and as soon as I had killed the engine, I was told to report *immediately* to Captain Dalton. He would like to have a few words with me.

I dragged myself over to Headquarters and reported to the C.O.

"What in heaven's name happened over at Battalion?" he asked me.

I explained the whole fiasco as he sat there listening intently, his hands folded.

"So you had no way of knowing you were addressing an officer?"

"An *officer...no sir!*" I replied nervously.

"He's the Battalion Commander. I know the Major from the Point and he is really hard-nosed, but I think I can get him on a technicality because he wasn't wearing his uniform at the time. In the meantime, don't go anywhere near that CP under any circumstances. Dismissed... and Donald, don't sweat it."

"Thank you, sir!"

I snapped him my best salute, executed an about face and left. I looked at my watch and noticed it was 12:30 in the morning. I had just turned 20 years old. What a birthday present. I often wondered if the Captain had known it was my birthday. That's the kind of person he was.

After that, I was a real saint... for a while.

Two weeks passed since the incident with the "Major in the Shower," when I was called to the orderly room again. Entering the building, I was told by the First Sergeant to take a seat and start repenting my many sins before the C.O. lowered the boom on me. By the time the Captain came in, I was a nervous wreck.

As I entered his office, he told me to sit down and start writing. I didn't get the drift of what he meant.

"Sir, what am I supposed to be writing?" I asked quizzically.

"Your mother contacted the Red Cross because she doesn't know if you survived the attack and she's sick with worry."

"Well, sir, I was so busy I hadn't had time to think about it."

"You can take the time now and I'll see that it gets mailed. Make sure that you write at least once a month from now on or I'll *really* be upset. Do we understand each other?"

"Yes, Sir!"

During the rest of the war, most of the time, I kept my promise.

Around March 1942, they took the anti-tank platoon out of Headquarters Company. As a result, several of my buddies and I were transferred to the newly formed Anti-tank Company. I was promoted to Corporal and squad leader. I didn't like it at all. If I could have seen into the future, I would have liked it a hell of a lot less.

We had all new officers. Most of them weren't worth a damn. My new men were draftees, except for a few National Guardsmen. They had very little training and no idea about what was going on. We started from scratch and tried to shape these men to the Army way of doing things, with very little time to do it. With a few exceptions, these enlisted men became some of the most heroic and courageous soldiers anyone could ever hope to serve with.

Our new C.O. wasn't a good leader. He never talked to the men except to chew them out. The non-coms were trying to teach them, at the same time showing some compassion. Most of these kids were right out of school, bewildered and homesick. The last thing in the world they needed was an officer constantly berating them.

We tried to instill some confidence in the men by practice firing our 37s at a 6 X 12 sheet of half-inch steel plate rigged on a skid and towed behind a truck, to simulate the silhouette of a Japanese tank. The tiny armor-piercing shells bounced right off the metal and whined off into the distance—so much for instilling confidence in our anti-tank guns.

We went into combat with a weapon that we had no confidence in—against tanks they weren't worth a tinker's damn. Later, when we used canister rounds at close range against Japanese infantry, the guns were excellent. The shell created a beehive effect, similar to a giant shotgun shell. Expanding as it traveled away from the muzzle, it spread hundreds of small pellets that ripped apart anybody in the way. They were superb for antipersonnel defensive positions. Our only problem would be acquiring enough of them. We could never have too many.

In May 1942, in the aftermath of the Battle of the Coral Sea, we were stationed on the beach and saw the aircraft carrier *Yorktown* returning to Pearl Harbor. It made us very proud to see her, flag rippling in the breeze, but also sad because of the loss of so many men suffered in the battle. She had been seriously damaged by Japanese dive bombers at the same time as the *Lexington*. The "*Lady Lex*" had been sunk, but the *Yorktown*, listing and burning, was saved by the heroic actions of her crew and brought home to fight again. With her hull blackened by fire, *Yorktown* appeared to be very seriously damaged. We wondered how long it would be before she could see action again.

The day after she docked, I drove one of our officers down to visit with his brother, a member of the crew. He told us the story behind the actions at sea. The ship was a mess, swarming with workmen and sailors, each with a specific job to do. Welding torches spat sparks everywhere as damaged pieces were cut away and replaced. A short time later, we drove back to our positions sobered by what we had seen. Amazingly, after only three days of round-the-clock work, the *Yorktown* steamed away from Pearl for Midway Island. Only temporary repairs could be made in such a short time, but the sailors and civilian workmen performed miracles just getting her ready for sea again. Some of the civilian workmen had stayed aboard and sailed with her, sharing her fate. She never returned.

We worked on beach defenses and patrolling for over a month, then started training for amphibious landings in July.

Training began on dry land. A 30-foot-high platform was built with a large landing net hanging down to within three feet of the ground, a ramp on one side. This trained us for the height and feel of the actual landing nets in the coming invasion of enemy held islands.

Pulling on our full field packs, cartridge belts (with first aid kit, full canteen, and bayonet) and helmet, we marched up to the top of the ramp, forming four lines. Facing the railing, we lined up eight abreast. When the whistle was blown, eight men climbed over the railing and down the swaying net. At the bottom was an outline of a landing craft traced on the ground. We were each assigned a certain space to stand to reduce any milling around.

Some of us were assigned to visit with a Marine Raider Battalion in August. They trained us to kill the enemy with a garrote, stiletto, brass knuckle dagger, helmet and anything else available in hand-to-hand combat. A rock, helmet, rifle butt, bare hands, dirt or even spitting in the enemy's face could be used as a weapon. Face-to-face with the enemy, the man who reacted more quickly, stayed alive.

We trained in foxholes at night waiting for the Raiders to infiltrate our positions. The Marines were specially trained to fight at night, silently and quickly. Instructors were patient—and experts with knives. During training, we didn't even know the Raiders were close until they jumped into our holes and pressed razor-sharp knives against our throats.

On Guadalcanal, we crawled out into the jungle after dark and used these silent tactics to kill Japanese in their own positions with our daggers, leaving the bodies to be discovered by their comrades at first light...just as they did with us. We learned that the Japanese had a particular fear of being killed with knives by "gaijin" or "barbarians." Evidently, they believed that their soul would not go to the Yasukuni Shrine unless they died honorably in battle.

Although they feared being killed in a knife fight, the Japanese relished fighting with the bayonet for some reason—part of their training that they excelled at. (Their propensity for bayonet attacks instead of firing their rifles in close combat saved my life more than once.)

Of course, we didn't know all this until we were in combat. It was on-the-job-training in the most lethal sense.

To simulate combat conditions as best they could, Raiders would take rotten, butchered cattle and splash the putrid flesh, guts and blood in our foxholes. We stood in the slippery, stinking mess all night long while we were fired on. Training in the pouring rain, day or night, toughened everybody up a notch. There was a stiff schedule of physical and mental training. Because the Marine Raiders were so physically fit and superbly adapted to that type of fighting, many of our people ended up in the aid station with concussions, sprains and knife cuts. The training we received from those men would save our lives countless times on Guadalcanal and in the Philippines.

In September, we moved into an embarkation area with wooden cabins. It was a real treat to get out of those damned tiny pup-tents. We knew we would be leaving Hawaii very soon and worked like a well-oiled machine, confident that we were ready to face whatever was asked of us—in spite of our officers.

One lieutenant was a certified nut who wore two pearl-handled six-shooter revolvers, swaggering around like a frontier gunfighter. He told us that when he drank at home, he had to go into the deep woods by himself because he always shot up wherever he was.

In October, we were taken out to one of our ships to make a practice landing on one of the nearby beaches with live firing—naval gunfire and strafing by planes. We scrambled over the railing of the ship, as we had done in training on land, climbed as quickly as we could down the nets and into the landing craft. As we stood in our heaving boats, all hell broke loose.

Scores of planes plastered the beach with bombs and machine guns. Shells from the ships screamed overhead impacting on the beach in front of us, huge geysers of sand erupting from the explosions. The noise was deafening. Large shells were blowing the barbed wire defensive positions all over the beach.

The first landing craft hit the beach and two teams dashed ashore to finish demolishing the remaining barbed wire entanglements with Bangalore torpedoes. These were sections of explosives in long tubes that fit together, were fused and then detonated to blow up beach defenses. We landed next, staggered up toward the beach crest into deep sand and furiously began to dig in. Machine gun and rifle fire rang out and men fell like flies. Officers yelled at us to "get up and knock out those goddamned Jap gun positions." Jumping up, hurling grenades, we charged the machine guns, rifles blasting.

It was a damned good thing that it was just a dry practice run. The bombs and shelling were real enough but the small arms fire was all sound effects. Combat landings were still in their infancy as far as planning, technique and equipment were concerned. They weren't even remotely close to the finely-tuned versions that were to evolve just a year later. Everyone was still learning, from the landing craft coxswain and Army private to the admirals and generals planning the whole invasion. Nobody really knew what to expect. We were told we could expect up to eighty percent casualties in the first waves to go in—just about average for a contested landing. This shocking revelation was definitely not a morale booster.

Still, some of the men saw it as a lark, spinning around and falling as the rest of their comrades assaulted the make-believe Japanese machine gun nests. Soon enough, they would be assaulting the real thing in the deadly jungles of Guadalcanal. The men pitching forward wouldn't be getting back up, joking and laughing with their buddies after the action was over. They would be dead.

The next day we went to the offshore training area and practiced getting down the landing nets more quickly. As we started down, the guy above me slipped and kicked me in the head. Stunned and thrown off balance, I lost my grip and fell over backwards. My feet caught in the net and I landed on the railing of the landing craft. I hit my shoulder and neck, breaking the rifle slung across my back. They finally got my legs free and laid me in the bottom of the landing craft. After three hours, they got me to the hospital.

My neck and shoulder were X-rayed, revealing a fractured right shoulder and damaged neck and arm ligaments. I was sent straight back to my outfit. My driver rigged a rope and pulley so that I could keep moving my right arm. Without the contraption, I could only move it a tiny bit. The Battalion medic marked me for "quarters" and I was relieved of duty. Every day I went to the aid station for therapy.

After two weeks, I could still only raise my arm out straight, no higher. When the time came to ship out, the doctor had decided to scratch me from the list because my shoulder and neck were still not healed. I told him I was going "rock-happy" and there was no way in hell that I was going to stay behind while my outfit shipped out. Fortunately, our medic was standing there at the time and after much heated and expressive wrangling back and forth, he convinced the doctor that they would get me ready on the ship for whatever was coming. The doctor eventually relented and put me back on duty.

The night before we embarked on the transport, we were sleeping in our cabins, which were quite close to a large ammunition dump. Without warning, there was an earth-shaking rumble and a shattering explosion. We grabbed our weapons and I was the first one to the door. As I stepped outside, there stood our lieutenant, his pearl-handled pistols aimed squarely at my chest. He was stinking drunk and had a wild, dangerous look in his eyes.

"What the hell are you doing out here you sonofabitch?" he bellowed. "Get your ass back inside and stay there!"

As he turned to go, I raised my rifle and debated whether or not to take him out. I couldn't just shoot him in the back. After he turned and staggered to another cabin, several pistol shots rang out. He had shot one of our men. There were two more shots as he shot another man. Our chaplain came running up to help the wounded men. The lieutenant shot him, too.

Finally, a soldier stepped out of his cabin with his M-1 Garand. He raised his weapon, took careful aim, and shouted; "Turn around, you rotten piece of shit!" When the crazed lieutenant turned, firing wildly, the soldier calmly stood his ground and emptied a full clip of eight rounds at him. The lieutenant was thrown backwards by the impact of the slugs and collapsed to the ground, dropping his pistols.

The only officer to show up was Major Dalton. He asked what had happened and we told him the whole story. The medics worked on the three men but it was too late. Nobody wanted to touch the lieutenant. They were content to let him breathe his last in the dirt. Because I listened to my conscience, three men lost their lives.

All the other company officers including our company commander were under arrest for being drunk and away from their posts. What a hell of a way to be heading into combat. We were going to have to go in on an invasion with officers that we didn't know or trust because all of the ones we trained with had let us down and were under arrest, except Major Dalton. The next day we grimly boarded our ship. It was a journey straight into the "Green Hell" of Guadalcanal.

CHAPTER 2

To the Shores of Paradise

Even as a young boy, I wanted to be a soldier. I had visions of war being an exciting and glorious adventure. Three of my six older brothers had already served in the Army in the 1930s. One was stationed in New York, another in Panama and the third in Hawaii. I decided on the Hawaiian Islands because it was a foreign place said to be primitive, exotic and exciting. It was a far cry from living in Providence, Rhode Island. As far as I was concerned, the farther away, the better.

In 1939, my brother Paul, twenty years old, joined the Army and was stationed in New York. My brother Frank would join in 1941 at nineteen. I turned eighteen in January 1940. I requested and received a discharge from the Rhode Island National Guard, (Coast Artillery) and joined the Regular Army on May 14, 1940. Boarding the transport U.S.S. *Leonard Wood* in New York, we sailed on June 29. I was on my way to Schofield Barracks in Oahu, Hawaii.

We sailed down to South Carolina, where we picked up more recruits. On the hull of our troop transport, enormous American flags were painted to identify us to any prowling U-boats or Nazi surface raiders in the area. Many merchant ships, American vessels included, had been torpedoed and sunk with heavy loss of life along the East Coast, even though we weren't at war yet. As soon as the sun set, the flags were illuminated with powerful spotlights leaving no doubt as to the nationality of the ship. We were also shepherded by Navy escorts as we proceeded down to the Panama Canal.

As we entered Limon Bay and passed Colon and Cristobal, the entrance to the Panama Canal, we counted four destroyers, two cruisers and three submarines. The ships greatly impressed us, for we didn't expect to see such a collection of our warships.

The entrance was similar to an immense lake, where ships waited to be assigned a spot in the queue, preparing to enter the locks. On both sides, heavy jungle grew right down to the water. Huge vine-covered trees towered above the river banks as we passed Fort Davis.

Approaching the first set of locks, named Gatun Locks, we were entertained by hundreds of screeching monkeys racing through the trees. They swung from branch to branch, scampering along the heavy vines, chattering and watching us as we lined the railings to admire their agile antics.

I had studied the Panama Canal in school, but to actually be there was an unforgettable experience. As we slowly approached the first lock, all we could see was a monstrous wall ahead of us. It seemed as though our ship was going to crash right into it. Just then, the gate swung open and we sailed right into the open lock. The huge gate then closed behind us, leaving the ship enclosed in a gigantic cement box. The walls of the lock were higher than the mast of our transport. Water was slowly pumped into the lock and our ship gradually began to rise.

After a while, we finally were able to see the top of the lock wall just above us. Then it was even with the ship's railing as we looked into the eyes of the people standing on the lock wall. It was a weird feeling watching people at the same level we were, for we were standing on a ship's deck. There was no forward movement, only the gentle rising of the ship on the water as it filled the lock. Soon we towered above the people on the lock as we reached the top.

Large cables were attached to the ship and hooked onto small engines called "donkeys." They huffed and puffed as they laboriously towed us into each of the three separate lock chambers until we were at the same level as Gatun Lake, the highest level of the canal. The gate in front of us swung open and the tiny engines, running on small railroad tracks, headed slowly back down the canal. It was impressive, to say the least. After the ship cleared the lock, the cables were disconnected and we proceeded on our way.

Sailing through the canal, we passed some incredible scenery. Whole mountains had actually been sliced apart for the waterway. There were heavily jungled and forested hills with large flocks of colorful birds wheeling gracefully overhead. We passed Gamboa, Darien, St. Pablo, Gaillard Cut and Gold Hill until we reached another set of locks, Pedro Miguel. After lowering the ship down to the next level, we proceeded to the Miraflores Locks, the last before exiting to the Pacific Ocean.

Our transport stopped briefly at Panama City for a few hours of shore leave. What an eye-opener that was! Especially for those of us who hadn't experienced the all-night, every-night action that was the rule in a wide-open city. It was a wild-west frontier town multiplied a hundred times. There were no doors on any of the buildings because everything was always in perpetual motion. You could be screwed, blued and tattooed in a heartbeat.

The Military Police were all over six feet tall and must have weighed in at over two hundred and fifty pounds. They carried large night sticks weighted with lead and web belts with .45 Colt pistols in holsters with long leather thongs with large knots tied on them. Every time we stopped to gawk at the night life, they came up behind us, whipped the knotted cord across our asses and told us to keep moving. We were learning fast that if the Army gave us a little something exciting, it would soon be spoiled by people with misplaced authority.

After trying to keep a few steps ahead of the MPs and still have a good time, we returned to the dock about 11 o'clock that night. While we stood on the dock watching the ship being loaded, we noticed three Army caskets being run up the conveyor. We asked one of the men stationed there what had happened to the three soldiers in the caskets. He didn't know but told us that they lost four or five people a week in the city from brawling and knife fights.

My brother Carl had told me he really hated it when he was stationed there in the thirties. Now I knew why. It must have been pretty unsettling to actually be stationed there. But, all in all, it was a fascinating experience we talked about for months afterward.

Once we were through the canal, we sailed up the West Coast to San Francisco. Disembarking there, we were ferried over to Angel Island, in the Bay near the infamous Alcatraz Prison. While there they let us spend a day in San Francisco, where the Golden Gate Exposition was being held on Treasure Island.

A group of us casually strolled along the streets of China Town, taking in the sights and looking for anything interesting. After spending most of my meager allotment of cash on sight-seeing, lunch and a few drinks, we came upon a shop that was filled with Oriental figurines. There were hundreds of different carved wooden pieces. It smelled of old wood, tung oil, dust and strange fragrances. I wanted a small reminder of my visit, but I had little left to spend except for what I needed for transportation. It was getting late and near closing time. I decided to check out this last shop before I headed back.

I noticed a small, dusty figure on a dimly-lit back shelf that seemed to beckon me from the midst of hundreds of tiny, round wooden faces. The store owner told me that it was a "Hotei" or "God of Happiness." His oversized, drooping ears supposedly indicated that he was a good listener. He looked like a small "Buddha," with arms stretched out and his bald head tilted to one side. He had an incredible carved smile and an enormous belly that you were supposed to rub for luck. There had to be a reason I was strangely drawn right to that one figure from the others that surrounded it. I didn't know why. I wasn't superstitious at the time. But he just looked—lucky. I tucked him securely in my pocket and rejoined my buddies.

While waiting to ship out, we pulled our first KP. The dining hall seated about eight hundred men for each sitting and there were two sittings for each meal. We started at five in the morning and worked until about ten o'clock at night. We should have slept like lambs at night but the bay, which had very thick fog in the evening, was constantly swept by the monotonous bellowing of a large fog horn on Alcatraz Island. It was so loud that the noise rattled our building and shook our bunks all night long.

The next part of the voyage began as we boarded our ship and sailed for Hawaii. Many of my fellow passengers were destined to be stationed in the Philippines. They were there when the Japanese attacked the Islands in 1941. Almost everyone on the ship would be either dead, wounded or a prisoner of war within two years. The U.S.S. *Leonard Wood* was later sunk by the Japanese.

As we pulled up to the dock in Honolulu, July 26, 1940, the first landmark we saw was the Aloha Tower. The Pan American *"Pacific Clipper"* was riding a light swell on the water nearby. She was one of the flying boats that flew regular routes from California to several islands in the Pacific in the thirties. Coming in to dock was a beautiful cruise ship, the *Luraline*. (She was later converted into a troop transport).

Assembling outside the terminal, we were greeted by Hawaiian men and women performing traditional dances, accompanied by ukuleles and drums. Hula girls in long grass skirts placed beautiful leis strung with brilliant flowers around our necks.

Army buses drove us to our assigned outfits. Mine was the 35th Infantry Regiment stationed at Schofield Barracks, about eight miles inland from Honolulu. At the time, the 35th was a part of a "square" division, containing four regiments known as the 24th Division, Hawaiian Command. It was later reformed into a "triangle" division known as the 24th Division with three regiments: the 35th, 27th and 19th, Hawaiian Command. In those days, they didn't send recruits to training camp. We went directly to our new outfit and were trained there.

We drove past Pearl Harbor, filled with warships, then through Pearl City, where the workers from the sugar cane fields lived in shanties. We drove by the gigantic Dole pineapple cannery and the seemingly endless fields of pineapples and sugar cane.

Clouds of smoke billowed from the fields. We were told that they were burning the cane fields before harvesting. Narrow gauge railways with small locomotives and cars carried the workers into the fields where they cut the cane stalks with large machetes, then loaded it into the cars for shipment to the sugar mill, where it was processed into granulated sugar.

The buses drove past Wheeler Field, the Army Air Corps base, then to Schofield Barracks. We didn't realize then what was in store for us. Our lives would suddenly be shattered and changed forever on December 7, 1941.

As soon as we got off the buses, reality set in: This was going to be our new home. It looked like a goddamned prison compound. The cement barracks were three stories high, covered with ivy. The second and third levels had a porch with iron railings. There were four buildings forming a quadrangle with a street in front of each building. It formed four quads: Engineers, 35th Infantry, 27th Infantry, and 19th Infantry. There was also a company of Missouri Mules and mule skinners (mule handlers) that trained for mountain transport of supplies and small howitzers, a hospital, firing range, motor pool and tank shed, where the light tanks were parked. Beyond the firing range was Koli Koli Pass, where enemy planes came through on the morning of December 7. A short distance from our barracks was the Army Air Corps base, Wheeler Field.

As we looked at each other, I imagined we all had the same thought. Have I made a mistake volunteering for this? It was too late now. The visions of frolicking with beautiful hula girls in grass skirts on warm, sandy beaches now dashed.

Shocked from our unhappy musings by someone barking like a dog, we all turned in that direction. There stood two old soldiers. One was a square-shouldered monster about six-foot-six with five stripes on each arm and a death-dealing scowl on his face. His partner was five-foot-two, also with five stripes on each arm. They were the meanest looking men I had ever seen. We all believed that we were about to enter six weeks of purgatory. My brothers had told me what to expect, but it didn't help one bit. Hell hath no fury like a frustrated drill sergeant in his twentieth year in the Army.

The first day of training with the "six week miracle workers" was a day of revelations. We all wore the same blue denim fatigues and floppy hats and barely understood anything that our Sergeants said to us. They yelled everything at the top of their lungs, which must have been the size of dirigibles.

The larger one (Monster) screamed something which we couldn't identify. He stood red-faced and fuming as we fearfully milled around looking at each other. Then the Pygmy started in on us.

"Are you ridge-runners and shit-kicking farmers *deaf* or just *stupid?* A simple yes or no will suffice. We don't want to over-tax any IQs here!" he bellowed.

No one dared answer or even move. We were too terrified. We stood there with our eyes bugging out—a mistake because Drill instructors, like dogs, smell fear.

"Oh, we are so sorry to start youse people with such a *tough* problem. Let's strip down to those shorts and do some pushups. *Now get down on the deck and start!*"

I thought, "Please Lord, give me the strength to make it through the next forty-two days and nights with these two sadistic lifers!"

We performed pushups until every single one of us collapsed, groaning and gasping on the ground. Then we marched up to the firing range, not to fire our weapons, but to get a bag lunch and some water for our canteens. No one was allowed to smoke all day.

Following more calisthenics and running, we were sent back to the barracks to recuperate. Our first night in training, they let us sleep all night. We shortly discovered that this was a luxury which would seldom be repeated.

In the morning, everyone shaved, showered, dressed, made up their bunk, put out the laundry and formed up in the company street in forty minutes. After formation we did calisthenics for thirty minutes and then ate breakfast.

At the table, someone said, "Hey, pass the grease." The Monster at the table went ballistic. He jumped to his feet, leaned over, stared down the offender with pure, unadulterated murder in his eyes and said slowly and deliberately, "Private, don't you *ever* use slang at my table *again.* When you want something, you had better say... *please!* Now move your worthless ass into the aisle and give me ten! If anyone else decides to violate the rules of my table, he'll be *sorry!*"

Five minutes later, a corporal at the other end of the table requested the maple syrup and as it was being passed down one of the guys took it and emptied it on his pancakes. Then, all hell broke loose. The corporal who had asked for it jumped up and then the guy who had short-stopped the syrup also jumped to his feet. In a flash the two drill sergeants at the table sprang to their feet like leopards, grabbing the two men before they could take a swing at each other. They were both slammed forcefully back into their chairs before we could put our forks down. The entire mess hall went silent as everybody froze.

The Monster icily hissed at the two, "You morons are going to learn that we don't tolerate anyone actin' up in such a boorish manner!" Then he sat down and finished eating. The rest of us wondered what sort of fearful punishment awaited those poor guys. We were about to find out.

Nothing else was said about the incident all day during training. We were hoping against hope that our sergeants had forgotten about it. That evening after chow, we were ordered to assemble at the rear of the barracks. There were piles of picks and shovels on the ground behind the drill sergeants and large wooden stakes in the dirt marking a huge circle. The Monster told us, as a team, we were not only responsible for our own actions, but also for every member of the team. If one man screwed up, we would all suffer the consequences.

Behold, lesson one.

"So, start digging!" he growled and stalked off toward the barracks.

We knew that if we didn't get the hole finished, we wouldn't get any sleep that night. And that meant we wouldn't be in shape for the next day, and more punishment.

Behold, lesson two.

After a few seconds of standing around and looking at each other, we all grabbed the nearest pick or shovel and started digging. After digging constantly for three hours, we were all nursing bleeding, blistered hands. The Monster came back and told us to stop. He leisurely walked over to the edge of the enormous excavation and proceeded to pace around it, stopping to study the neatly carved edges, without the slightest expression on his face. Then he slowly turned around and dismissed everybody except for the two instigators from the breakfast incident. They had to stay and re-fill the hole.

Behold, lesson three. And this was only the second day.

It wasn't all harassment. As we improved under the steady guidance of our Sergeants, they eased up on us. Actually, we became good friends. But we never asked for anything after that without saying "please."

After surviving recruit training, I was assigned to Headquarters Company motor pool as a driver. Soldiering in Schofield Barracks was no picnic. You couldn't get a promotion because all of the non-coms were lifers and wanted to stay in Hawaii. The officers loved the top sergeants because they ran the whole regiment, giving the officers time to play golf or drink at the Officers' Club. Quite a few of the officers regarded enlisted men as peasants. Playing football and boxing for your outfit was one way to earn your stripes; otherwise, you remained a private.

When I signed up for Hawaii, it wasn't a state and was considered to be foreign duty. I would serve only two years, instead of the usual three, for stateside service. Traditionally, after we had been on Oahu for six months, we picked out a pineapple field that was just being planted and say, "That's my field." It would take a pineapple eighteen months to ripen.

"When they harvest those pineapples, I'm out of here!"

I sweated out my field for a year.

When the Japanese attacked on December 7, I had only six more months to go. When they harvested my field, I left, but in the opposite direction.

The Hawaii we knew then was very beautiful, peaceful and laid back. There weren't any high-rise buildings yet. You could stand on Waikiki Beach in Honolulu and look all the way up to Diamond Head and see only palm trees and one small hotel. On a rare two-day pass we would go to Honolulu and see the Waikiki Theater. It was beautiful, with trees growing inside it. We bought lunch and then strolled around the city. At night we stayed at the YMCA, then continued our exploration the next day, had a few drinks, then caught a bus back to Schofield. After all, we couldn't do much else on a private's salary of twenty-one dollars a month.

The biggest farce at the time was the first day of the month: pay day. Ten men were detailed to pick up the payroll from the small bank branch on the post. They were issued Thompson sub-machine guns with full drums of ammunition. Two more men were given a large push cart, similar to the ones used by street peddlers. In addition, there were four officers, each with a sidearm, escorting the rest of the detail.

The small force formed up and marched over to the bank, two blocks away, tossed the payroll money bags into the push cart, then delivered them to each company headquarters. Who did they think was stupid enough to rob them? We were on an island a thousand miles from anywhere.

But here was the real humor of it all. We had to line up alphabetically in front of a long table with four seated officers. The first officer said in a very solemn voice, "Anderson, Donald E. You owe fifty cents for the American Red Cross. You also owe fifty cents for the Old Soldier's Home in Washington, D.C. Move down."

The next officer repeated my name and serial number.

"You owe eight dollars for laundry. Move down."

Officer number three called out my name. I replied, "Here sir!" He asked me what my serial number was. "6149959, Sir!" "Well, 6149959," he said, "you owe six dollars for the post theater. Move down."

I still hadn't even seen any money yet. They kept marking my pay sheet and passing it down the line.

Finally, I got down to the last officer. He looked up at me sternly and said, "Well, Private Anderson, it looks like you have been living way beyond your means. You owe seven dollars for the Post Exchange."

I looked him straight in the eye and said, "Sir, I guess next month I won't go to the movies and I'll stop brushing my teeth." He gave me a week of KP for that remark. It's a good thing I didn't say what I was really thinking.

Every Saturday morning, there was an inspection of quarters. We were assigned a bunk, a foot and wall locker. Our few worldly possessions were neatly arranged in a certain order in our tiny areas. At the foot of the bunk, our field packs were laid out, fully loaded, and carefully cleaned. Everything had to be done just so—or else. Our bunks had to be made up in a very precise and military way. When Captain Dalton came in for inspection, he took a quarter and flipped it onto the blanket. If the blankets were tight, the coin bounced back up and you passed; if it didn't bounce—extra duty.

After checking the bunks, he would pull out his infamous white handkerchief and wipe the bed rails, checking for signs of dust. If there wasn't any there, he would move on to the window frames and check them, too. If there was any sign of dust or dirt, the whole squad room lost their weekend passes. If no dust was found, we would all grin, but not for long; it was on to the rifle rack.

Each man had to pick up his weapon and "present arms." The bolt was pulled back and held out for inspection. The officer grabbed the rifle and proceeded to check the weapon for any sign of dirt. We used to spend many hours cleaning our rifles. They had to be well oiled to prevent rust from forming, especially inside the barrel. But for inspection, the weapon had to be washed clean, dried and polished. After checking the weapon, it was handed back. If it was found to be clean enough, the inspecting officer moved on to the next man in line.

Captain Dalton was an expert in detecting lint from a polishing cloth. That was how he became known as "Dusty Dalton,"—not coined out of disrespect. Most of us came to think the world of the soon-to-be-famous Captain, later General Dalton.

As a young lieutenant, he was thrown from a horse and suffered severe back injuries. He endured the agony of long months in traction. During his grueling recovery, he studied military tactics from the beginning of history, a factor in his becoming such an excellent combat officer.

Every month we were required to stand guard duty. Our names were posted on the bulletin board a few days ahead of time so we could prepare ourselves. The morning we were to go on guard, we had to be ready in starched sun-tan uniforms, jungle-style pith helmets, spit-shined shoes and rolled down socks. Our rifles had to be absolutely spotless. We waited in the barracks and listened for the bugler to play the "guard mount call," and then assembled in the company street.

There were usually about fifteen men in formation, plus a Sergeant-of-the-Guard and an officer, called an OD, (Officer-of-the-Day). The officer, accompanied by the sergeant, slowly walked down the ranks, minutely inspecting each man and his weapon. They pulled up our trouser legs to check to see if our socks were rolled down. They had us lift up one arm to see if our shirt had any sweat stains which meant that it wasn't freshly laundered. Weapons were thoroughly checked for dirt or oil. The man who looked the sharpest was picked as an orderly and didn't have to walk a post. He basically ran errands for the officers and sergeants for that day.

After inspection, we were assigned to different guard posts. We walked these posts only between four in the afternoon and eight in the morning. Shifts were rotated two hours on and four hours off. Some of the guard posts were very spooky, the Cossack Post being the worst. It was at the rock crusher up at Koli Koli Pass in the mountains, smack in the middle of nowhere. Usually the screw-ups and malcontents were assigned there as punishment.

Another was the warehouse complex. It consisted of several corrugated sheet metal buildings sitting atop 4-foot-high foundations about 100 feet long with large loading platforms on the sides. We had to climb a set of steps onto the loading platform, walk along checking the doors as we went and then continue to the end, down the stairs and proceed on to the next one. The only lights were sixty-watt bulbs over the doors. The rest of the area was totally dark. All the while, we carried rifles with a bayonet mounted with a full clip of ammunition and a round in the chamber, safety on.

The metal buildings expanded during the heat of the day and contracted at night while cooling. They creaked, groaned and moaned at odd times, making it a nerve-wracking post to walk. Needless to say, nobody liked to walk this particular post. Occasionally, an OD would see how close he could get to a guard before he was detected (actually hoping to catch someone either sleeping or smoking).

One night, my sergeant warned me that Lieutenant "Sneaky Pete" was going to catch himself a napping goof-off or an errant smoker. About three in the morning, it was as black as pitch with thick fog swirling through the area. I was determined to outwit this particular officer, so I stood about five feet away from one of the buildings. This position enabled me to see the faint glow of the light bulbs illuminating one of the loading platforms and still remain unseen myself. All I had to do was wait.

Shortly, along came the sneaky lieutenant tip-toeing around the building to snare an unfortunate victim. I let him pass by, snapped off the safety on my rifle and didn't say a word. I silently moved away and walked around to the other side of the building. I could hear the lieutenant, now becoming quite nervous, whispering, "OD....OD....don't shoot!" I stayed stock-still where I was and hollered as loudly as I could.

"Sergeant-of-the-Guard…Intruder on Post Two!"

I snapped the safety on my rifle back on and waited for the sergeant.

When he arrived, I explained what had happened. We both went looking for "Sneaky Pete" but he had rapidly cleared the area. The sergeant was wearing a big grin on his face. He turned to me and said, "I think the OD went back to change his skivvies. You did a good job Private!" He spun on his heel and left, still smiling. That was my first compliment in the Army, and I always cherished it.

A wonderful day to escape the grinding, monotonous Army routine and the homesickness that we all experienced was a once-a-year tradition simply called Soldier's Day: free keg beer, roasted pig on a spit, "three-finger poi" and a beautiful beach—everything you could wish for except a girl to share it with.

Trucks picked us up for a day at the soldiers' beach on the north end of Oahu. The Hawaiian Luau with exotic hula dancers featured "Hilo Hattie," whose famous line was; "When Hilo Hattie does the Hilo Hop, all the traffic comes to a stop." After seeing her dance, we knew why!

The women in Hawaii wouldn't get within a mile of us, so we inevitably wound up at one of the "temples of pleasure" in Honolulu. There was one solid block of them in the center of town. "The Cottage" had mostly Asian girls, while the "Honolulu Rooms" featured American girls that had left home for Hollywood but hadn't hit the "big time," instead settling for a lesser fame in Hawaii.

One pay day, we visited one of the "temples" when the Fleet wasn't in port. Along with my buddies, Shirault and Moody, I waited patiently at the end of the long line of soldiers, all of us dressed in civilian clothes. Several minutes after we arrived, a matronly woman with some teenagers walked up and got in line behind us. The three of us kept looking at each other and wondering if we should politely tell her what the score was. All the soldiers in front of us were snickering and making crude remarks to each other.

Finally, the woman tapped me on the shoulder and politely inquired what time the show started. I told her it was a continuous performance. She asked me what the premise was. I told her it was strictly about money and pleasure. She said that it sounded very interesting and educational. The three of us decided that we had milked the situation long enough. Before I could explain the real situation to her, Moody loudly blurted out, "Lady! This is a *cat house!*"

I thought she would be upset—but she was very cool. She just corralled her brood, thanked us kindly and strolled away.

On the weekends that we didn't have details, we spent time reading in the library or visiting the post movie theater. All the officers sat up front and the enlisted personnel had to sit in the rear. After experiencing combat, we discovered that this procedure was usually reversed.

At other times, we were able to visit the post beer garden or go for long walks around the Island. Moody, Bennett and I had lunches made in the mess hall and hiked up into the mountains, a great way to get away from the system for a while. We really got sick of so much discipline and regimentation, seeing nothing but other GI's. At the time, we hadn't the slightest idea about how bad it was really going to get. A fateful countdown was underway, and we were blissfully unaware.

Every so often, at one, two or three in the morning, a bugle alert would sound. We jumped out of our bunks and quickly dressed, dragged on our full field packs, grabbed our weapons and ran down to the company street in eight minutes flat. Trucks would pull in; we mounted up, moved out to our beach positions and stayed there for two weeks. The guys who didn't keep their packs in order were in big trouble for two weeks thereafter.

While on beach defense training, we practiced firing our 37s out over the ocean at towed targets. Most of the firing was done by the non-coms. Being lowly privates, we got to pick up the empty brass shells and clean the weapons. After the war started, those hard-nosed, rated men wrangled transfers to permanent training companies that stayed in Hawaii for the duration. As privates or corporals, we were then promoted and deemed worthy to lead other men into battle.

During our beach training, Command decided to integrate the Tank Company into our two week exercises. The problem was that no one notified—us. We were all asleep in our pup tents when suddenly we were jarred awake. Roaring engines, sirens and then brilliant gun flashes and grinding, shrieking tread noises were heard as the tanks approached our bivouac area.

As I desperately tried to scramble out of my pup tent, I became tangled up in my mosquito net. As I was rolling out, a light tank straddled me, crushing my tent and all of my gear. Lying under the tank, between the treads, I prayed he wouldn't change direction and mash me into pulp. All of a sudden, I heard whistles blowing and a red flare burst overhead. I saw its flickering red glow on the ground in front of the tank's hull.

The tank driver immediately shut down the engine and the crew popped out of the hatches. When they saw me lying on the ground between the treads, they almost fainted. It seems that someone had dropped the ball and hadn't informed our outfit to clear out of the area the previous day. I never did get reimbursed for all my flattened personal belongings. A few days later, we lost one of our men when he fell from the back of a moving truck. It was one bad week.

The mule skinners joined us several times during exercises. The mules were very adept at climbing the narrow trails in the mountains and equipped with special pack saddles designed to carry our mountain guns, small 37mm howitzers. Broken down to traveling components, the guns consisted of the barrel and slide mechanism, a set of two trails and two large wooden-spoked wagon wheels.

It would take many men to haul these heavy guns up a mountain, hence the mule "pack trains." After spending two years with these lovable darlings (temperamental as hell and biting at the slightest provocation), we never did take them with us. Some genius sat down and figured out that the mules would require so much food, water and bedding straw, that it wouldn't be feasible to commit them to combat. Also, they wouldn't be able to endure the diseases and harsh climate in the jungle. Consequently, we became our own mules. Corps Headquarters discovered that the Army had over five hundred dollars invested in each mule, but each enlisted man cost next to nothing—a calculation that did little for our self-esteem.

As we boarded a transport, we didn't know where we were going— although the rumor was Australia.

Guadalcanal
Solomon Islands
1942

CHAPTER 3

The 'Canal

As we waited to board our ship, we were issued heavy winter overcoats, which told us that we were going southwest. Intelligence knew that the Japanese would somehow find out about the wool coats and think we were going to the Aleutian Islands. Unfortunately, it didn't work. Tokyo Rose always knew where we were going before we did.

Leaving Hawaii, we had three troop ships escorted by two cruisers and three destroyers. All the soldiers had leis hung around their necks. According to tradition, we were supposed to toss them into the water; if they floated ashore, then you would return someday. We all tossed them overboard. (A large number of men from these ships returned to Hawaii and were laid to rest in the national cemetery called the Punch Bowl, overlooking Pearl Harbor).

Our ship had so many men aboard that we could not all be topside at one time. We were divided into three groups, each having a strict schedule. The transports and escorts constantly zigzagged to foil any enemy submarines. Cruisers kept their observation float planes in the air during the day to spot subs or enemy vessels.

Several times, the destroyers peeled off from the convoy, a "bone in their teeth," and proceeded to drop depth charges on suspected subs. Their sleek gray shapes cut the water at high speed. Their sterns, digging into the water, would seem to disappear under the roiling foam. We watched as the crewmen worked at the fantail, dropping and firing depth charges, the explosions spewing massive gouts of water that sent rippling shock waves through the thin hull of our transport. Destroyers raced around our ship like hens watching over their brood, circling constantly, their guns manned and ready.

New Caledonia, an island roughly twelve hundred miles from Australia, was our first destination. We proceeded to sit there for days on end but no one was allowed off the ship. With little to do, we spent much of the time going to and from chow. At the designated time, everyone lined up in a queue that wound around the ship two or three times. After standing in line for hours, you received a dry cheese sandwich for lunch. At dinner, the procedure was repeated and a sandwich, maybe an apple, was handed out. Then you would try and find a space to sit and eat. There were no mess halls with tables and chairs—just a metal bulkhead to lean against, if you were lucky. Everybody else had to stand wherever there was an opening.

Lines formed for drinks at the water fountain that was only turned on at certain times. Sometimes it would be turned off just as you got your turn after waiting for an hour, because they had to conserve fresh water. It was miserable. After fighting in the dripping, foul jungle, sick with malaria and yellow jaundice, covered with slimy leeches, soaking wet, hungry, filthy and frightened, I would think fondly of those long, safe lines, and stale cheese sandwiches.

Our convoy finally left New Caledonia and headed for Guadalcanal, code-named "Cactus." Was it prophetic that our Regiment, the 35th Infantry, was nicknamed the "Cactus Regiment" before the war? We were bothered by the fact that we were sent with only three destroyers and no cruisers (cruisers were the only escort we had that were equipped with their own planes).

We sighted Guadalcanal early on December 17, about nine in the morning. The 35th Infantry was the first regiment of the division to land on the island. I was still having problems with my shoulder and right arm. Every so often, my arm would go numb and my right hand would spasm open for a few minutes. I was hoping that it wouldn't happen as I approached the railing to climb down the landing net for our trip to shore.

As I climbed over the railing, loaded down with all my equipment and rifle, I was having real trouble trying to get my stiff shoulder and arm to cooperate. I was carefully trying to get down the net without falling off, when I heard the landing officer, up on the deck above us, yelling down the side of the ship at me.

"You there, get your ass moving! You're holding up the whole goddamn line!"

There wasn't much that I could do except try and keep moving without losing my grip and dropping down on top of the men already in the landing craft.

"Get that sonofabitch off the net or I'll shoot him myself!" screamed the officer, who was now brandishing a Colt pistol in his right hand.

I glanced down to see how far I would have to jump to avoid getting shot. About ten feet below me, I saw men from my squad standing in the swaying landing craft with their rifles raised and pointed at the officer leaning over the railing high above.

"Like *hell* you will!" yelled one of my men as he and several others drew a bead on the blustering officer with their rifles. He holstered his pistol and proceeded to harangue other unfortunates near the top of the net. He was evidently under orders to keep the landing going as quickly and smoothly as possible to avoid any delay in unloading into the boats. They expected the enemy to attack at any time and needed to get everyone off the ship in record time. He wisely decided not to challenge men who were going into the teeth of the unknown, heavily armed and not in the best frame of mind.

As I dropped heavily into the landing boat, my men lowered their weapons and grinned at me, throwing the officer a jaundiced eye and a few choice words and hand gestures. We pulled away from the ship and headed in to the beach.

No trucks or heavy equipment were available because we were originally supposed to go to Australia. The ships loaded with most of our equipment were already there. The USS *Republic*, a troopship carrying the 172nd Regimental Combat Team originally destined for the 'Canal, accidentally hit two "friendly" mines as they approached an anchorage in the Fiji Islands, and sank with all their equipment on board. We had taken their place.

As we moved toward our designated sector on the narrow beach, we'd been told of the plight of the men from the First and Second Marine Divisions that we were relieving. They had been fighting "tooth and nail" on the Island since August. It was now December. Fighting the enemy for months with meager support from the South Pacific Command had decimated their ranks.

The top Brass couldn't "get their act together." As a consequence, thousands of Japanese were able to land on the island and reinforce the remnants of the original garrison without serious interference from either the Navy or the Marines, who held only a small area about four miles across. Elements of the Japanese Second Battalion, 28th Infantry Regiment landed first. They were followed by the infantry and artillery units of the 24th Infantry, 124th Infantry and the Second Division, along with the 17th Army Headquarters. The Japanese continued to reinforce these units with more men as the battle progressed and swallowed up their resources.

Without proper supply, the Marines ran short of food, medical supplies, weapons, planes and everything else but raw courage. They were determined to defeat the enemy or die with no thought of surrendering. Having already discovered captured Marines in the jungle (tied to trees, tortured, mutilated and left to die) they knew the brutal nature of the enemy. If the beachhead could not be held, they would take to the hills and fight a guerrilla war until help eventually arrived.

The average age of these men was about nineteen years old; some, as young as sixteen or seventeen. Using Yankee ingenuity to overcome their supply problems, these "green" troops taught the Japanese a deadly lesson: don't ever push a Marine into an impossible situation—when they perform their best. Since the war began, the enemy had swept up everything before them. When the Japanese met the Marines in combat on Guadalcanal, it became a fatal lesson for untold thousands of the emperor's best warriors.

Waiting on the beach, we watched the lines of sick, exhausted Marines slowly file past. Farther down the beach, groups of Marines were being transported in landing craft out to the ships anchored in the roadstead. Filthy, ragged uniforms hung from their bodies, ravaged by wounds, disease, malnutrition and the intolerable strain of months of constant combat. Many didn't even have shoes, but every man gripped a clean weapon. Their gaunt faces were bearded and dirty, eyes sunken and red-rimmed. This marked the first time that we had seen men with what came to be known as the "stare." They shuffled by, putting one foot in front of another, as if unaware of their surroundings.

But they weren't beaten. They were being relieved after having won a hard-fought victory under the worst conditions imaginable. The Japanese had been handed their first major combined defeat on land, sea and in the air— literally stopped dead in their tracks. They would no longer advance south towards Fiji, New Caledonia, New Zealand or Australia. For them, only retreat, death in combat, suicide or starvation.

Now it was our turn to fight the Japanese in the steaming, mosquito-infested jungles of Guadalcanal. We all hoped that we would measure up to the example set by our predecessors.

Only the Lord knows why someone, unknown to this day, told the Marines that we were jungle-trained troops. It was the first time that any of us had even seen a jungle. We were able to talk to some of the Marines as they waited for the landing craft to pick them up from the beach. They gave us a few pointers before they left.

"Don't ever just wound a Jap—make sure he's dead. They send out a few men pretending to surrender. When we get up to meet them, the Japs drop to the ground and their men behind them open up on us."

"The bastards booby-trap their own dead and wounded. If you want to make it out—do whatever you have to. No pity. From now on it will be kill, kill, kill in that order."

"It's a battle to the death from here on in. You guys had better set aside any of your Sunday school teachings or you won't make it through twenty-four hours."

"Keep one bullet in your pocket…just in case. You can't surrender to 'em. When we found our guys, we could hardly tell who they were—tied 'em to trees and cut 'em to pieces—"

"For the duration, think of yourself as a killing machine or you won't make it back."

How could we not remember those words.

My outfit formed its bivouac east of the Lunga River, to relieve the Marines in that area. We dug foxholes and slit trenches for sleeping and protection against air raids. We stretched shelter halves over the top to keep the rain out—or so we thought. That night, we had our first air raid since Pearl Harbor. Most of the bombs were dropped near the airfield, the ridge near the jungle (called "Bloody Ridge" by the Marines who fought there) and the main bivouac area inland from the beach.

The enemy planes droning high overhead were unopposed, as there were no night fighters available at this point in the war. Everyone raced for his position and waited for the onslaught. When the planes reached their release point, bombs screamed down out of the darkness, whistling louder and louder until they impacted seconds later. The ground rumbled and shook as the explosives tore up the surrounding area. Red and yellow flashes lit up the darkness, allowing hellish, flashing glimpses of the blasted jungle, followed by the sharp, pungent stink of cordite and burned vegetation. Finally, the Japanese left after dropping their bomb loads and droned off into the distance.

The next day, we were sent down to the beach area to unload landing craft coming in from the ships offshore. There was no dock on the beaches, so the ships had to sit out in the channel and transfer everything into landing boats. As they came in to shore, all the cargo had to be manhandled onto the beach and carried to dumps inland. There were "daisy-chains" of men lined up for hundreds of yards, passing supplies hand-to-hand, all the way down the line to the palm groves off the beach. Everything that came in over the beaches had to be transported, moved, and carried by hand. From bandages to anti-tank guns, we pushed, lifted, rolled, and stacked all of it without the use of vehicles.

Air raids were among the worst possible experiences. Several times a day, Jap fighters and bombers would come in strafing and bombing the beaches and the ships just offshore. We would be out in the water, up to our waists or shoulders moving supplies, when the planes started in. The "Zero" fighters flew in quickly, hugging the waves, and then opened fire; they strafed the beach, landing boats and men moving supplies in the water. As the bullets and cannon shells churned the waves on impact, the planes flashed past, banking away for another run.

Everyone tried to get out of the water as quickly as possible—no easy matter when there were waves fighting you and the soft sand sucked at your feet. The shock wave from an exploding bomb in the water could easily crush your guts from a near miss. Hundreds of struggling soldiers slogged through the ocean to reach their gun positions or trenches while our anti-aircraft guns blasted away at the planes overhead. Our ships opened up, as well as machine guns from the beach positions, depending on how low the Japanese were flying.

Jap bombers would fly high over us, sun reflecting from their fuselages and wings, and drop their loads. The bombs grew larger every second, whistling down at you with increasing speed. If the first one hit a distance in front of you, the rest would hit closer and closer until the concussion lifted you right out of the slit trench, slamming you back down to the ground, knocking the wind out of your lungs.

If the planes were in formation, bombs would straddle you, the blasts knocking you senseless. Noses bled, eyes became bloodshot and ears rang. When you got up out of the trench your whole body felt like Jell-O and you would keep shaking for about an hour until it subsided. But we were the fortunate ones; some of the men around us had lost limbs and suffered other terrible wounds from concussion and shrapnel.

In the meantime, not very far away, there were men fighting and dying in the jungle. We would soon relieve them.

I was amazed at the tiny size of the beachhead. Standing in the middle of it, I could see both ends clearly. Gazing up at Mount Austen, where the Japanese were dug in, we knew they had excellent observation posts enabling them to see everything that moved on both the airfield and the beach. It made me feel naked. We could also hear the fighting going on nearby. The sound of artillery and small arms fire rattled through the jungle and out to those of us manning beach positions. The narrow strip of sand began to draw more attention from the Japanese.

There were two Army divisions on the 'Canal; the American and our 25th Infantry known as the "Tropic Lightning" Division. (The division patch was a lightning bolt on a taro leaf.) The 25th Division's code-name on Guadalcanal was "Lightning." Our general became known as "Lightning Joe Collins." He had never seen combat but didn't let that slow him down. He was so outstanding, that in 1944 he was sent to Europe to take over an Army division bogged down near Cherbourg, France.

In August 1942, after capturing the unfinished airstrip, the Marines formed a tiny perimeter and concentrated on using abandoned enemy equipment to complete it. The airfield would be their only source of air support for a long time.

Across the strait was the island of Tulagi. After the Japanese had been killed in a fierce fight, it became a haven for ships damaged in the Slot, the narrow passage between Savo Island and Guadalcanal. There were so many ships sunk off the Islands, both Allied and Japanese, it was called Iron Bottom Sound. In fact, we were told, the magnetic compasses of ships passing over it were affected by the mass of sunken ships. Over the next six months, the oil-slicked, shark-infested channel closed over the funeral pyres of many exploding, burning warships.

Initially, the Japanese Navy came down the Slot at night and landed troops at the northern part of the 'Canal. Their warships shelled the airfield and beach area, then retired back up the Slot. This occurred on such a regular basis, the Marines nicknamed it "The Cactus Express," later changed to the "Tokyo Express." American vessels sailed into the roadstead during the day and unloaded. They would then "get the hell out" before the Japanese came down the Slot again at night and blasted everything with impunity.

Many important naval battles were fought in the Slot with ships lost on both sides. At first, the U.S. Navy took a beating. As the see-saw battle for control of the sea offshore continued, the combat on the island also dragged on, neither side able to strike a decisive blow.

Basically, the Marines had been dropped off and left to fend for themselves, forced to use ingenious methods to keep themselves going. The airfield, Henderson Field, named after Major Lofton Henderson, a hero killed at Midway, needed every bit of inventiveness had to keep planes in the air. Fuel had to be hand-pumped into every plane, a time consuming process. With few spare parts and even fewer planes, mechanics worked out in the open in all kinds of weather, subjected to bombs, bullets, malaria, bad food, and snipers. As they tried to sleep in tent-covered foxholes, warships of the Japanese Navy steamed down the Slot and then blasted the hell out of the island.

After flying and fighting all day, the Marine pilots helped to re-arm and refuel their planes by hand. Then, after a meal of wormy rice, they would also try and grab some elusive, shell-interrupted sleep. For the thousands of "mud marines," life was even worse. With clothes and shoes rotting off, insufficient artillery, terrible food, and no sleep for days on end, they had to hold back the increasing number of Japanese trying to re-capture the airfield.

Both sides realized that the airfield was the key to the entire effort. The enemy needed to knock it out and hold off the United States Navy until the "soft" Americans either starved or surrendered. The Marines had to hold the tiny mud strips in order to keep from getting wiped out; they required the "flying artillery" to help keep the enemy ships and planes at bay during the daylight. The night was a different story. Our aircraft usually didn't fly at night and were sitting ducks for the nightly rain of explosives, courtesy of the Imperial Japanese Navy steaming down the Slot.

Conditions became so bad that the Marines started calling Guadalcanal, "Operation Shoestring." They had to use the Springfield '03, bolt action rifle, and had little in the way of ammunition. Fighting in the swamps week after week, they were forced to eat Japanese rice full of maggots. They were a tough outfit and I saluted every one.

Evidently, the Japanese believed that there were only a few thousand Marines on the island. The first enemy outfits sent in were decimated after a tough fight in the Marine positions. Following this defeat, more and more Imperial soldiers were sent in to take back the Island.

Before new attacks could be launched, the Japanese had to cut trails through miles of heavy jungle to position their troops close enough to the Marine lines to enable them to achieve surprise and recapture the airfield. When the uncoordinated attacks finally began, they were disjointed and unsuccessful even though they temporarily captured an important ridge near the airfield. It was recaptured after a counterattack by courageous Marines with rifles, bayonets and grenades. The Japanese suffered very heavy casualties, especially among their officers and noncoms.

After their defeat, the Japanese soldiers were forced to retreat through the same jungle they had attacked through..

The battle settled into a semi-static contest between two exhausted fighters. Both sides built defensive positions while they reinforced for an inevitable, decisive showdown. One of the epic battles of the war, the future course of the Pacific conflict revolved around a postage stamp of an airstrip on an island considered unimportant only a few short months before.

During the first week, we kept moving along the beach, only two hundred yards from Henderson Field. In an attempt to keep planes in the air, a small number of bombers and fighters as well as a few observation planes and an occasional PBY flying boat brought oxygen bottles for the fighters and other desperately needed supplies.

When Japanese bombers flew over, we were in the middle of the battle. Flying above the effective ceiling of our anti-aircraft guns, the enemy planes released their loads, the bomb trajectories arcing down to their targets. They screamed in, impacting over a large area—exploding around the airfield, supply dumps and our beach positions. When they attacked the vulnerable shipping offshore, our ships would unwittingly rake the area with fifty-caliber machine guns, 20mm and 40mm or larger anti-aircraft guns in their efforts to knock down the wave-hugging enemy planes.

Our supply vessels dumped large drums of high octane aviation gas and regular gasoline over the side and let them float to shore with the tide. We waded in up to our chests and pushed the barrels into shore, where other men rolled them through the wet sand into the fuel dumps in the nearby palm groves.

One day I was in the water up to my waist when Jap planes came in without warning. I attempted to run but couldn't make any headway. There were five Zeros up there ready to slaughter the chickens in the barnyard. What really worried me was that I was surrounded by barrels of high octane gas. One shell and that would be it.

Luckily for me, the Japanese went after the ships on their first pass. The planes ran in, firing as they banked, jinking and side-slipping, trying to keep the turning ships in their sights. Two of their number fell to the ships' anti-aircraft fire spitting streams of tracers. The first was hit and fell off on one wing, cart-wheeling into the ocean in a towering spray of oily sea water. The second plane was hit in the engine, shattering the canopy and probably killing the pilot. The plane burst into flames, shedding pieces as it curved in a great descending arc and crashed in an oily, burning slick near one of the destroyers.

Three others quickly climbed and banked around for another run. By this time, I was madly scrambling out of the water. I dove behind some fallen coconut trees as they came in again—so low, I expected them to crash. I could see their tracers, seemingly aimed straight at me.

The shells hit the floating gas drums, which blew up with a tremendous flame-spout, blasting burning fuel over the water's surface. A few men didn't make it out; their smoking bodies floated sluggishly in the waves. After the Japs had run out of ammunition, they pulled up and flew away, back the way they had come. The price of retaking this island was getting higher by the day.

Our daily meds were intended to ameliorate some risk. The medics gave us Atabrine tablets every day to prevent malaria. Some of the guys threw the pills away because it was erroneously believed they caused sterility; however, the pills did cause the skin to turn a sickly yellow. We stayed under our mosquito nets at night. When using the latrine or when enemy planes came over, we wouldn't be covered, so thousands of malaria-carrying Anopheles mosquitoes descended on our unprotected bodies, biting constantly. It was a constant battle to see which would get us first: hungry, buzzing mosquitoes or enemy planes.

Quite a few nights, a single Jap plane would cruise overhead. "He" was known by many names; "Washing Machine Charlie," "Charlie" or simply, "that sonofabitch," among others. Several different planes regularly made the trip down to harass us. They were all called "Charlie." One pilot in particular had a perverse sense of humor. The engine on his plane was de-synchronized so that its irregular sound was annoying as hell, preventing everyone from sleeping—which, of course, was his intent. Leisurely flying back and forth, the pilot would sometimes get on the radio frequency of the anti-aircraft guns and taunt us over the loudspeakers.

"Okay, fellows, don't get in your holes just yet, I'm going to look around for awhile… I know this is going to frost you. I learned all this at Pensacola, Florida, courtesy of the U.S. Navy, class of 1938. Maybe I'll toss my ring down to you, but not tonight!" he would say, confidently.

There weren't any night fighters then, and the guns couldn't nail him, either. He would cruise around for about forty minutes and then come back on the air.

"It's time that I earned my pay. Everybody get in your holes. Here it comes!"

A bomb or two would whistle in from the blackness.

Some nights, the air raid siren sounded and all of the action took place at Tulagi, across the channel. We had mixed feelings about that. We were thankful it wasn't us but were sorry it was them. It was always quite a sight with the guns firing tracers, thousands of them crossing the blackness, shells bursting and bombs exploding. The colorful anti-aircraft shells waved back and forth following the planes like someone spraying water with a garden hose. It looked like an insane Fourth of July fireworks display with live bullets.

Finally, on January 4, 1943, our battalion, (the Second Battalion) moved up to the front lines to relieve units of the 132nd Infantry on Mount Austen. This area was called the Gifu Pocket, (or Gifu Strong Point), situated between Hills 31 and 27. It turned out to be the toughest and most heavily fortified sector in the entire campaign.

CHAPTER 4

Into the Green Hell

A great deal of terrible combat remained, but conditions were vastly different. Thousands of fresh troops, both Army and Marines were ready to go in and wipe out the Japanese still holding out on the island. We had planes and plenty of artillery, unlike the Marines who had held on by their fingernails. It would be costly but there was no alternative. The Japs weren't going to give up. The only way to finish the campaign was to go in and kill them one by one.

We moved closer to Mount Austen. Before going into combat we carefully test-fired all our weapons. On the 6th of January 1943, we started up the jungle slopes. The mountain was approximately 1,500 feet high, a mass of gullies, steep jungle-covered ridges and swollen rivers. The only road was the Wright Road, a rough, uneven jeep path being cut along the ridges to provide a faster supply route. There were few trails save for those from the recent passage of native bearers carrying supplies to the front lines.

Our company was assigned to escort and protect these native bearers, our only means of supplying our men fighting in the dense tracts of jungle. The natives were wonderful people. Exceptionally strong, they carried heavy water cans, boxes of rations, cases of grenades, mortar shells, rifle ammunition, medical supplies and everything else needed to keep our outfits operating in the trackless jungle without complaint. On the way back from the front, they gently carried our wounded back with them.

The supply route was the only lifeline for our men. Even when Jap snipers fired on us, the bearers showed no fear. That's more than I could say for myself. The only thing that really bothered them was being in the jungle after dark. I couldn't blame them. We tried not to exhibit fear or show undo concern while we were with them, especially when we were being fired upon.

It took several exhausting hours to get up to the positions just behind the front lines. Most of the way was a combination of steep climbing and slipping in the wet, decaying jungle vegetation. The temperature was always in the nineties and the humidity close to one hundred percent. Everything was perpetually soaked. Much of our time was spent crossing streams, climbing vertical rock walls covered with dense needle vines that tore our clothes and exposed flesh—and cutting our way through the thick jungle.

And there were the leeches, floating in the streams or dropping off leaves and vegetation. They freely sucked our blood after injecting an anti-coagulant. When satiated, they dropped off to digest the blood; then they waited for a new victim. If we tried to pull one off, the body would often tear away, leaving the severed head, streaming blood, still attached to the flesh. So, one by one, we had to burn them with a lit cigarette until they dropped off.

It was common to find dozens of the filthy things after crossing a stream or struggling through the steaming jungle. Taking turns, we checked each other often, removing the slippery, squirming creatures and stepping on them. Bloody sores quickly became infected. The remaining, dripping wounds refused to heal and began to fester in a matter of hours, leaking blood and yellow pus.

Our filthy bodies and slimy, rotting coveralls stank because we couldn't bathe. Most men broke out with cases of jungle rot or became dehydrated from excessive sweating. Some men suffered from heat stroke from not taking their salt tablets. Men began to stagger, turned slowly around and around, stumbling off the narrow trails into the jungle or simply passed out while their eyes rolled back in their sockets, skin hot and clammy. Jungle ulcers ate away flesh until the bones showed through the ragged, slime-encrusted sores. More men were lost to illness than to the enemy.

The Marines had told us to wear our helmets without the straps secured under the chin: Concussion from an exploding shell nearby could break your neck. The straps were either, tied over the helmet's rim, left dangling or taken off completely. While walking, the helmet shifted around on your head and slid over your eyes. Helmets were heavy and hot as hell. We were literally being stewed in our personal "steel pots."

Carrying our casualties down from the front line, we required ten to twelve litter bearers to reach the jeep road being cut along the ridge lines by bulldozers. As bearers, we traded places every few minutes, allowing each other to rest from the tremendous exertion. It was back-breaking, but absolutely essential that the wounded be treated as soon as possible at an aid station in the rear. Pure hell for the casualties, many soldiers didn't survive the ordeal.

On nights when we were late starting back without wounded to carry and the sun had set, (we were still high up in the hills), the natives would run at top speed so that they wouldn't be caught in the jungle when it really got dark. Loaded down with all our combat gear and weapons, we were unable to keep up and protect them from ever-present Japanese snipers invisibly waiting in the underbrush or trees near the barely discernible trails. They used smokeless powder in their bullets. We couldn't identify their firing positions by the telltale smoke usually left behind when a weapon was discharged. If the natives succeeded in getting too far in front of us, away from our protection, the Japs would undoubtedly kill them before they reached the relative safety of the rear area.

This routine ended for us on the 13th of January, when we were called down to our company CP. We were told to get everything in order. They were sending us in to replace the Second Battalion, who had suffered heavy casualties from disease and the fierce fighting.

Dug in on the northern slope of Mount Austen, the Second Battalion had replaced a unit of the Americal Division on January 9. Overextended lines and a lack of manpower had taken their toll. The positions were under constant sniper and mortar fire, inflicting casualties on the already under-strength outfit. Combined with malaria, yellow jaundice, dengue fever, fungus infections and heat stroke, they were in danger of being overrun by a concerted effort by the enemy. We were the only "reserves" available.

While stationed on the beach near the airstrip, we watched as the aerial dogfights and the naval battles offshore unfolded, as the enemy attacked our shipping in the channel and plastered Henderson Field. Before the enemy arrived, our planes would take off from the strips on the other side of the coconut palms, where we had our gun positions. We heard them revving up, then racing down the length of the dirt runway to lift off, skimming over the treetops and straining to gain altitude as quickly as possible.

One morning, we sat in our beach positions, watching the planes scramble after the air-raid siren sounded. A heavily loaded dive-bomber began his take-off run down the airstrip. It sounded as if his engine was off-pitch or beginning to misfire as he built up speed. When he was three-quarters of the way down the runway and hadn't lifted off, everybody scrambled for cover. Usually, if the aircraft didn't get to a certain speed before it approached the palm trees at the end of the runway, it either plowed into the trees or stalled and crashed into the sea. Our positions were just on the other side of those same trees at the end of the runway.

As the plane got closer and closer, his engine screaming and whining, we all dove for the nearest foxhole. It was obvious that he wasn't going to make it. He had already committed to the take-off and couldn't back off. It was already too late.

As I tumbled into my hole, the plane lifted off at the last second, barely clearing the palms. He passed directly over us, his sick engine straining and popping. If he could just bring it back around and land—.

Then the engine quit.

The aircraft dropped like a stone and nosed into the sea just beyond our positions. The men on board were blown into oblivion as the plane hit the water and exploded in a terrific blast. Pieces of the plane and crew dropped all around us, as we crouched in our holes to escape the flying debris. Even as the pieces of the plane were settling to earth, the take-offs continued apace, the fighters and bombers flying through the drifting smoke of the crashed dive-bomber.

After the planes had taken off, everybody prepared for the incoming air raid. The nearby anti-aircraft gun crews checked their weapons, training them back and forth at high elevation for high or medium altitude bombing attacks or low-level fighter sweeps that tried to knock out our planes on the airfield or the huge supply dumps in the palm groves down the beach.

The ships offshore up-anchored and moved farther away from the island to gain maneuvering room before the enemy made their appearance. Warships, usually destroyers, went to full speed, their gun batteries swiveling and elevating as they tracked the incoming Japanese formations.

Our fighters lit into the enemy before they reached us, white contrails twisting and turning in the deep blue sky. Jap planes fell to earth, trailing plumes of smoke and flame as they descended over several miles and crashed into the sea. As the fighting grew closer, we heard the stuttering sounds of fighters' machine guns as they made pass after pass on the bombers or chased enemy fighters high above us, twisting, turning, diving and climbing, trying to eke out an advantage before firing.

We seldom saw parachutes unless one of our pilots bailed out. He would free-fall until he could safely open his chute at low level. Opened any higher, pilots would be easy targets as they fell through the air battle. Destroyers fished the pilots from the water even while continuing their own firing. The enemy planes, if they didn't explode outright, screamed down to the water in long, curving death-dives, trailing a miles-long smear of flaming fuel. Most plunged straight into the ocean, leaving very little wreckage. Some tried to steer their disintegrating aircraft into the frantically maneuvering ships below.

The exploding shells from the ships pocked the sky around the attackers as the bombers and torpedo planes made their runs. Occasionally a Jap plane received a direct hit and simply disappeared in a bright orange-red flash, a shattered wing or piece of fuselage leaking smoke and slowly fluttering to earth.

After a raid was over, we cleaned up the damage around our positions as our planes came back from the fighting, some trailing smoke, leaking fuel, riddled with bullet and cannon holes, damaged engines running erratically or dead altogether. A few didn't make it to the fields and dropped into the palm groves just short of the strip or into the water offshore. Some crash-landed on the runway when their wheels wouldn't come down, gouging and tearing the metal Marston Mat to shreds.

Often a plane landed, taxied to a stop and sat there with the engine idling. When the ground crews raced to the plane to check on the pilot, they discovered that he had died from his wounds after saving the aircraft. Many didn't come back at all. They took off and simply disappeared, never to be seen again.

At night, bombing started all over again, always more terrifying in the pitch darkness. There were no lights at all showing on the island, of course. Everyone alone with his own fears, though we were in a gun position with other men, we often couldn't even see the men in the position next to us.

At night, fear grew indescribably, almost unbearably. We could hear planes coming and the bombs whistling down, but we couldn't see them. The tremendous noise and muzzle flashes from the anti-aircraft guns and exploding bombs combined with the eerie glow from gasoline fires and tracers from the ships offshore—a mere prelude.

Now we prepared to move up into the mountains and jungles to engage the enemy: close-in, hand-to-hand combat. War became essentially personal. Down and dirty, often with no spectators and usually no back-up to help. We had our one rule: Do whatever you had to do to survive. Kill the enemy, no quarter asked or given.

Until now, the war had been pretty one-sided. The Japanese had been doing unto us at will. We were nervous, having never been in close combat. All of us wondered how well we would perform—or survive.

I had always been taught, "Thou shalt not kill." My parents were not violent people. Combat asked me to ignore every rule that I had lived by. Now it would be kill or be killed, life or death, no middle ground. I had never killed another soldier close enough to look right into his eyes as he rushed me with a rifle and bayonet. Close enough to feel the fear and smell the sour stink of our filthy, sweating bodies as we struggled to kill each other.

Japanese training included some troubling add-ons: they thought nothing of killing the enemy, especially defenseless wounded. They had butchered men, women and children from China to the Philippines for years. Their savage history was replete with merciless warlords and *Bushido*, the Warrior's Code: unthinkable to surrender to an enemy in battle meant failure.

In turn, we would kill them by any and all means available—or perish. Now we shared our enemy's concern for failure. Could we find the moral and physical strength to defeat the enemy? The stakes were too high to consider that option. If we failed, the Japanese would win. For us, that was unthinkable. We had to win—any way we could.

The Marines on the beach told us what to expect from the Japs so we were prepared but also more apprehensive. As they considered mercy a weakness, it was despised. Having no place in the life of a warrior, mercilessness made the Japanese soldier difficult to defeat. They fought fanatically as hard as they could, and then willingly died for their Emperor rather than shame their families by surrendering. The more enemies they took with them, the better. Their spirit would then go to the Yasukuni Shrine, where they would be revered as Gods for all time. Their soldiers had been taught this since they were children. It was ingrained, so there was only one way to defeat them in combat: to make sure we came out and they didn't.

There is nothing that can really get a person through the test of combat. You have to trust in yourself, your buddies, your training, luck and the presence of your guardian angel. I firmly believe that everyone who survives in combat has one that looks over him through the whole experience. It's the only way to explain how anyone can go through that much suffering and torment and still come out on the other side. If you survive, parts of you die and are changed forever. The "new person" is a shell of the person you were before. The innocence of youth is permanently destroyed and replaced by horrible memories that play back over and over, every day, for the rest of your life. You can never be the same again.

Since the beginning of the war, the Japanese had been touted as invincible jungle fighters who swept all their enemies aside. They were excellent soldiers who could endure terrible privations, a kind of mystique that had grown up around their abilities in the early part of the war. Extremely tough adversaries, they were men, nonetheless, who had to eat, sleep and fight the jungle and disease to survive. We had to be tougher and luckier in order to make it through.

We had listened to the fighting since we landed, but we would move up on the line the following morning. Everybody kept busy—getting ready in his own way. Some honed their combat knives or machetes on whetstones until they were razor sharp. Others checked, cleaned and re-checked their weapons and equipment until they were satisfied that everything was ready. The dripping "Green Hell" of the jungle was patiently waiting for us to enter its dank, perilous embrace.

Oh, how I hated to see the sun go down that night. It was time to sleep—but who could? I tried to appear calm as I sat on a coconut log slowly honing my combat knife and rubbing the stomach of my little wooden "God of Happiness" still with me since China Town—back in 1940. His polished wooden smile was a comfort that I relied upon when things got rough. I discovered that he really was an especially good listener. I carried him throughout the war and I could rely on his comforting smile.

The following morning, loaded down with as much as we could carry, we trudged up the dark, barely discernible trails. The triple-canopy foliage was so thick that the sunlight rarely penetrated to the jungle floor. It was a bone-torturing process of stumbling and clawing our way through a hazy twilight world of decayed, mold-covered mush, tangled vines and sharp thorns. Slipping and sliding, we struggled through the dripping undergrowth, teeming with slimy leeches. Weighed down with our weapons and ammunition, we stopped every so often to rest for a few minutes and pick the bloody leeches off each other. Then, it was back to climbing.

We chopped much of our way through the jungle with machetes. The vegetation grew so quickly that trails cut in the morning, had to be re-cut on the way back down—the same night. With all the noise we made, I wondered how the hell we were going to keep the Japs from knowing where we were. But there was no alternative.

When we arrived at our destination, we occupied positions in the "secondary line" on a slope just above the jungle next to the main supply trail before relieving the unit on the "primary line." The next morning Japanese snipers opened up from the thick jungle just below us. Their clear field of fire meant we had no effective cover except for a few foxholes. Down near the trail when the firing started, I couldn't reach the foxholes.

As the rounds zipped past me, I ran for the rim of the slope to return fire as best I could. Running in a crouch, with one hand steadying my bouncing helmet and the other gripping my rifle, I made it to within ten feet of the rim. My right arm suddenly went numb again, my hand jerked open and I dropped my rifle. It fell between my feet and I went down like a ton of bricks. My helmet flew off and I tumbled over the rim and rolled down the sloping hillside to the jungle, over a hundred feet below.

Bruised and dazed, I lay still at the base of the slope, where the grass stopped and the jungle began. My weapon and helmet were at the top of the rim and I was at the bottom. If I began to climb back up the slope, the snipers would nail me before I got twenty feet. I could hear the sharp reports of their rifles potting away at my company. Without a weapon, I decided to lay low until the firing died down.

Suddenly, I heard one of the guys from my squad yelling near the top of the rim.

"Anderson's been hit!"

"Corporal, you okay? Where are you hit?"

I didn't want to yell back for fear the Japs would hear me. I lay there trying to think of a way out of my predicament.

Then, everyone above me opened up on the snipers, spraying the trees and the surrounding jungle with a blizzard of small arms fire. Rifles, BARs and machine guns blasted the nearby foliage. The noise was tremendous. Bullets ricocheted down through the trees and zipped into the dark jungle. A strangled cry came from behind me, as a sniper tumbled down from his perch and crashed to earth.

"Get Anderson the hell out of there!" somebody shouted over the din.

I looked up to the rim and saw someone jump up and start to crab-scramble down the slope after me.

"Stay down! Keep up your fire!" I yelled up the slope.

The soldier climbed back and resumed firing. After a few minutes the firing died down and I was able to climb back up the slope, retrieve my helmet and rifle and rejoin my squad. The entire area was carpeted with spent brass and stank of burned powder.

"What the hell happened? We thought you were hit," asked a corporal.

"My arm went numb again, I dropped my rifle and tripped over it," I replied, rubbing my tingling arm.

"Goddamn it, you were lucky as hell. That's all I can say," he said shaking his head.

No more sniper shots for a while, it was time to move up and relieve the outfits up on the line. When we finally staggered into the positions, it was quite dark. Everybody was soaking wet, filthy, exhausted and dripping blood from thorns and leeches. The whole area smelled like a rotting dump. It reeked of old garbage, overflowing latrine trenches, wet mold and putrefying corpses. A cold, slashing rain swept through the tiny clearing in blinding torrents. Foxholes and bunkers were overflowing with slimy mud and thick with insects. Invisible creatures could barely be heard slithering around in the pitch darkness. We couldn't see a goddamned thing.

With little to tell what was out in front, we did know that the Japanese were "out there." The men we were replacing motioned at the jungle to indicate our field of fire and whispered to us to make sure we took care of the machine gun in our hole. They showed us where the ammo boxes were and asked if we knew how to use the gun. We would need it, they muttered. When I asked them where the Japs were, they said that they were close enough to hear us talking. An involuntary shiver crawled right down my back as I peered out into the downpour. The two GI's promptly left, slipping and sliding down the barely visible trail to the rear. In seconds, they disappeared into the inky jungle.

We knew we were replacing G Company at night because the Japanese would hit whenever there was a relief taking place. If we could make the switch in the dark, there was less chance of getting attacked. If the enemy had any idea that an inexperienced "green" unit was being moved into a position, they would hit us for sure. Everything had to be done as quickly and quietly as possible.

We were all petrified. But it was our first chance to take revenge on the Japanese for what they had done at Pearl Harbor. Firing our rifles at sounds all night, we probably didn't hit any enemy, but we felt better than simply sitting there in the pounding rain and slimy mud letting the terrible strain play on our frayed nerves. The incessant drumming of the rain pelting my helmet, the alien rustling of the jungle, and the distorted, jumping shadows, kept me wide awake all night. Visions of mud-camouflaged Japs slithering through the slime like vipers, sliding into my foxhole to slit my throat, kept me on my toes.

Nobody slept. The downpour continued to fill our foxholes as we spent hours staring fearfully into the night. The sides of our hole finally collapsed from the water eating away at the edges, leaving us miserably crouching in a pit of cold, soupy slop.

In the morning, we were royally reamed by Battalion Headquarters for wasting our ammunition. Finally briefed on the situation, we suffered an additional drop in morale upon discovering that the enemy had been only about twenty or thirty yards away from us. The jungle was so dense, we could only see about five to ten feet in front of our bunker. If the enemy decided to attack us, they would be all over us before we could spit. What the hell good was a ten foot field of fire?

Still, no one knew how many Japs we were facing, what kind of pillboxes or weapons they had or exactly where they were. Every night, they moved around, probing our lines, a situation not likely to improve anytime soon.

Our first day in the line, about 7:30 in the morning, we suddenly heard a flurry of shots off to our left. There was a terrible, blood-curdling scream and someone started yelling for a medic. Our first casualty, Birdie Nevell—one of my pals from high school—had been shot by a sniper. The bullet ripped through his thigh and then tore into his groin. Just a few moments later, one of our staff sergeants was shot through the head and died instantly. He had over twenty years in the Army and lasted only a few hours in combat.

Shortly thereafter, Lieutenant Daley came over and told all the squad leaders to get the men lined up. We were going to attack along with F and G companies, just like in the Great War. Fix bayonets! Over the top!

We thought so hard it must have been audible, "Oh, *shit!*"

Lieutenant Daley was a new, 20-year-old butter bar (second lieutenant), just in from Officer Candidate School, (OCS), at Fort Benning. He had been with us for only two days. All we knew about him was that he had just become engaged the previous month and had a lot to live for. Someone was waiting for him back home.

We were ordered to push about a hundred yards into the jungle—a short distance anywhere but there—more like a hundred miles. We moved very slowly into the dank foliage, trying to be as quiet as possible. "Wait a minute" vines wrapped around my equipment, my shoes sinking into the thick, mushy carpet of decaying vegetation as I crawled forward. From exertion and fear, rivers of sweat soaked my coveralls. The nerve-wrenching tension, combined with the suffocating humidity and the weight of my gear and weapons, sapped my strength in short order. My meticulously-maintained rifle, which I was struggling to keep free of fouling dirt and tangled vines, was slippery with sweat and water dripping from the vegetation. I had to constantly free myself from the clinging vines, peering into the jungle at the same time for camouflaged Japanese. The jungle was literally swarming with voracious leeches, but they were the least of my worries.

I couldn't see anything. Visibility was two feet or less. I could barely breathe because of the stifling closeness of the jungle. I felt as if I were being buried alive in a wet coffin full of moldy leaves—a combination of the terrible humidity and ratcheting fear. Here I was, trying to cut my way through the jungle and the Japs were just sitting inside their heavily-camouflaged bunkers unseen in the thick undergrowth. All they had to do was wait for me to unwittingly move into their sights. And squeeze the trigger.

After advancing only about twenty yards, there was a sudden, ripping burst of automatic weapons fire. Every nerve in my body sparked like an electric shock. From a low crouch, I dropped to the ground. I still couldn't see anything through the dark green wall of dense foliage. Stinging sweat ran into my eyes, distorting my vision. For some reason, I began to get an unbearable, pounding headache. Then, I realized that I had been unconsciously holding my breath as I strained to hear what was going on. I slowly, quietly, let the air drain from my lungs, fighting to control my body.

"Anybody hit?" A ghostly voice close by, called out.

"Lieutenant Daley!" Another disembodied voice shouted unsteadily.

Several men crawled over to the lieutenant but he was dead, killed instantly by the first rounds. Then the Japs opened up in earnest. We pulled back under heavy fire, bullets clipping the vegetation all around me. Shredded leaves and bits of branches and tree bark rained down as the rounds snapped past, mere inches over my head. The quick-firing Nambu machine guns were expertly camouflaged and totally invisible. We had no choice but to back off slowly, squirming backwards on our bellies.

We couldn't bring Lieutenant Daley's body back because of the heavy firing. Raising our heads would have been fatal. Japanese bullets swarmed us like clouds of angry hornets. His body was recovered several days later when we finally took the area. The only thing we could do was bring back his weapon and ammunition, so the enemy wouldn't get them.

Looking around for officers, I noticed that our new company commander had disappeared. Here we were up to our ears in heavily-armed Japanese and there weren't any officers around. One of our staff sergeants took over and told us to spread out and hang loose until more officers were sent up. We went back to our foxholes and waited. In the meantime, we kept busy removing the bloody leeches from each other and cleaning our weapons.

Finally another Second Lieutenant showed up and told us we were going to go in again, right away—into the breach. Then he said that anyone who didn't think he could make it should report back to the aid station. Four men got up and took off—two of them noncoms. We just stood there gaping at the lieutenant in disbelief. We wondered what possessed him to say something so ludicrous. We were about to go in to attack an enemy position, and he was sending able-bodied men to the rear because they "couldn't take it?" Goddamn it! Every man sent out of the line reduced our chances of coming out alive!

Shortly, two men arrived with a flame-thrower and two spare tanks of fuel, but they both flatly refused to go into the jungle with us. They were so frightened, neither one would budge. They wouldn't even speak, but stood there shaking their heads in abject terror, their faces giving voice: No goddamned way were they going to go in there!

Totally disgusted, one of my men, Private Driggers, swearing and ranting at the men for being cowards, grabbed the equipment. He asked the operator to show him how it worked. Then hoisting it on his back, he strapped it on. Another squad member and I hoisted the heavy spare fuel tanks and grimly headed back into the jungle.

This time we crawled, spread farther apart. We were learning as we went along. Our unit was an anti-tank outfit, and though not our specialty, it would be soon. Carefully crawling through the airless jungle, the weight of the heavy metal tank strapped on my back shifted back and forth, grinding my dirt-encrusted coveralls into my inflamed skin. The hot, moldy stench of rotting vegetation was sickening. The only sound was the brushing of the foliage and my labored breathing as I wriggled and squirmed my way through the thick vines and tangled brush.

I imagined that the enemy could hear every beat of my pounding heart as I snaked ahead, a few inches at a time. The metal tank of flame-thrower fuel seemed to weigh a ton and had to be sticking up, signaling the waiting enemy my exact location. I tried not to think about what would happen if they drilled it with an incendiary round.

Sliding on my belly, I crawled about forty yards. As we closed in on the suspected Jap positions, (I still couldn't see anything but jungle), we prepared to open fire. My helmet kept sliding down over my eyes as the jungle constantly swiped my face with clingy tendrils.

Pvt. Driggers readied the flame-thrower. He had to open the valves for both the compressed air and liquid fuel, allowing them to form their volatile mixture. Fuel sprayed out under pressure as the igniter triggered; flaming fuel would engulf the surrounding jungle, incinerating any unfortunate enemy soldiers in its fiery path. The heat from the flame could also singe the operator if he wasn't careful. More than one soldier had lost his eyebrows from blow-back.

Just as Driggers rose up to fire, the Japs shot him squarely in the chest. I heard the heavy, sickening impact as the bullet tore into him. He grunted once and then collapsed heavily to the ground. Immediately, all hell broke loose. Bursts of fire ripped the leaves inches above my head as I desperately clawed the stinking, wet earth, trying to get a little lower. The sharp bite of cordite smoke hung around me as I lay there, terrified.

Slugs began ripping through the fuel tank on my back with jerking, dull, metallic sounds...*thunk...thunk...thunk...thunk*. More bullets tore through my combat pack, impacting in a small tree just behind me, ripping out jagged chunks of bark and splintered wood. The fuel mix from the riddled fuel tank instantly streamed down my back and sides, soaking through my coveralls, and pooling on the jungle floor around my churning guts.

My head to one side, pressed against the slimy carpet of decaying leaves, I glanced ahead into the jungle. I could barely see the movement of two enemy machine guns, about four feet apart, just ahead of me. I was lying in a slight depression directly under their line of sight. We must have crawled right into one of their cleverly camouflaged firing lanes and hadn't even noticed. I could feel the blast from the nearest Nambu, as it minced the jungle vegetation all around me. I was sure they would lower the barrel a few inches or one of the Japs would simply stick a pistol out of the gun port. My mother would get a telegram from the War Department.

"We regret to inform you that your son..."

I thought, *"Dear God."*

For a split second, I could see it clearly, and then my mind went totally numb, and I felt paralyzed. I thought that I must be hit in the head. I couldn't move or think or even breathe. I was close to despair. I couldn't move forward or crawl back until I got the fuel tank off my back. I lay there gripped by fear until my training took over. I knew that I had to do something or I was going to stay there permanently. I had a sudden vision of myself lying there wounded, unable to move, as the Japs crawled out to finish me off, crawling over the jungle floor closer and closer—the gleam of knife blades scraping through the leaves. I had to move.

"Driggers must be dead," I thought. "He's not moving. I'm all alone. I can't turn around because vines are partially wrapped around the fuel tank. I can't fire my rifle because it's underneath me and I can't free it. The bunkers are too close to use a grenade; the blast would kill me as well as the Japs—"

I ran down my limited options as rationally as I could while bullets continued to tear through the jungle around me. The noise was deafening. I mentally checked off each option as on some deadly shopping list of wrong choices.

"If the fuel ignites, I'll burn to a crisp." I thought. "Do something, goddamn it!"

Fortunately, the Japs were firing regular bullets and not tracers.

Just then, I heard Driggers moan and knew he was still alive. Somehow, I had to get over to him and drag him out of the line of fire. I managed to squirm out of the harness holding the useless, fuel-dribbling tank on my back. My companion with the other spare tank had also had his riddled. We were both soaked with the oily, stinking fuel. He dumped his tank and we both crawled over to Driggers. The machine guns couldn't depress low enough to finish us off, thank God. It was only a matter of a few inches. But it was enough.

"Don't worry, we're going to get you out of here," I whispered softly into Drigger's ear as we lay side by side.

"They shot me—they shot me," he rasped, as he struggled with the excruciating pain.

"You're okay—you're okay. You're going home—you'll be okay," I whispered, trying to help him and still keep one eye on the jungle, in case the Japs came out after us. I kept whispering, trying to keep him from going into shock. I was scared shitless, but my training made my body do what my brain balked at. We had to get the flame-thrower off his back before we could move him. We couldn't leave it for the enemy to pick up and use against us. And at the time, we had only a few, ourselves.

Luckily, Driggers was lying on his side. The weight of the tanks had twisted him as he fell. We slipped them off and gently laid him on his back. I checked the flame-thrower and saw that bullets had ripped into both tanks from the side and blown off one of the valves. We were all lucky that the fuel hadn't ignited. Finding it useless, we left it there. It was vital to get Driggers out as quickly as possible. We were able to slowly drag him out of the direct line of fire. His limp body seemed to be cemented to the ground. We could move him only a few inches at a time.

Rounds whipped by, just over our heads. The horrible, tearing sound of the quick-firing Nambus washed over us as we struggled, groaning and swearing, to get back far enough to treat Driggers before he bled to death or went into severe shock.

"Hicks! Get a medic and a litter! Make it quick!" I yelled into the jungle.

We turned our attention to Driggers.

I tore open his coveralls and jersey with my knife. He had a nasty, sucking chest wound. Besides the blood he was losing, we could hear air being sucked through the ragged bullet hole in his chest every time he breathed. The bullet had evidently punctured one of his lungs. I wiped my sticky, bloodied, hands on my coveralls; then I sprinkled sulfa powder into the wound and applied two square compresses. I tried to feel his back for any exit wound, so that he wouldn't bleed to death, but the bullet was still lodged in his lung or back.

The stretcher bearers still hadn't arrived, so I sent my companion to get more help. We couldn't move him much farther. We were both totally exhausted. I couldn't get enough air and I felt dizzy and sick to my stomach. Most of the firing had stopped, but we were still in deep trouble. The Japs were just waiting for one of us to show ourselves, and they would instantly fire at the movement.

Unfortunately, as we were pulling back, our passage caused the underbrush to shake and quiver. Our own men, thinking we were all dead, mistook us for the enemy. They knew that the Japs had stopped firing and feared that they were going to attack at any minute. They opened up with everything they had, except grenades, only because we were too close to the foxhole line. Now the shit had really hit the fan. We were going to get killed by our own people.

I began screaming at the top of my lungs.

"Cease fire! Cease fire! We're bringing in wounded! It's Anderson! For Christ's sake! Anderson! Cease fire!"

The firing tapered off and stopped.

Several men crawled up dragging a litter. It still took quite a while to drag Driggers out. We didn't dare get up, the Japs would have taken us all out if they opened up again.

We finally got him out safely by slowly sliding the litter through the tangled foliage a few inches at a time. Nobody knew what had happened to the lieutenant who was supposed to be leading us. He had simply vanished. We never saw him again. The medics took Driggers out and told me they thought that he was going to be all right. But his war was over.

I sat, shaking, on the edge of my log bunker, soaked with stinking fuel, my hands and coveralls smeared with my friend's blood. As I tried to collect my scrambled wits, a buddy of mine knelt down beside me with a look of concern on his face. He stared at me for a few seconds.

"Are you all right?" he asked,

"I think so. Why?" I replied.

He pointed to my combat pack, shaking his head in disbelief.

Completely shredded by bullets, the pack's contents were riddled. There were even bullet holes through the loose back of my coveralls. I took my pack off staring at it in amazement. Then my blood ran cold, as I realized how close I had come to shaking the Reaper's bony hand.

Trying to salvage what I could from my pack, I noticed that my lucky "God of Happiness" was still there. Quite a few of his toes and fingers had been blown off, but he was still smiling. I gratefully rubbed his belly for continued luck and put him safely in the breast pocket of my coveralls until I could get another pack.

Colonel Dalton came up to see us and get the latest details on what had happened. Except for Lieutenant Daley, who had been in the jungle with us when he was killed, the colonel wasn't very pleased with our new officers, to say the least. We were told later that our company commander had turned up two days later in a chow line near Henderson Field. The higher-ups sent him back to New Caledonia. The attacks were called off; the line companies were still taking heavy casualties. More creative thinking was needed before we were sent back in.

The men from the line companies were really suffering. They had been up on the line much longer than we had and were in much worse shape. Our hearts bled for those poor guys. They were more experienced than we were. They had great officers leading them, but their casualties were also a lot higher. Hardly any replacements were coming up to bolster their rapidly dwindling numbers. Most of their men were sick with malaria. Unless they had a fever with a temperature of at least 104, they stayed in the line.

Our training hadn't prepared us for this kind of fighting. We had been trained to fight tanks and personnel in cities or open country. Except for the few days training we had received from the Marine Raiders in hand-to-hand combat, we were as green as a bullfrog's ass when it came to fighting in the jungle. We had to learn fast or die even sooner. Within the first hour, we had two men killed and two wounded. It was a bad start, but it could have been much worse. Fortunately, the Japanese had cooperated and pretty much left us alone. They didn't have to attack because they were quite safe sitting right where they were. Their ingenious bunkers were immune to destruction from everything except a direct hit from a bomb, heavy artillery shell, grenade, satchel charge or a fiery blast from a flame-thrower.

Heavy artillery couldn't be used in that kind of thick, triple-canopy jungle with any effectiveness because of the proximity of our own troops and the position of the artillery batteries in the rear. The shells exploded in the upper canopy as they dropped through the trees, creating air bursts that were more dangerous to us than the Japanese. Bombs couldn't be dropped with the accuracy needed to insure destruction of the maze of underground warrens. Planes would never be able to spot the positions from the air; the jungle all looked the same.

The enemy's bunkers were built into the root systems of enormous trees with only tiny firing ports exposed to direct fire. To blow them up with grenades, you had to crawl up next to them, pull the pin, let go of the handle for a second or two and then stuff it into the port. A few more grenades were insurance. Emptying a .45 Colt or Tommy gun into the hole didn't hurt either. Most of our heavy weaponry had been thwarted by the primordial jungle and the ingenious use of natural camouflage by the Japanese.

For all our technological advances over thousands of years, it sometimes boiled down to the primal instinct of men fighting any way they could: the sour smell of the enemy, the bitter, coppery taste of fear, and the raw adrenaline-pumping savagery of personal survival. The utter weariness when it was over, hardly changed since cavemen first walked the earth. Only weapons changed—sometimes they were the same bare hands and stones.

My emplacement was a "hardened bunker." It consisted of a hole in the ground about 5 by 5 feet square and 4 feet deep, covered with a layer of logs above ground, logs on two sides of the hole, all then buried under a heavy layer of dirt. Inside was a water-cooled thirty-caliber machine gun mounted on a tripod. It belonged to G Company but was "on loan" to whomever was using the hole at the time. We kept it scrupulously clean at all times. Our survival depended on it.

The men we relieved knew we would need the gun, although my buddy and I weren't very proficient with it. There was one belt of ammo in the gun when we arrived. There were also two additional ammo cans in the hole—a total of about 450 rounds in all. We spent all day checking on the men and their equipment. Everything was saturated with muddy slime making for a major effort simply to keep the weapons clean.

While we were preparing to come up the day before, we were given enough rations to last three days. We received three tins of milk crackers, three tins of greasy Spam, a three pound bar of what was described as "high protein semi-sweet chocolate," (commonly called a "D" bar, which usually gave you a terrible case of the runs) and a carton of Chelsea cigarettes. The food tins were stamped "1919" and the chocolate bar was so hard that we broke it into pieces with our helmets and stuffed it into our canteen cups with water, waiting for it to soften enough so it wouldn't break our teeth. We set the cups on the edge of our foxholes and let the constant rains fill them, which didn't take long.

Our cigarettes became damp and moldy from the high humidity and matches never lasted very long. They simply disintegrated. Everybody took extraordinary measures to keep things as dry as possible. Most of the guys who didn't smoke before they landed, including me, were now chain-smoking, lighting their damp, stale cigarettes with unsteady hands.

Our bunkers and foxholes were full of slimy, stagnant, muddy water. God knows what kinds of bugs were floating around in there with us. We were always soaked to the skin. All day long, snipers took pot-shots at us. Bullets tore through the area at the slightest movement. We couldn't see a goddamned thing. We knew that the enemy was all around us. And that was about all we knew. Basically concerned about what was happening around our own hole and the positions on either side of us, we considered that the big picture. I didn't give a shit about what was happening anywhere else, anyway. We were too busy trying to keep each other alive.

As bad as this seemed at the time, these turned out to be our best days in combat. Actually, I should call them the least terrifying. We suffered relatively few casualties and our hearing became more acute—more acclimated to the myriad, confusing sounds of the jungle. That was the good news. The bad news? The relative lull in the fighting wouldn't last long.

Our first full night in combat began with a smothering darkness settling in around us like a blanket, leaving us unable to see anything, except a few outlines where the jungle fused with the night sky. No one dared leave his hole for fear of being mistaken for a Jap infiltrator and being shot by his own men.

This night almost turned out to be my last.

About two in the morning, I heard something outside our hole. It came from my side of the bunker. My buddy was sleeping while I stood guard. I gently woke him up, telling him that I was going to check out a noise. It was probably nothing, but he should get on the gun just in case. He immediately took his place at the machine gun, checking the ammo belt to be sure it wasn't twisted or muddy.

I put both hands on the logs covering the top of the hole at the rear entrance, slowly pulling myself up about half-way out. There was a very faint, eerie glow in the sky at the time, but it was dark and quiet close to the ground where I was. I saw something glint for a split-second and at the same time heard a loud, sickening, heart-stopping...*SSSWIIISSH*...that barely brushed my head.

Instantly, just to my right, ear-shattering shots exploded in the still night air.

BANG...BANG...BANG...BANG!

The blinding muzzle flashes were right in my face.

"What the hell..." I thought. "This is it...*I'm dead!*"

There was a heavy, splattering...*THUUMMP*...that sprayed my face and side with warm, sticky mush. At the same moment, I dropped back into the bunker. My buddy was going out of his mind, thinking that I had been shot.

"Where are you hit? Where are you hit?" he kept shouting.

I tried to get my eyes to focus and my ears to stop ringing. I saw flashes. I finally convinced myself that I wasn't shot. There were no bullet holes that I could find. I sat in the hole and slowly regained my vision and hearing.

At dawn I glanced out the back of the position and my blood froze. A Japanese officer lay dead on the side of our bunker, only a few inches away. His face was a ruined, bloody pulp, his jaw blown off and the back of his head, disintegrated. Blood and most of his brains and skull were splattered over the top of the bunker and on my face, hair and coveralls.

The soldier in the hole next to mine had already taken the dead officer's saber. He told me that the Jap had infiltrated our position and was standing over me in the darkness. Obviously, he had seen me rise out of the hole and swung his razor-sharp saber at my head. He literally missed me by a hair; the sound of raindrops on my helmet had kept me from hearing well, so I had removed it.

A split second later, the guy in the next position a few feet away, alertly spotted the glint of the descending blade, aimed his Colt .45 automatic at the silhouetted Jap, and fired four rounds. They say that "a miss is as good as a mile." The Jap, an Imperial Marine, was at least six feet tall. He was hit squarely in the head and throat from five feet away. He was dead before he hit the ground. Needless to say, I was glad to let the man who saved my life keep the saber. It took four of us to drag the heavy corpse through the muck into the jungle and cover it with slimy jungle flora.

After several days in the position, I decided to go down to a nearby brook and bathe because I just couldn't stand the filth and smell any longer. We hadn't been able to wash up for longer than I could remember, and my coveralls stank to high heaven. They were still saturated with the putrefying remnants of the dead Japanese officer's body. I had flies on my bloody coveralls, buzzing and crawling all over me.

I grabbed my weapon and a piece of hard GI soap, walked down to the brook, laid my rifle on the bank and dropped my revolting coveralls. Then I peeled off my greasy undershirt. My skin was as white as a ghost and severely wrinkled from being constantly wet. The outer layer of skin came off with the undershirt. I didn't even want to think about what my feet looked like. We never took our shoes off. I didn't take them off now. I just stood there in the water thinking about getting clean.

Just as I soaped myself up, a single shot rang out and a slug plowed into the muddy bank next to my ankle. There I was, naked, with my coveralls down around my shoes, and my weapon out of reach on the bank. I immediately dropped into the stream like a sack of potatoes. Another shot ripped the air even closer than the first and damned near hit me in the ass.

I hollered for my men to open fire on the sniper.

"*Jesus Christ!* He has to be close by! Can't anybody see him? Shoot the bastard for Christ's sake!"

"Why wasn't anybody shooting at him?" I thought. "He's going to get me for sure if they don't get him first. Nobody's firing. Oh, shit! Come on! This guy is either a lousy shot or he's just making me sweat before he finally tires of his little game and lets me have it. *Fire*, for Christ's sake! *Fire!* Sonofabitch! I'm dead—*Goddamn it!*"

I'd never felt more helpless in my life.

Lying there in the dirty water, totally defenseless, waiting for the searing impact of the next bullet, I gritted my teeth, closed my eyes and prayed for deliverance. I made promises to the Almighty left and right. I prayed that the Jap wouldn't kill me—or hit me in a spot that wasn't absolutely vital—an arm or a leg: a million dollar wound.

Finally, one of my men spotting movement from the sniper's perch, calmly stood up in plain sight, took careful aim, and blasted away with his BAR. Firing at an enormous tree about a hundred feet tall, he emptied an entire clip into a patch of leaves about halfway up the trunk. The heavy slugs hit the camouflaged sniper, tore through his jerking body and ripped the bark from the tree.

The Jap started screaming and slowly pitched away from the tree, his rifle tumbling end over end until it smashed into the ground. He dropped about five feet and hung there, slowly twisting, upside down, tied to the tree branches by a piece of rope. His helmet, heavily camouflaged with leaves and twigs, was still strapped to his head.

Several other guys, seeing him fall, jumped up and fired at him with rifles and Tommy guns. Then, everybody opened up. The sniper jerked and spun violently as hundreds of bullets literally chopped his body apart until the rope broke that was holding him in the tree. The little that remained of him plummeted to the ground—one less sniper. Nobody bothered to check the mangled corpse. There was no need. He was left where he fell. The jungle would do the rest.

I got up and quickly finished my bath. My squad couldn't resist a few comments about my "lily-white ass making an excellent target for every Jap within rifle shot." The meager benefits of my bath didn't last very long. My coveralls still smelled like I had rolled around on the slimy, stinking floor of a slaughter house.

Later that same day, one of the men in my squad started to crack up. He kept coming to tell me that he had to get out of there. He wasn't going to kill anyone anymore. I asked him what the matter was; he hadn't killed anybody yet. He hadn't even fired his weapon. I couldn't reason with him. He just wanted out. I tried to calm him down and sent him with three other men back to Battalion Headquarters to pick up ammo, rations and water. I thought that maybe a few hours away from the line would straighten him out.

Only three men came back; the complainer was gone. My men told me that he had picked up a heavy case of grenades and deliberately dropped it, crushing his own foot. He had crippled himself to escape combat. By doing that, it meant that his buddy, still with us on the line, would be all by himself at night in his gun position.

I put the spare man in an adjacent position with two others. But now there was a gap because of the empty bunker. If there was a hole in the line, the Japs would be sure to find it. Night was their time to feel out our positions before they attacked, trying to get us to open up and reveal ourselves so they could toss a few grenades at us. It worked both ways. In front of our holes, we sometimes we placed trip wires tied to cans with empty brass or rocks inside. When one of them rattled, a few grenades were lobbed in. Nobody fired at night unless we were being attacked.

That night, after dark and before the moon rose, three Japanese silently infiltrated right through the spot where the empty hole was. We were expecting them. They crept silently toward us. Two Japs crawled toward our hole, knives drawn. When we heard them sliding through the mud, they were too close for us to use our rifles. We weren't supposed to fire anyway, because it told the enemy exactly where your hole was.

Without making a sound, we grabbed our knives from the side of the hole. My buddy took one Jap and I crawled out after the other one. We left their bodies outside our hole until morning.

The third Jap was killed by another soldier nearby. There was a brief sound of a scuffle, swearing in English, then a horrible, muffled yell, a few seconds of expelled breath, like someone being hit repeatedly in the chest with something, and then a terrible, agonized, gurgling groan.

Then silence.

The sound of a body being rolled in the watery mud—then silence again.

We were fortunate that we hadn't accidentally killed each other. The fight was at the edge of our hole, in pitch darkness, side by side, flailing arms and legs, cursing and clawing, slashing, gouging and stabbing, before it was over.

We owed our lives to the tough Marine Raiders who showed us how to stay alive in combat by going for the kill with a knife and surviving. I really have to give them credit for kicking our asses back at Waianae. They taught us the most valuable lesson of all: how to stay alive in combat.

The next morning, after first light, we stripped the dead Japanese of anything we could use. Diaries, documents and unit identification were sent back to Intelligence for examination. Any flags, or "belts-of-a-thousand-stitches" which the Japanese soldiers wrapped around their bodies to ward off enemy bullets, were stripped off and packed away for trading with the rear echelon troops for food, cigarettes or clean socks. Then the putrid bodies, already swarming with ravenous flies, were dragged into the jungle.

Soon after, we got our new regimental colonel, Stanley Larson. He immediately got things moving. We didn't know it at the time, but he would be one of the most outstanding officers we ever had.

On January 15, GI's from Intelligence came up and began broadcasting to the enemy to surrender. After what we'd seen of the Japanese, we knew it wouldn't do any good—really just a waste of time. They kept at it for three straight days. I had seen only one prisoner during this entire time. That was it—one soldier, and not much of a return; as far as we were concerned, not worth the risk. Our life insurance policy was shooting each body with a Tommy gun or rifle to make sure none of them were "playing possum."

Usually, the "intelligence boys" didn't bother asking us to take prisoners. Even though they knew the Japanese were usually very helpful, and talked like magpies when they were taken to the rear, (because their officers never told them not to—they weren't supposed to be captured in the first place, so what was the point?), they also knew what the Japs did to American wounded and prisoners.

At about four in the morning on January 16, my buddy woke me. It was my turn to stand watch. It was absolute hell trying to stay awake. We were all worn out and totally exhausted. We were becoming morose from being tired, cold and soaking wet all night, every night. Terrible cramps set in from crouching in the decaying, clammy dugout that was always full of muddy water. Swarms of mosquitoes, insects, centipedes and large spiders crawled on us day and night. Our nerves were stretched dangerously thin from constant fear. At night, jungle noises drove us crazy, and we couldn't stop trembling from the cold, driving rain.

My friends, who had been killed, seemed to visit each night and talk to me. They were dreams, but it seemed so real, that it screwed my mind up for hours on end. I tried to convince myself they were still alive, but, of course, they weren't. They weren't coming back but they still lived with me in my feverish dreams. I began to suspect that they might be the lucky ones.

Just as it started to lighten a bit, I must have been in an exhaustion-induced trance because I kept hearing a strange new sound. It was very scary. My head was resting against the barrel of our machine gun and the dirt on the lip of the bunker. I finally focused my bleary eyes and nearly died of fright!

A foot from my face was a huge lizard.

The indigenous reptiles grew to a length of four or five feet and were about two feet tall. The natives told us that they wouldn't bite unless they were startled, but their large, knife-like teeth were extremely dangerous. If the attack didn't kill you, the infection from the bite would. They ate almost anything, especially rotting corpses.

The monster flicked its tongue at me, a low hissing sound escaping from deep within its body. I didn't dare move because they were as fast as lightning. I wouldn't have a chance to fire my weapon before it grabbed my face in its sharp teeth. I wanted to call to my buddy but thought better of it.

I sat there, motionless, staring into those cold, unmoving eyes. Its muzzle was dripping with bloody fluid and its teeth were jammed with shreds of slimy, rotting flesh from feeding on the bloated bodies of dead Japanese during the night. I felt its unspeakably foul breath on my face: cold death. Sweat streamed down my face, burning my eyes, but I didn't dare to blink.

All of a sudden, the world exploded.

The lizard disintegrated before my eyes. My buddy had woken up, seen the creature near my head, slowly raised his rifle and fired from the hip. I didn't know whether to thank him or to punch him. The rifle was only inches from my ear when it discharged. He didn't even hit the lizard. The muzzle blast only startled it and blew it away from the edge of the hole. When I looked out, it was slowly walking around, looking for something else to eat.

After several minutes, it slowly disappeared into the jungle where we had left the Japanese bodies. I could hear it digging in the rotting corpses, crunching bones and tearing flesh, until it was satiated. Then it disappeared into the jungle.

Again I had a splitting headache and my ears kept ringing, but I was still in one piece.

CHAPTER 5

Devil's Den

We received word on January 17 to pull back about 250 yards because a firestorm of artillery and mortars was going to be laid on the entire Gifu Pocket. Artillery began registering on the target early in the morning. Single rounds exploded around the target area, like a dog pissing on trees, marking territory. So far, it was mostly barking, but the bite was not far behind and the jaws were about to snap shut.

Once again the language experts tried to get the enemy to surrender. They broadcast their pleas in Japanese over loudspeakers set up on the ground and in trees. They droned on and on in that peculiar sing-song tone, expecting a response that would never come.

"Surrender and you will be well-treated. Your commanders have abandoned you. You are fighting a war you cannot win." Over and over, "Lay down your weapons and come forward with your hands raised. You will be treated well. We have food, water and cigarettes. Come out and save yourselves!"

No dice. We could have saved Intelligence the trouble. We all knew that they wouldn't give up. Why the hell should they?

What we didn't know was that the Japanese Army had already decided to evacuate as many soldiers as possible from Guadalcanal and send them back up the line to other islands. The remainder of the troops facing us, were from the Gifu Prefecture in Japan

What we discovered later was that the Japanese still able to travel on their own were given the option of making their way to the coast. They would be taken aboard destroyers and transported north. But they refused to leave their friends behind to face certain death from combat and starvation. They were resigned to die there as a rear guard in order to buy time for the rest of their comrades to escape the noose drawn tighter each day by the U.S. Army and Marines. There would be no way to escape once they were surrounded. We found most of them were suffering from starvation and disease. Many more were wounded. They had no medicines or bandages and very little food. We were dug in near their only source of water. The only thing they weren't short of was ammunition and courage. We had to admire their bravery and tenacity.

Units of our 35th Regiment worked their way around the Gifu heights, totally surrounded by almost impassable jungle and accessible only by a few narrow trails that were well covered by mutually supporting automatic weapons. The Japs had built reinforced, heavily camouflaged bunkers all over the place, so well disguised that we literally had to trip over one before we saw it. If one was knocked out, an adjacent one could cover its field of fire. It was an ingenious maze of superbly built pillboxes, bunkers, skillfully-cut firing lanes, booby traps, snipers, mines and invisible spider holes—foxholes with camouflaged lids.

To build bunkers, the Japanese dug around the base of a tree, covering it with layers of logs, forming a large rectangular hole. Then the logs were covered with dirt and carefully replanted with vegetation that quickly reclaimed the bare earth, completely wiping out any trace of the excavation. Inside the bunkers, Nambu machine guns rigged with string were sited to fire on a fixed traverse through a nearly invisible firing port. When we approached, pulling the string would fire the gun.

Tunnels connected some of these bunkers underground. If a grenade was thrown into one, the gunner was already in a different place, firing from somewhere nearby. If the tunnel wasn't collapsed by the initial blast, the gunner could start firing again from the same position after the first unit passed on.

The only sure way to destroy these tunnels was to collapse everything by using tanks or satchel charges. Or we'd go into the tunnels, slowly crawling through the darkness, waiting for a booby trap or a rifle to explode in our faces. Desperate struggles underground were won by men armed only with a knife, a Colt pistol and more courage than one could imagine. They were the predecessors of the "tunnel rats" of the Vietnam War.

The slopes of the Gifu presented a nightmarish defensive position. Every square inch seemed to be covered by machine guns and knee mortars. The ripping sound of a fast-firing Nambu machine gun was usually the last sound you heard just before tripping over a bunker aperture, hidden under a tangled mass of slippery tree roots.

Cries of "Medic!" echoed through the jungle, mingling with the crackling of rifle fire, grenade explosions, mortar blasts, and the tormented screams of wounded and dying. When bunkers were blown with satchel charges and grenades, shredded vegetation rained down as well as branches, splintered trees, dirt and stones. Pieces of bodies were everywhere, even hanging in the shrapnel-splintered trees. Each position had to be totally demolished before tackling the next one. Each Japanese was checked to make sure that he was dead. Tommy gunners sprayed each body, head to groin, just to be sure. A liberal use of ammunition and a healthy dose of caution were always good ways to stay alive.

The Japanese had prepared the Gifu to be defended in a 360 degree arc. There was no direct way in. We began to wonder if there was any way out, besides being wounded or killed. In the maze of bullet-swept jungle, there was often no way to tell where the firing was coming from. Cross fires were everywhere. Bullets zipped by from every direction. Some were ours; some, theirs. Undoubtedly, some of our casualties resulted from friendly fire.

The only way to stay alive in the close confines of the jungle was to employ as much firepower as possible. The Tommy gun used by many of our men could clear jungle at close range better than anything else. With Japs all around us and extremely limited visibility, accidental shooting of each other was inevitable.. The only alternative to taking heavy casualties during assaults was to pull back and plaster the hell out of it with artillery and mortars.

Other outfits of the 35th ringed the Jap positions with hastily prepared foxholes (the line companies had been losing too many men trying to pry the Japanese out one at a time, fighting day and night). With these kinds of cleverly-sited bunkers, one enemy soldier could hold us up for hours or days before he was killed, causing heavy casualties. Some of the Japanese were found chained to their weapons. There was no question of the enemy surrendering. The only question was, would the artillery be able to knock the bunkers out?

What we needed were delayed fuses on the artillery shells, allowing them to penetrate the bunkers before exploding. Even then, it would have to score a near-direct hit to destroy them. Often, shells burst close to an enemy position, but didn't significantly damage it. Air bursts took out tree-tied snipers, but had no effect at all on the ground bunkers. Many were impervious to any kind of shell fire. They were too well-built. They would have to be destroyed by the infantryman—as usual.

About one o'clock in the afternoon, everything that would fire was concentrated on the Gifu. The area became an indescribable, screaming nightmare of explosions, smoke and red-hot killing steel. The noise and concussion were so bad that it numbed the mind and body and we were 250 yards away from it. This lasted for about an hour and a half.

There was unimaginable destruction.

Gigantic trees were uprooted and blown to bits. Whole areas were laid waste: stripped, chopped, shredded, minced and flattened. Smoking shell holes combined to create one large crater after another. Fires started from the hot shrapnel, spread out of control through the area, consuming everything in their paths. Thick, rolling clouds of choking smoke from the fires and explosions blotted out the sky. Any observation of the target area was utterly impossible. A forest of explosions blossomed in the jungle as the systematic destruction continued. We hoped it was doing as much damage to the Japanese as it was to the surrounding jungle. Everything was being pulverized by the rain of shells, grid-by-grid, yard-by-yard, foot-by-foot.

We got the word to return to our positions. The sharp, choking stench of blasted and burning vegetation and dismembered bodies enveloped us as we sat nervously in our holes, ready to attack. We waited and waited and waited. Normally, an advance was begun immediately after the artillery preparation was finished, in order to keep the enemy from regaining his senses and regrouping for a coordinated defense or counterattack. But this time, we just sat there—waiting.

Without transition experienced in other parts of the world, night suddenly swallowed us after interminable delay filled with nervous anticipation. The mountain chill signaled the jungle's unfurling of nightly song: noises mysterious and strangely hypnotic. On cue, the Japanese began their nightly probing, sometime lighting firecrackers to draw fire or imitating the calls of animals or birds to communicate with one another. A call from one side of our position, answered from a different location on another side—and occasionally from behind our holes.

Every so often, a Jap would call out somebody's name or imitate a wounded GI, calling for help, from out in front of our holes. We knew that if anybody was captured by the enemy, there was no way we would be able to help him.

After a second sleepless night, and expecting an attack any minute, we got some good news. Tanks were being sent up.

"Tanks? How in the hell are they going to get tanks up to us?" someone wondered aloud.

Sure enough, a single light tank managed to struggle up to our positions. (The others didn't make it.) It slowly clanked and roared its way up, slewing and sliding on the mushy ground, dragging a stinking cloud of blue exhaust. The tracks were clogged with broken foliage and mud. The tank commander popped up from his hatch for a few seconds, looked around, shouted something to the soldiers crouching next to his vehicle, and then disappeared back into his turret.

Infantrymen moved up with the tank on three sides to protect it from enemy suicide attacks. Moving forward at a crouch and leapfrogging, the infantrymen pointed out suspected Jap gun emplacements to the tank's crew. Many of the pillboxes and bunkers had been stripped of their cover by the previous day's barrage but hadn't been significantly damaged or destroyed. Japanese machine guns and rifles fired on the tank as it slowly advanced on them, bullets ricocheting off the thin armor, throwing sparks on impact and then pinging away into the jungle.

As each emplacement was identified, the turret turned slightly and the 37mm cannon fired, sending a high explosive round into the bunker. The explosion of the shell in the confined space was successful: bits and pieces of dirt, roots, guns and bodies blew out as each one was hit and silenced. Smoke poured from the shattered apertures as ammunition caught fire and cooked off, sounding like a Fourth of July fireworks display—underground.

The idling tank switched to a new target and blasted it with several rounds, firing its bow machine gun loaded with tracers to pinpoint the enemy. Covered by the crouching infantrymen, it blew up the Japanese gun positions one by one. It pulled back when it ran out of shells, infantrymen covering it closely from both sides as it slowly clanked out of sight. In its wake, it left shattered, burned-out bunkers full of dead Japanese. Later in the afternoon, it came back up to a different spot and destroyed more bunkers and their occupants.

Around two o'clock in the morning on January 23, I thought our end had come. We were all so tired, soaking wet and dazed from all the shelling on the previous day, we dozed off. We hadn't slept for days and our nerves were worn raw by the constant fighting. It was impossible to stay awake, a deadly combination.

Terrifying screams and rapid firing jerked me awake. Grenades were exploding all over the place. Tracers zipped over our heads scoring the night with bright, jagged, overlapping streaks. It took only a few seconds to realize what was happening. We quickly regained our senses. The Japs were trying to break through our thinly held line. They had been probing, trying to find the weakest spot to break out of the trap. We were that spot. They hit us along with F Company, dug in next to us. Now the "fat was in the fire."

Somebody was desperately shouting into a radio nearby.

"I need flares, right now! Do you hear me?"

They began popping overhead, causing grotesque, dancing, phantom shadows to flicker over our positions and the surrounding jungle. The attacking Japanese came straight for us, suddenly appearing from the jungle, then disappearing in a different direction as they ran through our positions. Ragged, disjointed firing all along the foxhole line became a torrent as everybody opened up on the screaming enemy.

Hysterical, saber-waving Jap officers exhorted their comrades with shrilly-screamed oaths. Soldiers charged us, the light from the flares reflecting eerily on the long bayonets locked on their rifles. Colored tracers from both sides sliced the air at crazy angles, disappearing into the night. Dark, snarling figures struggled together, cursing, slashing and killing.

Nerve-stripping screams echoed through the night as men hacked each other to death with anything they could find—sabers, bayonets, machetes, axes, bowie knives and shovels. Mutilated men fell where they fought. Muzzle flashes from rifles, shotguns, pistols and Tommy guns sparked and blinked brightly along the ground, as GI's fired at the Japanese. The enemy answered by bayoneting anyone in their path.

The Japanese swarmed toward us, bayonets red with blood as they jabbed their long rifles into the foxholes around us. We fought for our lives as they seemed to come from every direction.

We fired our machine gun as fast as we could—to hell with burning out the barrel. Our tracers disappeared into the bodies of the attackers, spinning them around, as we traversed the killing ground in front of us. We ran through our last belt, the hot, ejected shell casings covering the bottom of the hole. We both picked up our knives and rifles and scrambled out of the bunker.

We pitched the last of our grenades into the mass of screaming Japs, their torn bodies silhouetted by the flashing explosions. They still kept coming. Both of us fired our rifles until we were down to our last clip.

As clearly as if he were standing next to me, I heard the voice of a young marine I had spoken to on the beach, the day we landed in the island.

"Don't *ever* hesitate. Do whatever it takes. It's you or them. No mercy, no compassion, no second thoughts. They may wind up being your last. Make *sure* that they don't get a second chance at you. And make *goddamned sure* you keep one last bullet for yourself. After seeing what they did to our guys—no way in hell will they ever take *me* alive."

I brought up my M-1 and fired the last clip into the enemy until I heard the metallic *"ping"* as the empty clip ejected. Throwing down my rifle, I pulled my Colt, as two Japs charged. Their helmets were camouflaged with fresh foliage, uniforms ragged and filthy, and they were screaming in a high-pitched, sing-song. Both gripped rifles with long bayonets locked on the barrels.

As they ran full tilt, straight at me, I aimed at the first man, and hit him in the chest. He crashed to the ground, rolling over and over, his equipment flying out from his body.

As if in slow motion I swung my pistol to the right as the second Japanese closed in determined to stick me in the guts. He didn't fire his rifle though only yards away.

In the bright flare light, I could see him clearly—his face smeared with dirt and sweat, eyes firmly fixed on mine, bayonet level with my stomach, screaming at the top of his voice. I steadied the pistol with both hands and squeezed the trigger. The Colt kicked and rose, as I emptied the remainder of the clip into him, only three strides away from me. He was thrown to the ground as if he had run into a stone wall, his rifle flying from his hands and skidding along the ground, hitting my right foot.

A bloody nightmare ensued. After emptying our rifles and pistols, we fought hand-to-hand. Everybody used whatever they could pick up. Empty rifles were used as clubs. Men were hacked apart or shot. Bodies flew through the air amidst ear-splitting explosions. Everywhere the air filled with choking clouds of cordite smoke and whining, slicing shrapnel from exploding grenades. Butchered men fell everywhere as the riptide of attacking Japanese broke on our positions.

When the enemy stopped coming, I froze where I stood, shaking and shocked, still alive. Men stumbled about, groaning. The wounded, their blood staining the soaked earth, were attended by the few medics who hadn't been bayoneted or killed as they tried to bandage our wounded during the fighting, never hesitating to risk their lives to help a comrade—even after they were hit themselves.

We all expected another attack, but stood there numbly holding whatever weapon we could find, waiting for the enemy to hit us again. They didn't.

Flares were still drifting overhead, sporadically lighting the area. I picked up the rifle of one of the Japanese that had charged me and wiped the dirt from it. I sat on the crumbling edge of my hole to examine it. The rifle was in good condition and smelled of fresh oil. The bayonet had been recently sharpened. Curious about why he hadn't just pulled the trigger when he had the chance, (he could hardly have missed me from just a few yards away) I pulled the bolt back. It ejected a clean round. The action was crisp, the barrel unobstructed by mud. The trigger mechanism didn't seem to be damaged.

I walked over and knelt down beside him. First, I checked for grenades. Then, I removed his torn helmet to see if there were any papers or documents tucked inside. I removed a few photographs and letters, but considering the damage the bullet had caused when he was hit in the head, I didn't think they would be of much use to Intelligence. One of the smeared photos was of a young woman dressed in a kimono, holding a fan, with Japanese characters scrawled vertically along one side. He was wearing a bloodied "belt of a thousand stitches" wrapped tightly around his waist. I started to check his pockets and found ten rounds of rifle ammunition. Why hadn't he fired?

This *Banzai* charge had been their last attempt, evidently deciding to break through or collect "ten lives for the Emperor" before falling in battle. We stood knee deep in dead Japanese. The stench was unbearable. A light, undulating mist had formed over the ground in the still night air, mixing with smoke, the sweet, sickening smell of blood-soaked dirt and torn flesh. Each wounded man suffered his own torment; groans broke the silence.

The wounded Japanese were immediately shot; it was much too dangerous to approach them. They would kill any medic or other GI that came to help them. Live grenades were often carried by the enemy as they charged in. Sometimes they were killed before they could throw them. They would have to be disarmed before the body was moved. Often, they would booby-trap their own bodies before dying by tying explosive charges to their chests. Fortunately for us, they had died before activating the fuses.

As dawn arrived, we took stock of our situation. Ninety of the enemy had been killed. The piles of mangled corpses were searched and then taken to a large pit scooped out by a bulldozer. As we dragged away the bodies, our coveralls and shoes were soaked with the viscous, stinking, bloody remnants. We policed the area and removed the broken weapons, equipment and scattered remains. Everything was thrown into the pit, crawling with flies and squirming maggots, then covered with dirt.

Our wounded were evacuated and the dead carried out, leaving the shaken survivors to man the shrinking line. The battle cost our battalion sixty-four killed and forty-six wounded. The Gifu had finally been broken. The mist-shrouded slopes were ours, but the price had been high. The entire area had been reduced to a smoking, blasted, maggot-infested, burned-out wasteland.

Our outfit spent the entire day reorganizing, restocking ammunition and trying to clean up the mess from the battle. There was a constant stream of officers and noncoms from the rear coming and going all day long looking at the area, collecting souvenirs and asking questions. Some had gone around examining insignias cut from the uniforms of the Japanese before they had been buried. Others simply walked around looking for something to "pick up." I could imagine how long any of them would have lasted on the line, during the fighting. Their uniforms were clean and in good condition. They were clean-shaven and well-fed. Their web gear was freshly scrubbed and some had brand-new Colts that probably hadn't even had the safety off since they had qualified at the range back on Hawaii.

These men always showed up after an action had taken place and the fighting was over. My people sat on the edges of their foxholes and watched with a jaundiced eye, (quite literally) as they snooped around. When the "shit hit the fan," these same men were nowhere to be seen. They were always "back in the rear with the gear." They never asked about our casualties or talked to us. I thought they were vultures, showing up after the kill to get their share of the bloody carcass. It made me sick.

My buddies were exhausted, filthy, unshaven for weeks—their foul, blood-stained coveralls and shoes torn and rotten, smelling of death. I knew that I must look the same to them. Everyone was at the end of his endurance.

As exhausted as we were, we still had to re-supply ourselves with water, rations and especially, ammunition of all types. One of the worst things you can hear in the middle of a fight is, "We're out…!" I could still see the smoking muzzle of our machine gun traversing uselessly, as we realized there wasn't any more ammo for it, and the Japs were still charging. Then, all the grenades were gone, rifles and pistols. Finally, there was only one way left open—close with the enemy to kill him any way you could.

My stomach churned every time I thought about it, replaying in my mind as if in a haze, over and over and over:

The soldier's long bayonet leveled at my guts, dust and blood erupting from the impact of the Colt's bullets, hellish flashes of light playing across a ruined face as he collapsed to the ground… dropping my Colt, grabbing the machete, a blur of frenzied fighting, sobbing wounded, shots ringing out, dead men carpeting the jungle floor.

The following day, we were pulled out of the line.

It was a strange feeling, struggling back down the mud-clogged trails toward the airfield and our old beach positions. No one talked. Everyone exhaustedly slogged along like zombies, each man following one weary step with another. Men supported their buddies or carried their weapons for them. Many wore bloody bandages or limped along on bare, torn feet, eaten away with jungle ulcers or "trench foot." Most were either too tired or shocked to give a damn about anything. We all must have had "the stare." We were trying to figure out what it all meant—the sheer futility of it.

We had come to the 'Canal, a bunch of young kids, never having really loved or hated. Now we were old men of eighteen, nineteen and twenty. The cold fact was that we were all hardened killers. The smell of death lingered around our shuffling lines of men returning from the brink, changed forever. There was no going back. We had taken men's lives without mercy, and would keep on killing for as long as we had to. Even our own men in the rear areas stared at us with different expressions, seldom tried to talk to us or look into our eyes. They didn't want to be around us. It wasn't just because we smelled like dead animals. They feared us.

I silently prayed for redemption. Only time would tell. I felt as if something evil had entered my soul and I feared that more than the terrors of combat. The Army taught people how to kill day in and day out, but couldn't tell them how to live with it. It boiled down to survival—pure and simple. If I ever made it back home alive, would I be able to adjust? No one would ever be able to explain this to people back home. Others could never possibly understand unless they were there. Everything that happened was pushed, kicking and clawing, as far back into the dark recesses as possible.

The real trick was keeping it there.

CHAPTER 6

Dust to Dust

We were served a warm meal, but most of us couldn't keep it down. Our stomachs weren't used to warm food. After surviving on cold rations for so long, the change caused us to throw up anything else. We had trouble getting our shoes off because we hadn't removed them for weeks and our feet became terribly swollen. Immersion foot, jungle rot, leech infections, blisters, shrapnel wounds and a hundred kinds of disease sapped our strength, reducing our numbers alarmingly.

It was a sure bet, if the enemy didn't get us, the bugs would.

We left these same positions in early January to fight on Mount Austen, and the 24th Infantry, an all-black regiment, took over. After weeks of fighting in the suffocating heat and humidity of the dense jungle, the sunshine and ocean breezes were a magnificent tonic.

My outfit didn't arrive at the beach until after dark. Before we could relieve the 24th Infantry, our anti-tank guns had to be picked up, and taken to the beach positions. Water-proofed and put into storage, the guns stayed there since they were of no use on rugged Mount Austen.

After picking up our guns, we rushed back to and relieved the 24th, which moved back a few hundred yards as a reserve. As soon as we were in position, our guns were field stripped and every part cleaned of the cosmoline that had been applied to keep the parts from rusting. Cosmoline, a tar-like preservative, was very difficult to remove. The mechanisms were placed on the gun covers on the sand and in the pitch darkness, washed and cleaned, down to the tiniest pieces. The many hundreds of hours of practicing this very procedure blindfolded back in Hawaii had paid off.

We were almost finished when a battle suddenly flared up in the channel between us and Savo Island. Ships were firing and planes bombing and strafing something offshore. We could hear boats out in front of us but couldn't tell if they were ours. Our positions, which were right on the beach, were the first line of defense for that area. If there were Jap destroyers or barges coming in, they would hit us first.

We set new records for re-assembling our guns and waited in the dark. Many vessels were out in front of us, but we couldn't recognize any of them in the blackness—just noisy, dark silhouettes, gun flashes blinking like fireflies, weaving about in the darkness out in the channel.

Suddenly we heard a boat heading straight for us at full power. My gunner asked for permission to open fire, but I told him not to until I gave him the word. We heard something vaguely familiar about those racing engines.

At that instant a huge, dark object hurtled past us close inshore, parallel to the beach. Continuing on, it exploded in flames. One of our PT boats had been badly damaged in the fighting. We could see men leaping off the boat, silhouetted against the flames spreading over the plywood deck. Thank God we hadn't opened up on it in the darkness. All of the crew made it to shore but the boat burned and sank. Spectators to this off-shore battle, we didn't have to fire a shot all night. Still, our nerves were frazzled.

The following morning, soldiers from the 24th invited us over for chow. When they learned we had just come down from the fighting and didn't have anything, they gave us razors, shaving and bath soap, face cloths, towels, cigarettes and food. These men were some of the nicest people we had the privilege to serve with in the entire war. They shared everything with us.

In contrast, the Seabees and Navy wouldn't give us the time of day. They all did outstanding jobs, but those two branches of the service didn't care much for murderous, mud-slogging dogfaces, except when souvenirs were involved.

Then, the trading began in earnest.

Soldiers began a brisk business in trading homemade "captured" Japanese battle flags, shredded on the edges, with well positioned bullet holes or "blood stains" on them and other souvenirs, to sailors for food and cigarettes. We all had a good laugh whenever these "authentic" battle souvenirs were traded on the beach and then taken back aboard ships in the channel, probably accompanied by tall stories of how they had been single-handedly taken from the enemy by the proud owners.

On the 28th of January 1943, I turned twenty-one. I also came down with malaria. Happy Birthday. I was sent to the Battalion Aid Station for about a week. They gave me quinine and that was about all they could do for me. When my temperature climbed to near 104, they gave me rubdowns with alcohol.

Initially I had terrible chills, even though the air temperature was in the nineties. Then I developed a spiking fever and splitting headache. My ears rang like a loud, continuous doorbell. I was either sweating or shivering. On top of that, the Japs came over and bombed the hell out of us at night. As the worst of the malaria episodes subsided, I returned to my outfit on the beach.

After we had recovered somewhat from being in action, we went to find where our comrades had been laid to rest. We were upset to find that the cemetery was just a plot of land laid out and cleared of underbrush and overgrown vines, with no markers at all. We knew it was temporary but felt that it needed some markers on the hastily dug graves. After all, they were our friends.

We collected large brass shell casings and bartered with the Seabees to have them welded into crosses. Then we had cement boxes made and set the crosses in them. At Henderson Field we scrounged some sheets of aluminum and made name plates to go on the base of the crosses. We scratched the names on each one and mounted them on the boxes.

In a private, solemn ceremony, we placed the crosses on the graves and said a prayer for each one of our friends. It was all we could do for those brave souls. We hoped they would find everlasting peace after so much suffering. We said our good-byes and walked slowly back to the beach.

There was still fighting. It was now February 1943. "Dusty" Dalton had been promoted to full colonel and taken over command of the 161st Infantry Regiment. The Marines were sweeping along the coast, in attempts to kill the remaining enemy or force them to retreat to the tip of the island. They were supported by the Navy for extra firepower. Colonel Dalton was in his customary role.

We had Colonel Larson, whose leadership we trusted; nonetheless, we missed Colonel Dalton and worried about him. No "arm-chair warrior," but a genuine leader of men in combat, he led from the front, rather than by orders issued over a radio from some dank, musty underground bunker in the rear. I still believe that Colonel Dalton was held back by his "associates" from West Point because he thought of his men as people, and not as expendable pawns on a map overlay. We loved him because he never asked us to risk anything that he wasn't also prepared to sacrifice. His theories of leadership in combat operations were proven more effective and successful as the war ground on. And we would come to know that he was truly one of a kind.

The first of March, we started getting warm food each day. The cooks were challenged to make it palatable since everything they had was canned, powdered or dehydrated. There wasn't anything fresh to eat at all; from the Marines we learned that the Navy wound up with it.

What sustained us were packages from home. When a parcel came in, everyone shared what he received: cookies, fruit, cakes, candy, soap, shaving cream, sunglasses, foot powder—even handguns and small-arms ammunition or shotgun shells. (Men frequently asked for their six-shooters from home.) Every mail call might bring a small box of treasure from the States.

Except for isolated skirmishes, major fighting started to ease up in March and April. The airfields were enlarged and roads carved out of the surrounding jungle. Runways were extended and resurfaced with new Marston Mat, and revetments for the planes were constructed. Vehicles were landed and put right to work.

More and more aircraft were flown in for the move up the Solomon Islands Chain. Showers and latrines appeared. Swamps were drained by the Engineers, and heavy anti-aircraft batteries were installed over the area. Tent camps were built and mess halls set up. The Seabees even erected a movie screen.

Some nights as we were watching a movie, everything would suddenly black out. The anti-aircraft guns started blasting away, lighting up the area with their muzzle flashes. Several times, the searchlights picked up enemy bombers in their beams and we saw them dropping their bombs. Since we were not in our own area, we didn't know where the bomb shelters were. Instead, we headed for the nearest stagnant, mud-filled culvert on the side of the road and enthusiastically rolled in: the price to pay—just to see a movie.

CHAPTER 7

Jungle Juice, Typhoons and Cigars

During March, April and May, we had it fairly easy as we moved along the beach to make room for new outfits arriving and preparing for the next push north from Guadalcanal to Arundel, New Georgia, Bougainville and Vella Lavella. While waiting, we still manned beach positions. I continued to suffer bouts of malaria and yellow jaundice. I sat in my hole with a blanket. Some bouts were more extreme than others; I just couldn't shake the damned bug. The medics always had their hands full. There wasn't much they could do unless your temperature spiked or you collapsed. You just had to sweat it out.

Some of our more enterprising ridge-runners from Tennessee, Louisiana and Georgia managed to scrounge enough material from the airfield and Quartermaster to build a working still. The powerful concoction was promptly nicknamed "Jungle Juice," among other things. It was potent in the extreme, especially for men who hadn't had a drink in months. The actual recipes were generally kept a secret, except from the men who were making it. There were different versions: some used sugar and raisins, one contained potatoes or torpedo alcohol. It was nasty stuff.

One night, as we sat on coconut logs watching a movie projected on a makeshift screen, the entire area was suddenly raked by 20mm cannon fire. Everybody dropped flat, trying to keep as low as possible. Shells exploded on the logs and trees, and ripped through the tents all around us. Shrapnel was flying every which way; then the firing stopped.

After a few seconds, we peered over the tops of the logs and saw two idiots at an anti-aircraft gun nearby, whooping like Indians and dancing around the smoking gun. Fortunately, they had run out of ammunition before anyone had been wounded or killed. Both of them were fortified to the gills with homemade Jungle Juice. They had emptied a whole can by themselves. I couldn't figure out how they were still breathing, never mind standing.

For several days after this incident, the MPs searched high and low for illicit stills, but they never found them. After all, the men who had built them were professional moonshiners from the Blue Ridge Mountains. If there were three things they were good at, it was shooting, making whiskey and keeping their stills secret. The MPs were totally stymied. After a few days, they wisely gave up—stunningly outmatched.

One morning, as we sat in our positions one morning watching the planes taking off from the airfield and shooting the breeze, some fool had to say, "Boy, hanging around like this sure is getting monotonous."

Talk about bad luck. I wanted to hang him. Sure enough, at about three o'clock that afternoon, the air raid sirens started blaring and all of our planes took off from Henderson, hauling ass up the Slot. It seemed as if every plane that could still fly was already airborne.

Here we were, stuck out on the beach in shallow foxholes scraped out of the flat sand. No cover anywhere. The supply and warships, "up-anchored" and hauled ass as fast as their propellers would turn—a bad sign for us.

Crews on the anti-aircraft guns received word that over two hundred enemy fighters and bombers were headed straight for us. We hunkered down and started asking for divine intervention in a big way. No air raids had occurred for some time.

While all this was happening, something very strange was taking place. The ocean started getting rough, forming huge, foaming white caps. The wind rapidly picked up, whipping us with stinging salt spray. Shortly, water began running up the beach into our gun positions, flooding everything in sight.

The sky was almost as dark as night though it was only afternoon. Unsettled, we forgot about the air raid because the water began rising, soon up to our knees and getting higher and higher. Our anti-tank guns, and everything else we had, were submerged under a foot of thrashing, foaming seawater. There was no escaping with our equipment because we didn't have a vehicle. We were all scared out of our wits.

The surging waves were now up to our hips. Our tent, which was firmly anchored with long stakes, collapsed and washed away. We had no option but to stay in our positions, holding our personal weapons and wait for the storm to subside. All our ammunition was ruined except for what we had on our cartridge belts, which we hung around our necks to keep them out of the sea.

There wasn't a shred of shelter anywhere near us. We stood shivering, soaked, and beaten by the wind and waves—as though we were in the middle of an ocean only three or four feet deep, waves washing against us, flowing inland. Nothing could be seen in any direction—only black water with white, foaming caps. The terrific wind lashed at us with increasing force, threatening to blow us clear off the island into the sea.

We stood there all through the night, scared to death.

Toward morning the wind died down, and the water receded. As daylight arrived, it was obvious that we had just survived a typhoon. The sea calmed, and the sky began to brighten a bit. The island was a mess. Landing craft were driven up the rivers; tons of supplies had been destroyed, aircraft damaged, trees stripped, uprooted and swept away, weapons and equipment damaged beyond repair.

Our foxholes were flooded, and much of our gear had washed away during the night. To overcome the setback, we buckled down to clean our weapons before rust set in. We finally found our tents and some of our personal items that had washed into the tree line. Everything else was gone for good. I never heard that idiot complain about being bored again.

On guard duty two weeks later, I sat on the trails of our gun, leaning over the shield looking seaward and thinking that I'd never see home again. Our troops were taking a beating in North Africa and we would need to fight on every godforsaken island in the Pacific before invading the home islands of Japan itself. Who the hell could possibly be lucky enough to survive that long? It sure looked bleak.

I had come on duty at 4 am. Just as it began getting light, I thought I saw tiny specks coming up over the horizon. I couldn't make out what they were. I woke up two men and had them check it out. They both agreed there was something out there, still too far away to recognize.

Finally, when it became full light, the spots became sticks. Then, there was a whole forest of sticks. Holy shit, it was a convoy of ships! I grabbed the phone and furiously rang up headquarters.

"We've got a lot of goddamned ships heading straight for us and we don't know if they're ours or theirs!"

After a minute or so, they came back on the horn.

"Wait one—do not, I repeat, do not take any action until authorized by GHQ or SOPAC HQ."

"Well, I don't know who belongs to all those initials," I thought, "If I see a red meatball flying from those masts, I'm going to start my own battle. Headquarters can kiss my ass!"

A few minutes later, the word came down.

"Those are our ships coming up from New Caledonia," reported the voice on the radio.

It seemed that someone could have told us to expect a convoy. We were all pretty disgusted.

All the time we had held this post, we had watched our planes taking off and landing on Henderson Field. Most made it back safely, but some would bank around low over our positions, trying to get a straight approach, start in for a landing and then crash into the palm trees just short of the runway. First the explosion, then a cloud of black smoke would rise into the air, followed by the crackling of flames and sometimes a secondary explosion from ammunition or a hung-up bomb. The crews didn't stand a chance. The palm trees bore burns and scars from the previous months.

We were able to go down to the airfield, one day, to talk to the ground crews servicing the planes. The mechanics let us sit in the cockpit of a B-24 Liberator bomber and answered all of our questions about the planes and their operation. We were quite impressed. Those poor guys really had a tough time when the Japs came over and bombed the runways. Every time the place was hit, the mechanics were smack in the bulls-eye. Their foxholes were on the sides of the runways, out in the open.

One spectacular night the enemy came over while our bombers were lined up on the runway, gassed and fully loaded, engines running for an early morning raid. As they warmed up their engines, the air-raid sirens went off. Even though engines were still cold, several airmen pushed their throttles to the wall and took off, straining for altitude. As the Jap planes droned overhead with bomb-bays open, our remaining aircraft were sitting ducks.

Hit by the falling bombs and unable to take off, one of our bombers was blown fifty feet into the air intact, exploding as its gas tank and bomb load caught fire. The flaming gasoline and burning debris cascaded into the foxholes and burned every man there to death. The rest blew up on the runway, their full loads cooking off in the tremendous heat.

We were about two hundred yards from the field when the planes were hit. The terrific concussion blew us off our feet as gigantic fireballs threw debris hundreds of feet in the air. Pieces of airplanes, men, vehicles, dirt, trees and burning fuel rained down all over the area. As bad as it seemed then, those brave men had the wreckage cleared and the airstrip operational by first light— an incredible feat.

Working twenty-four hours a day, stripped down to just shorts, through downpours, broiling sun, terrible humidity, insects, bombing and strafing, those guys were truly the unsung heroes of the campaign. They pumped gasoline, armed and loaded bombs, changed over-worked engines and tires or repaired radios. Without this support, the island could never have been held.

As we were leaving, from our visit with the mechanics at the airfield, the ground crews offered us a two-man life raft that had been salvaged from one of our wrecked planes—it even had two small paddles. The mechanics inflated and checked it for leaks; then we carried it out to the road. We were able to hitch a ride from some Marines in a supply truck heading toward our gun position. Needless to say, we had a lot of fun with our new toy. But, as it turned out, we should have left it at the airfield.

We got to talking about the things we missed the most. Sex was number one, followed by ice cream, fresh, cold apples, a glass of cold milk, bacon and eggs and a real cup of "Joe." A couple of guys wanted to get some cigars. The Seabees wouldn't sell us any, so we sat around trying to come up with a fool-proof idea to procure some. Why couldn't we paddle out to one of those ships offshore and ask them to sell us some?

My buddy and I collected two helmets full of "souvenirs" to trade, grabbed the raft and set off paddling on a sea as smooth as glass. The sky was a deep blue, not a cloud in sight. The ships didn't seem to be very far out, so we picked out a destroyer and headed for it.

We paddled for about forty minutes and were closing in on the ship when they sounded a damned siren that scared the living hell out of us. Then, a loudspeaker came on warning us to stay clear of the vessel or they would blow us out of the water. We hollered back that we only wanted to buy a few cigars. The ship's captain told us to haul our asses clear of the area or suffer the consequences. We shouted back our compliments to the Captain and our sincere condolences to his crew, accompanied with the appropriate, vigorous hand gestures.

Suddenly, the ship blew off steam and a klaxon sounded General Quarters. *Bong...Bong...Bong!*

Sailors were running all over the ship. We became concerned because we thought the destroyer was going to run us down, but that soon became the least of our worries.

As the ship got under way and sped past us, we heard the air-raid sirens on shore, blaring. We bounced around like a cork in the destroyer's foaming wake, as it circled around to the center of the channel, gun turrets revolving with raised barrels searching for incoming enemy planes. The ships near us were hauling up their anchors and starting to zigzag as they picked up speed. We were caught smack in the middle of an air raid!

Japanese planes began their wave-hugging runs as the ships were getting under way. The two of us were paddling furiously with our pathetic, tiny paddles, but no matter where we headed, it wasn't going to be fast enough to gain safety anywhere. We had no choice but to sit out the attack where we were and pray. Nearby a Liberty ship, hit by either a bomb or a torpedo exploded on the port side and began to burn. Debris fell back into the water as the vessel slowly turned for shore, vomiting a dense cloud of flames and smoke.

During the action, ships were firing in all directions, trying to knock down the enemy planes as they came in for their runs. The noise was deafening. Shells flew all over the place. Several Japs crashed into the water very close to us, sending huge geysers of water and burning fuel skyward. Enemy torpedo planes skimmed the water, aiming for the vulnerable transports and cargo ships moving slowly out of the channel.

One Japanese plane was hit high above us and started to smoke heavily as it headed down to the sea. It slowly nosed over, until it was almost vertical, picked up speed and streaked down leaving a huge trail of black smoke. Unfortunately, it was heading straight for us. We were powerless to escape the impact area as the plane's wings ripped off, the burning fuselage plunging down straight for us. I couldn't take my eyes off the blazing wreck as it knifed into the water nearby, showering us with sea water, nearly swamping our bobbing raft.

Now we were getting truly anxious. What a hell of a time to be floating around in the middle of all those ships, with the enemy bombing and strafing. At the same time, dogfights were above us; our fighters tried to shoot down the enemy bombers before the ships far below were hit and sunk. Planes were mixing it up in a mid-air free-for-all with American and Japanese fighters chasing each other, guns chattering and engines whining.

Aircraft came screaming down, some missing a wing or a tail, leaving a white or black smear of smoke, dropping toward the sea. Other burning planes carved fiery trails until they exploded, scattering thousands of pieces onto the ocean below. A few parachutes blossomed in the midst of the battle, surrounded by burning planes and the ugly blotches of smoke from the ships' anti-aircraft fire. The enemy pilots always rode their planes down.

The air battle dropped lower and lower, until the few remaining Japanese planes headed north to reach their bases before their fuel ran out. Our fighters chased them until the Japs disappeared over the horizon.

As it turned out, we were told the raid was one of the biggest mounted by the Japanese during Watchtower (as the Guadalcanal operation was code-named). We paddled like demons back to shore, surviving, but aging twenty years in just a few hours. And no cigars.

We had to hide our raft in the jungle because everybody was looking for the two fools in the life-raft, joy-riding in the middle of an air raid.

A few days later, we were hanging out, watching a Navy PBY seaplane land and taxi up to one of the small wooden docks nearby. The crew had picked up a Japanese pilot from the drink, north of Savo Island. We walked over, cradling our weapons, and volunteered to take him off their hands, but they refused. The crew put him right back in the plane until the armed guards came to escort him to the prisoner compound.

As we walked down the beach, we saw a few natives and struck up a conversation. They had helped us haul supplies up to the front lines. One of our squad figured he would teach these natives a few card tricks; "Take a card and don't show it to me—"

Thinking he had pulled this off and looking very smug, he grinned from ear to ear. One of the natives asked if he could borrow the deck. The "genius" with the cards said, "Sure," with a silly smirk on his face.

Well, you should have seen the look on his face as this native started rapidly shuffling the cards and proceeded to perform all kinds of complicated card tricks. Come to find out, he was from New York City. He had been in the Merchant Marine and jumped ship in 1936.

Following that lesson in humility and with no duty at the moment, we decided to check out the stockade holding Japanese prisoners. They certainly didn't look like the fierce soldiers we had encountered. They weren't. Most were conscripted Korean laborers shipped into the 'Canal by the Japanese to work on the airfield. They looked more than happy to be our temporary guests.

Often after chow, we wandered over to the airfield to visit with some of the mechanics who were working on the aircraft near our positions. They were cannibalizing wrecked planes and using the parts on other planes. It was amazing to see how they could rebuild a plane that had been riddled with shrapnel and bullet holes, still able to limp back to the airfield. Some of them looked like so much torn scrap metal with wings. Several times, pilots landed barely alive, but they brought their planes back. Then the overworked mechanics started working their miracles. It takes all kinds of heroes to win a war.

I was stricken with malaria for the 12th time at the end of June. My food wouldn't stay down, and I started to lose weight. Nothing would stay down, not even water. The medic sent me down to the aid station. It was set up in a low area under some trees and was fairly dark inside the tent. I staggered into the tent where the doctor confirmed that I had malaria again.

"Yeah, it's malaria. Give him some Atabrine and send him back to his outfit."

After the two minute diagnosis, I was on my way back to my gun position. I was still as sick as a dog. I couldn't walk straight, had a high fever and was in serious trouble, although I was sure that I could "beat the bug" as I had done so many times before. I didn't realize that I was on the verge of total collapse.

Back at my gun position, I was sitting in my hole when my men brought back the medic. He sat down next to me and asked what I was doing back at the beach, instead of the aid station. I told him what had happened and what the doctor had said. The medic jumped up, cursing a blue streak, and picked me up with the help of a few of my squad. I was supported between them and helped over to the medic's jeep, where I collapsed into the front seat. One of my buddies jumped into the back and held me by the shoulders to keep me from falling out during the wild drive back to the aid station.

I remember little of the trip, except for the truly magnificent swearing of the medic, as he maneuvered around jeep-swallowing potholes and oncoming trucks. I was quite sure that he cursed continuously through the whole trip, without repeating himself once. Truly, a gifted man.

We pulled up to the aid station and the medic ran around to my side of the jeep. He helped me into the aid tent and sat me down on a stretcher; then he walked over and grabbed the doctor. They came over to me and the medic angrily gave the doctor the third degree.

"Why the hell was this man sent back to his unit in this condition?" he angrily asked the doctor.

"He's got malaria, just like thousands of other guys on this island. We don't have room for him, anyway," replied the doctor.

"Goddamn it! Didn't you even *look* at him? He's running a temperature of a hundred and three and he's yellow as all hell! Take him outside in the light and take a good look at him for Christ's sake!" The medic was obviously not going to back down.

The doctor grumbled at him but helped me up and took me outside. The medic stood there holding me up as the doctor examined me more thoroughly. He lifted my eyelids, opened my mouth, felt my forehead and squeezed my throat and neck. Then he took my pulse. I was shaky and didn't think I could stand up much longer. I was rapidly losing what little control I had left. The color drained from the doctor's face as he looked at the medic.

"You're right. This man is in bad shape. It looks like malaria and yellow jaundice. Take him back to the Battalion Aid Station right away."

Then he turned on his heel and walked back into the tent without another word.

The medic started swearing again as they put me back into the jeep. The next thing I knew, I was in a tent, drifting in and out of consciousness. I thought that I must be dying. My temperature was up to 104 degrees and I became incoherent. They transferred me to the Division Field Hospital. I heard a doctor asking why they had waited so long before sending me down to him. I had malaria, yellow jaundice, and hepatitis—to boot.

The next time I woke up, I was in a large tent with stretchers lining both sides, filled with sick and wounded GI's. I was so weak that I couldn't even raise my head. A medic came by and told me to roll out of my bunk into the slit trench a few feet away in case of an air raid. The sides of the tent were rolled up and tied. I turned my head to talk to the medic, but he was already gone. Then, I blacked out again.

I awoke to loud noises and what sounded like people yelling and the pounding of running feet. As my mind cleared a little, I realized that the loud noises were explosions nearby and there were people running all over the place. Somebody a few stretchers down from me was screaming hysterically, and men were hobbling by me trailing filthy, bloody bandages.

The same medic ran up and told me that a Japanese submarine was just offshore, throwing in shells from its deck gun. A shell exploded close by as he yelled at me to get into the slit trench before I got my head blown off. Strangely detached and unconcerned, I remember just staring at the poor medic like he was speaking another language. I was so sick I just didn't give a damn.

The medic ran back and simply tipped my stretcher over, dumping me on the ground, and I rolled into the muddy trench, filled with water. I sat up with my back against the trench wall, with stinking water up to my chest, and fuzzily watched the attack unfold, brilliant red and yellow flashes winking in the jungle. The colors began to twist around my head and the sounds blurred together into an unbearable roar. Then, oblivion.

Somebody was shaking me awake, but I wasn't in the trench anymore. I was back in my stretcher, covered with a blanket and a cool cloth on my head. I felt a little better, but my mouth felt like it was filled with cotton and my ears rang unbearably. A medic was gently shaking my shoulder and saying something I that couldn't understand. As my hearing cleared up, I heard him asking me if I thought I could drink something. He gave me some warm water, but I instantly threw it up all over myself.

I blacked out again. Snatches of things blurred by me.

More explosions and screaming, everything dark, a strange banging sound, like someone slamming a door…

POM-POM…POM…POM

Eerie, whistling sounds, getting louder and louder, ear-splitting detonations, brilliant flashes of yellow and red light, rapid rushes of hot air blowing through the tent, horrible screaming, people running back and forth, more whistling, getting closer and closer—then nothing.

I opened my eyes and it was light again. The area outside the tent was a mangled mess. There were craters everywhere, trees uprooted, vehicles smashed and roads destroyed. But the hospital was spared. Jagged tears carved the top of the tent that hadn't been there before. Shafts of watery sunlight wandered in and out the holes.

Only semi-conscious then, I remembered hearing the scream of falling bombs, the anti-aircraft guns blasting away, the tremendous explosions and the yelling of the patients, defenseless in their beds. I think one of those voices was mine.

A medic came over and sat down next to me for a few minutes.

"Aren't you from the 35th?" he asked quietly.

I simply nodded.

"Weren't you at the Battalion Aid Station a few days ago?"

I nodded again. Couldn't he see that I was in no shape to play twenty questions?

"You're one lucky guy. The Japs staged an air raid last night and the Battalion Aid Station took a direct hit. Everyone there was killed. I'm sorry to have to tell you this. I didn't know if you had friends there. They brought them in this morning. They're over there, if you need to check for anyone."

He pointed to a long row of bodies covered with canvas and blankets. I managed to stand up and stagger over to them, struggling to see if I knew anyone. There were a few men that I recognized from the rear echelon and the aid station, but most of them were too badly torn up. Their own mothers wouldn't have known who they were. Some would never be identified.

The exertion and shock was too much for me and I blacked out again.

The next thing I remember is waking up and hearing a soft, whirring sound. I was in a white metal bunk with a soft mattress and cool sheets! Delicious, chilly air was softly coursing over me, like a breeze straight from

Heaven itself. At first, I thought it was another dream, but I wasn't killing anyone and they weren't trying to kill me. Except for being so sick, I was enjoying this absolute miracle.

I was on a hospital ship sailing for New Caledonia. When we arrived, I was rushed to the 11th Army General Hospital. The female nurses there were absolutely wonderful. I hadn't been able to eat or drink anything for days and had become dehydrated. First they gave me a bath, only in bed. I received an intravenous drip and some hard candy. The nurses told me to let it dissolve in my mouth slowly. By this time, I was down to a mere 125 pounds and was so weak that I couldn't sit up. I got a glimpse of myself in a mirror and was shocked by the ravaged scarecrow staring back. With a scraggly beard and yellow complexion from the Atabrine tablets and yellow jaundice I had contracted, I looked like a damned corpse.

There were a lot of patients much worse off than I was. Some of these soldiers had large, open jungle ulcers on their chests or stomachs. A few had massive areas of skin missing from fungus infections. There was a device rigged up overhead that constantly dripped some kind of solution on the open wound. It looked like Chinese Water Torture.

At least once a day, one soldier would start screaming; *"Get this fucking thing off me, you sadistic bastards…Jesus Christ, I can't stand it!"*

Of course he had been tied down so he wouldn't tear down the drip. It was absolute hell for him. He was going insane from it. A nurse would come in and calm him down. They were all very kind and compassionate and would turn the drip off for a few hours to give the poor guy a break.

As sick as I was, I kept thanking the Good Lord for my deliverance from beyond Hell. They kept me in the hospital for two months, while I slowly recovered. Then I was sent to a "repple-depple" (replacement depot), waiting to be returned to my outfit on the 'Canal.

New Caledonia was a giant trans-shipment point, handling everything you could possibly imagine for supporting a full-scale war. Because of the shortage of men, they needed every pair of hands they could get. Instead of sending troops on their way, some would be kept there to work on projects. I was such a lucky candidate.

Every morning, after breakfast, we lined up. They gave us each a paper bag with a dry sandwich with some kind of unidentifiable filling in it, then loaded us on trucks and drove out into the mountains and valleys to huge supply dumps with all kinds of equipment stacked everywhere—like a gigantic, open-air warehouse. Some dumps had conveyors that were a mile long. We stood on both sides of the conveyor, one crew unloading the trucks as they arrived, while the next crew pushed the cases and boxes along the conveyor. Then we climbed up to the top of the piles of supplies and kept stacking all day long.

In this climate, men often got heat exhaustion. The dust started blowing and clogged eyes, ears and mouths. Late afternoon brought rain, and we'd be ankle deep in mud. This was just what I needed after recuperating for two months in the hospital. I lost all the weight I had carefully gained. We wound up stacking supplies for a solid month.

One morning some of us who had been in combat were told to shave and shower and report to supply. We drew new khaki uniforms and prepared to leave in an hour. I thought: "This is it, I'm out of here! I'm finally going home!"

We climbed on the truck and were driven to the hospital. It turned out that the First Lady, Eleanor Roosevelt, was touring bases in the Pacific and wanted to talk to soldiers that had been in close combat with the Japanese. She was very gracious and observant, as she gently held our hands and talked to each of us. She said that when she looked into our eyes, it broke her heart. Much later, when she returned to Washington, she made a statement that said she saw great sadness in our eyes and something else that was very unsettling. She also stated that "these soldiers should be debriefed before returning to civilian life." I agreed with her 100 percent. When we returned to camp that afternoon, we had to turn in our new uniforms for our old worn-out coveralls.

Our two hours of fame were now just a fine memory.

Finally, the powers that be decided to send me back to the 'Canal. I boarded a ship and headed back to my outfit. Two days out, I had a relapse of malaria and had to be put in the sick bay. The captain of the ship detoured and dropped me off at Espiritu Santo, code-named "Roses." They didn't want me on the island because they didn't have malaria there. I was kept under a mosquito net and strict quarantine, until arrangements could be made to send me back to the hospital in New Caledonia. By the time a plane flew me back, I had to be kept in an Acute Case Ward for several days and then in a General Ward for several more weeks.

While I was in the hospital, I heard that the 77th Division was nearby. That was the outfit my brother Frank was in. I hadn't seen him in over three years. They wouldn't let me out for just a day to look for him and I couldn't walk out because the only thing I had to wear was a hospital "Johnny" with no back to it. I probably wouldn't have gotten very far running around in a white nightshirt with my ass hanging out. I kept trying to get somebody to check around for Frank, but they all had a very heavy work load and couldn't spare the time.

Finally, when I was discharged from the hospital and sent to the replacement center, I was able to sneak out on a truck and travel around. I found some men from my brother's outfit but he had already been sent on ahead to hit one of the Gilbert Islands. I was so damned mad and depressed. I didn't know if I'd ever get the chance to see him again.

While at the replacement center I learned that Colonel Dalton had been admitted to the hospital. I visited him the next day and we spent time talking about peacetime Hawaii. I told him that his wife had sent me a Christmas package from Vermont as she did each year. He asked me if I was still writing each month to my mother and asked if I needed anything. After a while a nurse came in and told me I would have to leave in a few minutes and walked over to another patient. Colonel Dalton smiled as we shook hands but neither of us spoke. I nodded, smiled and walked out of the hospital.

After being discharged from the hospital, I was put on a ship that had only a few men on board and we sailed all alone with no escort, which I thought was a bit odd. I asked one of the sailors where we were headed and he told me Auckland, New Zealand. At first I couldn't believe it. In fact, I refused to believe it until we pulled into the harbor.

New Zealand

1943

New Caledonia

1944

CHAPTER 8

Deliverance

The first thing we saw upon entering the harbor was a beautiful city filled with sparkling white homes, automobiles, and thousands of people on bicycles. I couldn't believe my eyes. I'd finally reached heaven. It was the happiest day of my life. I had tears streaming down my face from conflicting emotions. I was so sad and elated at the same time. The terrible nightmare was loosening its grip—if only a little.

My outfit had gone on to Vella Lavella, north of the 'Canal, the next step up the Solomon Islands ladder. I had been in the hospital for months and missed the fighting on that island. More of my friends were killed there, fighting in the jungle. Survivors were relieved and sent to New Zealand for rest and recuperation. The constant combat had taken a terrible toll on all personnel.

When I returned to my outfit, everyone thought I was a ghost. They believed that I had been killed in the air-raid that wiped out the Battalion Aid Station on the 'Canal. As I had been evacuated the next morning, and nobody told them, they had assumed the worst. Many of the victims from that tragedy couldn't be identified. I finally assured them it was actually me by telling them several of my unfunny quips.

The first thing they did to welcome me back was to lead me over to the mess hall to show me the huge walk-in cooler. It was a wonderful thirty-six degrees inside. All kinds of fresh food was stocked there along with giant cans of fresh milk. I drank a large glass full of the first cold, fresh milk I'd had in two years. Then, I was given a large apple—fresh, cold and crisp—another dream came true.

Auckland was cool and dry. Because it became quite chilly in the morning and evening, I was issued woolen pants and jackets. The change in the climate was wonderful compared to the oppressive heat and humidity on the 'Canal. It seemed as though I had come up from an unforgiving Hell and found myself in Heaven.

The New Zealanders were fantastic hosts. We were able to go to the city of Auckland every day. We were amazed at how much the place and the people resembled home, very comforting and restful. We spent a lot of time taking in the sights: the trackless trolleys, theaters, restaurants, dance hall, beautiful parks and the ferry rides in the sparkling bay.

I was invited to Christmas dinner with a family named Peters. They had a special Christmas cake that had coins in it. I still have the one that was given to me, a 1941 half penny. I was honored with an invitation to attend the sulky races with Mrs. Peter's brother, his wife and their daughter Audrey. It was very gracious of them.

Audrey was kind enough to show me around the city. We saw all the sights and went to the movies. She told me that the young man she was engaged to was off somewhere fighting the Nazis, and she missed him very much. He was very fortunate to have such a wonderful girl to come home to.

Audrey asked me if I would like to visit her family in Wellington, where they lived. They were in Auckland visiting and had to go back home the next day. I asked for a week's leave and it was approved by Colonel Larson. I told Audrey that I would see her in a few days and would take a train to get there.

But the Army had other plans.

I received my leave papers signed by the Regimental CO and the next day I was in a jeep taking me to the train station. As we were passing the Orderly Room, our Company CO stepped out and stopped us.

He was six-foot-five, about 225 pounds and loved to intimidate enlisted men. He asked me where I thought I was going. I told him that I was going on leave to Wellington and had a pass signed by Colonel Larson. He told me what I could do with the pass and then told me to go back and grab my gear. I was shipping out in six hours.

I was heart-broken to be leaving so soon. It was only right for me to leave first because my outfit had continued fighting on Vella Lavella while I was in the hospital. Several of my buddies had been killed there. That evening I was on another transport heading back to New Caledonia for the fourth time during the war.

Some men jumped ship and went AWOL. When they were caught and returned to the Army, they were assigned to a Graves Registration Company. Their job was to recover dead soldiers from the battlefield.

A plot was marked off for the temporary graves and the holes were dug. Fingerprints would be taken from each body (if there were any), a dog tag wedged in the soldier's mouth for later identification. The body would be searched for papers or personal items, then wrapped and buried. Many of the dead were horribly mangled and badly decomposed from the heat. Often, bodies would fall apart as they were being handled by these unfortunate men—with predictable results. Quite a few of these soldiers wound up shooting themselves, pawns of war in a most tragic sense.

The ship docked at New Caledonia at the end of January 1944. We were to be the advance in setting a new base camp before the rest of the division arrived later on. Camp was located several miles from the capital city of Noumea, the only city on the island. We moved equipment up from the docks, set up squad tents, a completely new motor pool, kitchens, orderly rooms, showers, latrines and all the other things needed for the everyday operation of an entire Infantry Division.

I was assigned to the motor pool section as a driver. I drove every kind of vehicle except tanks and self-propelled guns, called M-7s. Jeeps, command cars, wreckers and all manner of trucks were used on a daily basis. We hauled supplies, delivered vehicles, towed guns and artillery to the ranges, drove officers from one meeting to another, hauled ammunition and transported GI's all over the island.

Once again, we had to subsist on dry rations, working eighteen-hour days setting up the massive camp area. We received a half-day off each week, a brutal schedule. The hills and mountains in the training area looked much like New England except for cross-country training areas, physical training fields, artillery and small-arms ranges and gigantic supply dumps spread all over hills and valleys for miles around. Much of our time each day was spent driving to and from these different points, stopping only to load and unload people or supplies. Most days we ate our cold rations in our vehicles.

We visited a Red Cross canteen in Noumea where we could get coffee and doughnuts and relax a little. Stopping at a local restaurant, we couldn't get anything to eat because the language was French and hospitality, nonexistent. Soon we learned that the population was Vichy French and had no love for the Allies. Perhaps they'd rather have been left to the tender mercies of the Japanese.

Our entire outfit arrived in February and we started receiving replacements. The reason the division was sent to New Caledonia was to regroup from being in combat for a year and to train replacements. If the Army wanted to get us away from the distractions in New Zealand (of which there were many, indeed) they picked the perfect place. There wasn't going to be anything to distract us in New Caledonia. The people hated us; all parties glad to be left alone.

Veterans of the 'Canal had been instructed not to get too graphic about the close combat we had seen there. The officers didn't want the replacements to think too much about it until the last few days on the troop ship.

Small unit tactics training began with map reading and using a compass while moving cross-country. The next phase involved putting on full field packs, drawing three days rations, then heading out into mountains we had never been to. We covered thirty-three miles a day and ended back at the camp.

The toughest going was the forest. We had people out in front of us for a hundred yards and had to keep checking the compass, even at night. Spotter planes constantly circled overhead to make sure we didn't cheat. On the last day of the exercise, we got off course.

While we were standing there, trying to figure out exactly where we were, we heard a 90mm anti-aircraft gun firing. Suddenly, there was an uncomfortably close air burst. We didn't know from which direction they would fire again. Shrapnel severed tree limbs and foliage. There were no radios or phones to notify the gun position of our situation. I told my outfit to follow me, and we ran as fast as we could, back the way we had come. Thank God, we had only entered the outer edge of a firing range that wasn't even on our map. After all the combat we had been through, it would have been a hell of a thing to be hit or killed by a practice shell from friendly guns.

Every day there were gun drills with our 37s. I was promoted to buck sergeant in April. I didn't want to be a squad leader any longer after the 'Canal. After losing men in combat, I replayed every decision and asking myself, "What if—?" When I was about to go in to combat again, and looked around at all the new men that I knew were going to be depending on me to get them through it safely, I knew it wasn't up to me. It was up to Fate, but that thought was hardly comforting.

In May, all the men who had fought on the 'Canal were issued their Combat Infantry Badges. We were all very proud to belong to such an elite group of American soldiers. Most of the people who served during wartime didn't fight at the front. A very small percentage actually saw "the sharp end," combat. Even fewer survived it. Most of them probably couldn't talk about it, when they got home.

Long hours were spent each day trying to get everyone to act, and react, as a team. We were getting to know each other and how to work together. Every man not only knew his job and responsibility but he also knew how to take over another man's job in an emergency—plenty of that in combat.

Additionally, everybody had to get used to his weapons and equipment. "Range time" was very important to familiarize the new men with the characteristics and shortcomings of hand-held weapons, both American and Japanese. Each man had to be proficient with a variety of infantry weapons. If your weapon was damaged or out of ammunition during a fight, you had to be ready to pick up something else and continue fighting. Whether it was a rifle, pistol, shotgun or machine gun, weapons training could save lives; the M-1 Garand and M-1 Carbine were good examples.

The gas-operated Garand, which was unquestionably one of the best infantry weapons of the war, was a huge improvement over the old, bolt-action '03 Springfield that was in circulation before the opening of hostilities. It utilized a metal clip with eight rounds; after the last round was fired, the clip ejected through the top of the weapon with a loud *"PING!"* That was your signal that the rifle was empty—and time to push in another clip. The rifle fired as quickly as the trigger was squeezed. Unlike a Tommy gun or a BAR, which you had to fight to keep on target, the Garand was steady, fast and accurate. Of course, as with any weapon, you had to keep it clean; you depended on it to save your life.

On the 'Canal, we had discovered that, initially, the Japanese weren't used to facing the new weapon. Most of the rifles that the Marines were issued were the old Springfields; with their slow rate of fire, the Japanese would find it easier to assault a position. However, the first Garands were carried into combat on a large scale when Army units landed to reinforce the Marines. (It seemed that the Marines were always at the very end of the supply chain. They were supplied by the Navy and complained that they usually got what was left after everything else was handed out. The saying went thus: the Army got the artillery, the Navy got the chow, and the "Corps got the Shaft.").

We were in perimeter positions, dug-in with two-man foxholes, the proverbial "buddy system." At night, usually one man tried to catch a little sack time while the other man stood watch: two hours on, two hours off, and so on. When there was movement in the jungle or suspicion that we were going to be hit, both men were awake and on alert. We rarely saw the Japs creeping up on us. They would spend half the night crawling into position, just to pinpoint our foxholes before they attacked. By then, however, they would be so close that we had no chance to kill them all, and some ran right through our perimeter into the rear areas. And the night would simply swallow them up.

With two Garand rifles in each hole, there was the potential for a lot of lead going out into the jungle at a rapid rate. The problem was, if both men fired simultaneously, they would often run out of ammo at about the same time. The Japs began to count the shots from the hole from their positions twenty to thirty feet away. Hearing the "ping," they knew they had just enough time to jump up and charge across the last few yards to get at us with the bayonet before we could reload new clips.

After we had been attacked and infiltrated several times, we devised a little trick.

In each hole, one man would rapid-fire a full clip as fast as he could. His buddy would load a full clip and hold his fire. As soon as the empty clips ejected, the Japs would assume that all the weapons were empty and jump up and charge. The rest of us would open aimed fire as soon as the enemy was up and running toward us. The shocked Japanese would be shot in droves, as the massed fire from all those rifles cut them down within a few seconds. Then, the first group, already reloaded, would shoot the few Japanese that tried to get back to the jungle.

This worked for a short time until the enemy figured out what was happening. Then, they changed their tactics. Also, at times there was no chance to experiment. Every man had to fire as fast as he could to keep from being overrun. Often, the Japanese would jump up out of the dark and be on us before we could even fire. Most men kept a dagger, machete or Bowie knife at hand, just in case. As excellent as the Garand was, the close fighting in the jungle sometimes eliminated a rifle as an effective weapon unless it was utilized as a club.

The main advantage of the M-1 Carbine was its smaller size and reduced weight. Many men took the carbine when going out on patrol. Quite a few officers carried them, early on. After snipers began picking off men carrying carbines, a sidearm or maps, believing that they had to be officers, (nobody wore any insignia of rank on their uniform or helmet as they did in Europe), a wild scramble for Garand rifles ensued.

The real problem with the carbine was its limited "stopping power."

One day, on the 'Canal, we had been waiting on the side of a narrow jungle trail, while the point scouted ahead of us. As always, we were spread out at intervals with weapons at the ready.

Suddenly, a Japanese soldier armed with only a saber, stepped from the thick jungle onto the trail. Before anyone could react, he raised it over his head and severed the left arm of the GI nearest to him. As he lunged for another man, he was shot four times in the body at point blank range with a carbine, but he kept on raising his saber for another blow. At that moment, he was shot with one bullet from a Garand. That one round knocked him backwards, causing him to drop his weapon. Before he fell to the ground, he was hit twice more, killing him instantly. Then, a sergeant stepped up and riddled his body with a Tommy gun.

As the grievously wounded GI was taken back down the trail, the Jap's body was searched and then dragged into the jungle. He had been shot four times in the chest with a carbine from a few feet away and it hadn't slowed him down. One shot from the Garand stopped him in his tracks. It didn't take long for these deadly lessons to "make the rounds." Most of them had been learned at the cost of men's lives.

We also could have used a great deal more practice firing live rounds on moving targets with our 37s. Each man in an anti-tank squad was allowed to fire only three rounds at a target on the firing range. It usually took that many simply to determine the range, never mind hit the target with any speed. The most difficult task was judging distances over water or in the mountainous ravines and valleys.

Our 37s were not powerful enough to knock out some Jap tanks, as flimsy as their armor was. We were supposed to receive new, more powerful 57mm anti-tank guns, but never did. Regular combat boots were never issued to us during the entire war. We had to wear regular GI shoes and canvas leggings.

In the jungle, the hooks on the leggings would catch on vines, causing men to fall, alerting the Japanese to our presence. You could say that men were killed because of those damned leggings: the filthy water from the swamps soaked the canvas and caused leg scratches to get infected, nearly as dangerous as a wound. One could very easily wind up with a tag on your big toe from either.

When we went into the 'Canal, we were wearing one piece coveralls. When nature called, you had to strip off all your equipment and practically get undressed, which can get pretty hairy at times. And there was really a problem when most of us had dysentery. Some men simply cut a slit in the seat of their coveralls to facilitate nature's call.

At times we were issued a combat pack, containing three pairs of socks and underwear, a shelter-half with pegs, toilet articles, a blanket, three days of rations, cigarettes, matches and a poncho for rain gear. In addition, we had our steel helmet, weapon, cartridge belt, holding eighty rounds of copper jacketed ammunition, canteen, first aid kit, bayonet, Dagger with brass knuckles, binoculars, compass, map, at least two hand grenades and a pouch.

Of course, I always carried my "God of Happiness." He was still brimming with good luck, (I hoped). During the action on the 'Canal, he had been lying in the bottom of my pack, safely tucked away over my spine. Japanese bullets had torn through everything in their path until they hit him. They were deflected just enough to rip through my canteen on my hip instead of shredding my back. I never went into combat after that, without rubbing his belly for luck—or what I had of it coming.

After loading up with everything we needed, our officers briefed us on our next odyssey: a one hundred mile forced march with full field gear. We were to strike out on a training mission and cover over thirty-three miles a day for the next three days. We squad leaders were given maps and that was it. We were told to get going immediately and if anybody dropped out, they were to be left where they fell. We had to be back at camp no later than 6pm. in three days, or we would have to do it over again until we got it right.

I knew that the wizards who had dreamed up this exercise had never done this kind of field training before, and they weren't going to go through it with us this time, either. They hadn't been over the terrain we had to march through and had no idea where the obstacles were or anything else. There had been no direct recon of the area. We had been handed a map and turned loose with a few thinly veiled threats about the punishment for failure; the officers went back to their tent for a stiff drink and a cigar.

Nonetheless, we jumped to it and made it look like we were full of piss and vinegar. As we passed the Regimental CP, we were clicking along at one hundred and eighty steps a minute, singing that stupid "99 bottles of beer" song. (I still hate it). We marched for fifty minutes, rested for ten and then changed to route step. There was to be no talking in the ranks. Talking slowed down the pace and caused people to get short of breath. We didn't want anybody to drop out.

This was a basic "forced march," requiring a great deal of discipline to complete. It is excellent training if done properly. It has been used down through military history, especially by the armies of the Emperor Napoleon. On the 'Canal we had to walk everywhere we went, even when we could barely stand and had to lean on each other to keep going.

We had been trying to impress this on the new men so they would realize that it wasn't a lark, but serious business. There was an actual purpose for all this activity, it wasn't simply make-work. We had to keep going for twelve hours and everybody's ass was dragging. There were to be no fires or smoking after sunset. We had been off the road for hours and were now on a steep slope and still climbing.

Too tired to go any further, we called it a day. Guards were posted, everybody ate their rations, loosened their shoe laces and fell asleep on the rocky ground with shoes on. During combat, shoes were never taken off for more than a few minutes.

About two in the morning, it began pouring rain. We got up, put on our ponchos and lay back down in the water and slept some more. At five o'clock, everybody got up and prepared for the day's march. We were to be ready to move out on the next leg at six o'clock, sharp. Many men had terrible blisters needing treatment and some had cramped muscles; a few were just too tired from lack of sleep. At six o'clock, we moved out on schedule, just as the ubiquitous spotter plane flew over us at low level to check our progress and position—so far, so good.

The sun came out, drying us off after our soggy night bivouac. We couldn't keep up our pace because we were forced to use dead reckoning for our Direction of March. There were no more roads, just forests. We pressed on and hoped for the best. About two o'clock in the afternoon, our lieutenant told me to take one man and scout our right flank. I picked out Private Hanks and we headed out about a mile to see what was around the area.

About a half-mile out, we saw a house out in the middle of nowhere. It was the only structure we had seen since we began the march. There was no road or path leading up to it and it looked deserted. As we stood there trying to figure out what it was doing there, a voice startled us from behind.

"Hello!" shouted the voice.

We both whipped around in shock; we hadn't heard anybody come up on us. There stood a friendly old gentleman wearing Tyrolian shorts and blouse. He stood there with his thumbs in his suspenders, looking at us with a big smile on his face. We both shook hands with him and apologized for being on his property. I described our predicament to him. After I showed him the map, he shook his head and told me that it was all wrong. The whole thing was screwed up.

"If you move two miles west, you will find a logging road that will lead you to a main road. You will be able to make up the time you lost in the forest and won't have to take so many compass readings. Farther down, the main road also joins the road to your camp about thirty-five miles from here."

What a break! I liked to think that my little "God of Happiness" I carried in my pack had something to do with this unexpected good fortune. After thanking the old man profusely, we back-tracked to our outfit and set out to find the logging road. We reached the main road about eight o'clock that night after fourteen grueling hours. But we were on schedule and on course, thanks to a lucky happenstance.

Some of our people were really hurting with bleeding blisters, exhaustion and severe leg cramps. Some of these kids were just out of high school and had never walked over a mile or two before being drafted. But for their sake and ours, they were going to have to tough it out, even if we had to drag them back by their pack straps. It was up to us to encourage them and get them to believe in themselves, either gently or brutally, whichever was necessary.

At least the ground was drier and softer for our night bivouac than the previous night. We "older guys," 21 or 22, pulled guard duty while the tenderfeet recuperated. The next day was going to be the worst—but we didn't tell them that. After a long night, we roused everybody at 5am and I gave them a little speech to prepare for the day ahead.

"We started out with thirty-one men and we will finish with thirty-one. I'll be goddamned if anybody will drop out. That will *not* happen. *Nobody* gets left behind. When you people are in combat, *nobody* gets left behind, *nobody*. You and your buddies need to rely on each other to make it through."

I didn't think everybody believed this but it had to be said in a forceful tone of voice to keep up everyone's spirits.

We moved out at 6am sharp, some of us carrying two rifles and a few shouldering two packs, but there were thirty-one pairs of feet hitting the pavement and we were really tooling along. After ten miles, we began to have trouble. Our medic kept fixing bloody feet and strapping sore ankles. The heat of the day was building up, and we were all low on water. We had to take twenty minute breaks instead of ten.

Some of the rugged guys, mostly veterans, wanted to keep moving, as our orders called for us to leave the stragglers behind, but we continued loading the stragglers' equipment on to the tougher guys and kept moving. We were disobeying orders by not leaving the stragglers behind—but it was our team and we weren't going to leave anybody. We didn't ever do it in combat and we damned sure weren't going to do it here. What kind of example would that be? If we didn't support our people in training, how would they know we would support them when they were fighting for their lives against the Japanese? If we didn't look after each other everywhere, we might never survive in combat anywhere.

The men complained that we weren't going to make it back in time, their feet hurt, their equipment was too heavy—and what was the point anyway? We finally stopped at 4pm and formed everyone up in a big circle and read them the riot act.

"When we started, we were a team. As a team, we will operate as a team and return as a team, not like a bunch of goddamned civilians on a picnic! I don't give a rat's ass if we are not back on time, only that we march back in as a team! All thirty-one of us! Now you have one hour to rest, get your *shit* together and say a prayer. We have ten more miles to go and everyone will keep moving one foot in front of the other, until we reach camp! Am I *clear?*"

One hour later, we moved out and started to sing every song we could remember and then began to make up a few. We kept walking—more slowly, as it got dark. At around eight o'clock, a truck convoy came up the road but they were headed the wrong way. Even if they had been headed in our direction, we wouldn't be allowed to hitch a ride on them. We had to complete the whole one hundred miles on foot.

At ten o'clock, we saw the lights of the camp in the distance. We stopped to allow men to take back their rifles, adjusted all our equipment, and marched into camp as smartly as we could. Once inside, we marched to our area, dismissed the men and everyone collapsed on his bunk. The next day was supposed to be a day off, but the lieutenant and noncoms had to attend a critique at the Company CP.

Our illustrious CO complained that we were late and the spotter plane had reported us a half mile off course, two days in a row. I wanted to tell him that one of the citizens of the island didn't think the map we had was worth the "shit paper" it was printed on and if we hadn't met him, we would still be out in the boonies, like a few other teams that hadn't returned yet. But as they say, don't argue with authority because you can't win. Just spit when you get outside.

Our time was getting closer, and we would soon be moving out. We were given more shots against diseases we would be coming in contact with in our upcoming battles—two shots a day for three days. One poor guy got his first inoculation and dropped stone dead from an embolism. He never even got into combat. Of course, everyone was on edge after that, so we kept people occupied before shipping out. We might die in combat, from "friendly fire," enemy action or simply a shot of vaccine. It didn't pay to dwell on it. Fate knew. That was it.

Not all the days and nights on New Caledonia were tough. Some days, we had to spend only the morning hours doing gun drills; then we went down to the river to clean off the road grime from the 37s and ourselves.

After the work was finished, we played basketball or card games, wrote letters or just sat around drinking beer.

The beer was from Australia and came in quart bottles. It tasted all right, but was as warm as ant piss. I never played cards, because some of our brethren were dyed-in-the-wool gamblers—absolutely incorrigible. If there was a card game within a five mile radius, they would somehow get in on it. And they always won—always. There was a large movie screen nearby, but the movies weren't very good.

Once a month, names were drawn out of a helmet to see who would go home. To be eligible, you had to have at least ninety points. Some of us had over twice that amount and felt that the men with the most points should be the ones to go home first. That sounded fair to us. But the Brass didn't want combat experienced noncoms to leave, and possibly our names were never put into the steel pot.

One day, we had to get up in the dark, eat breakfast and load onto deuce-and-a-half trucks. We drove for three hours over bumpy, dusty, mountain roads to Tontuta airfield. We were joined by the rest of the division, approximately sixteen thousand men. We all lined up on both sides of the runway. By the time we moved into position, it was one o'clock and the sun was brutal, reflecting off the runway and beating down unmercifully. Men began to drop like flies, but no one otherwise moved.

At three o'clock, a shiny R4-D (the Navy version of the DC-3) cargo plane landed, some Brass dismounted and walked to a reviewing stand. My internal dialogue began, "This is all very rah, rah—"

Admiral Halsey or Nimitz—I don't remember which—contributed to the round of long-winded speeches. "You men will go down in *history*. You will march down the streets of *Tokyo* to final victory—"

As the Admiral finished, we could only imagine a noise, there being none.

Suddenly, one of the sixteen thousand soldiers yelled out, loudly as he could.

"Fuck Tokyo! Send me home!"

Right to the point; my internal dialogue was quite satisfied to stop with that.

We didn't arrive back at camp until almost dark. After Spam and powdered eggs for supper, we dropped onto our bunks, totally exhausted and thoroughly pissed off for having to go through such a grueling day just to hear some Admiral give us a half-assed pep talk. Many of us had already been in combat and didn't need somebody from the Navy giving us morale speeches about defeating the Japanese. If he wanted to ride a white horse through Tokyo some day to prove a point, let him. But we didn't give a shit about what was going to happen *after* the Japs surrendered—as if they ever would surrender. In combat, we were only concerned with surviving one hour at a time. Screw the rest of it. Let the Brass make flowery speeches to the people back home.

We didn't need it, but it probably helped us let off steam.

A few weeks later, we went through the same routine all over again, only this time, it was to see Bob Hope and his bevy of babes. He sure made a huge difference for the GI's in the Pacific and the rest of the world; the troupe helped us forget our misery for a few hours—just the tonic for thousands of homesick men. Was it our imagination that Bob Hope, with his big smile also sported maybe—a halo?

Scuttlebutt flew thick and fast about our destination. No one would know until we were actually on the transports, a few days from the landing. Though we didn't know, we figured that Tokyo Rose did. She would broadcast on the radio every night trying to break our morale, but it backfired, giving us opportunities for mirth. The latest music from the States would arrive over the air, songs that we couldn't even hear from our own side.

One of her recurring, purring themes began, "What is your sweetheart back home doing tonight? She is so far away. I'll bet she is sitting under the apple tree with your best friend, right now."

She would claim that the Glorious Forces of the Greater East Asia Co-Prosperity Sphere had annihilated the U.S. Forces on the island of Guadalcanal or New Georgia or some other island. Numbers of our ships sunk, planes shot down and soldiers killed were so far off the mark, that they brought hoots of derision and gales of laughter from all within earshot. Her stories would be embellished and spread throughout the ship.

"Didn't you hear? We were all wiped out months ago! I'm gonna write my Congressman and get my discharge. If I'm already dead, I want to be sent home."

So much for psychological warfare. Our next voyage began when we sailed, still destination unknown, on December 17, 1944. We embarked on the transports and began the long voyage to our next meeting with the enemy. All we knew was that we were heading north, back into combat. We tried to keep occupied by discussing tactics, telling stories, (some much taller than others), maintaining our equipment, or when our time on deck permitted, calisthenics or target practice and gun drill. Getting used to the rolling of the ship in the first few days was a little tricky for some of the men, resulting in many unclaimed (or reclaimed) meals.

The long days and nights were harder, though. Every man spent his time in his own way. A few had books or newspapers sent from home or purchased when we were in New Zealand. The dog-eared copies, usually missing their covers from use, were passed along from man to man. Veterans with nerves stretched thin, woke up at night screaming. I was revisited by the enemy from the 'Canal, as I tossed and sweated through the interminable nighttimes:

Visions of hundreds of screaming Japs attacking out of the wet, steaming jungle, long bayonets glinting like ice shards in the eerie moonlight, charging at us, as the last bullet leaves the smoking barrel of our machine gun…grenades exploding all around us…Jap officers waving long, razor-sharp sabers… tattered GI's rising out of their stinking, mud-filled holes…attackers impaled on bloody bayonets, clubbed to death with rifle butts, hacked apart with machetes and axes, torn to death with bare hands…

Still coming…

Frenzied fighting flowing around knots of struggling men, fighting for their lives…metallic click as a pin is pulled on a grenade…charging handle flying off as it's tossed…seemingly in slow motion…sailing through the air, wobbling, lands in the midst of the enemy, a brilliant, thunderous flash…bodies ripping apart…tangled, blood-spouting heaps…again…again…again…grenades flashing… men screaming…

Still coming…

Grenades, gone…rifle ammo, gone…Colts, empty…one bullet left, won't be taken alive…buddy looks into my eyes…we scramble from the hole, knives drawn…those long, bloody bayonets glinting like red, dripping ice shards in the flare light…

Still coming…

After weeks at sea, we learned where we would land in the Philippines, an island called Luzon. We were returning after three long years of brutal occupation by the Japs. We were one step closer to going home—but how long would it take?

Passing the island of Leyte, I knew that our troops were still fighting there, and my brother Frank, with them. I had missed him in New Caledonia the previous year while in the hospital. He was now twenty three. I hadn't seen him in three years. My brother Paul was fighting the Germans. I hadn't seen him in four years. I thought about them both and said a silent prayer for their safe return home.

I would never see Paul again.

Hundreds of ships composed our invasion convoy, stretching out for miles in every direction. The seas were so rough that the battleships almost disappeared in the troughs of enormous waves and the tiny destroyers would roll way over to one side, plunging bow-first into the maelstrom. After what seemed an eternity, they struggled back up to the crest of the next wave and start down the other side, their exposed screws churning the air and spewing spray until they re-submerged again.

Many of our troops were violently seasick and would be in terrible shape for the landing. As we approached the Mindoro Straits, darkness fell. We learned that the channel itself was only twenty miles wide, and the enemy supposedly had large guns emplaced on both shores. If they detected us, we faced disaster. Entering the China Sea, the storm played havoc with our convoy, and I thought our ship would break up in the heavy seas, but we made it through safely.

Approaching Lingayen Gulf on Luzon, the same beaches where the Japanese had invaded the island in 1942, the weather calmed and the seas moderated.

The Lord had definitely watched over us, but days of judgment waited.

Luzon
Philippine Islands
1945

CHAPTER 9

Warriors Go Forth…

As dawn broke, the black shapes of hundreds of ships around us slowly became sharper and more distinct. Battleships and cruisers, their main batteries searching out the ominous, darkened land mass in the distance, opened fire guided by unseen spotter planes acting as forward observers. The massive guns, belching enormous clouds of smoke, shook the surrounding vessels with their concussion. Shells, sounding like giant freight trains, streaked over the circling landing craft before exploding on targets inland.

Destroyers scurried about at high speed, laying a protective smoke screen around the ships, the thick, oily gray fog billowing from smoke generators on their fantails. As they passed alongside our transport, we could see the gun crews nervously scanning the skies overhead for enemy aircraft.

Without warning nearby warships opened fire at the sound of a diving plane. The gunners could only fire blindly in the smoke, yet the kamikazes could see the masts of the warships protruding through the murk, diving on them with deadly accuracy. Suicide planes had already taken a toll of our ships and men around Leyte, and no end in sight. We could see the sleek gray shapes of destroyers circling around us, guns blinking and flashing in the smoke, crackling like strings of monstrous fireworks.

Our deck officer motioned for us to grab our weapons and stand near the railing to disembark. Men arranged their gear before climbing down the cargo net into the waiting landing craft in a flurry of activity. I tightened my equipment, checked my weapons, slung my Garand over my shoulder and adjusted my helmet and pack. Soon we were all waiting nervously to go over the side to take our place in the ever-changing circle of waiting landing craft.

Veterans stood silently waiting, occasionally making a comment to a buddy, checking equipment or chain-smoking stale cigarettes. The replacements, though well-trained and coached by the veterans, had no combat experience to fall back on while the interminable waiting preyed on their nerves. Surrounded by hundreds of men, each was alone with his own thoughts and fears. The few of us who had already experienced our baptism of fire had mixed emotion as we stood waiting to disembark into the maelstrom of fire once again. I had a tight feeling in my guts. The trembling returned as the main batteries on a nearby battleship cut loose, shaking our transport.

We watched the new men for signs of uncontrollable fear. A few didn't look good, but some soothing words calmed them enough so they were able to make it over the side into the landing craft. We didn't tell them that the deck officer had orders to shoot any man that froze on the nets. I had already gone through that. Everything had to keep moving.

Men shuffled nervously about on the deck, slippery with puddles of greasy vomit. The rolling of the ship and the ever-present fear worked differently on each man. Some were violently sick and others simply waited at the rail with tight, blank faces.

Flashbacks of combat in the Gifu, on the 'Canal, flooded my mind.

The cold, metallic, coppery taste in my mouth returned.

The drifting flares reflecting on Japanese bayonets.

The screaming wounded.

The dead.

The wet, burrowing maggots.

I could still smell it.

The hair on the back of my neck stiffened. I lifted a damp cigarette to my mouth, took a last draw and dropped it to the deck, crushing it against the steel with my shoe. I wondered if I had the guts to go in and do it all over again. My mind said; "Yes, you can," but my legs needed convincing. The terrors and pain were still fresh, even after all the months that had passed since I had left the Island.

When the time came, we would all go in where our guardian angels would have their work cut out for them.

As clouds of rolling smoke enveloped the ship, shouts echoed along the lines of waiting men.

"Okay, let's go!"

"Move out!"

Ghostly figures, bent over with the weight of weapons and equipment, disappeared over the railing of the ship in a steady stream as shouting noncoms kept up a salty banter at the rail. Soon it was my turn as endless numbers of men lowered themselves into the landing craft to begin the long journey to shore.

I swung my legs over the railing, catching my first real glimpse of the rolling LCM, (a landing craft used for transporting small vehicles, such as a jeep or truck, to the beaches), far below. It had already been combat-loaded with our truck, loaded with rations, gas and ammo with our anti-tank gun hitched to the back.

Lowering myself down the salt-encrusted rope cargo net, I tried to keep ahead of the man above, so that he wouldn't step on my hands as he descended. The net shook and swayed with the movement of the ship, threatening to throw us off.

Nearing the point where I had to jump into the landing craft, I timed the maximum rise of the waves and dropped into the bottom of the craft unsteadily, but safely. I quickly moved to the opposite side of the landing craft and climbed into the truck next to the driver, trying to keep my balance against the heaving South China Sea beneath us.

I signaled to the coxswain that we were all aboard and he gunned the engines, pulling us away from the relative safety of the anchored transport into the "follow-the-leader" circling of tiny craft. We bounced and rolled in an ever-widening ring until the landing craft were all in line, then broke out to head for the distant beach.

The noise became an appalling, throbbing roar above the sound of the straining engines of our landing craft. Destroyers were firing as they swept by at high speed, their gun turrets turning as they blasted away at the attacking Jap planes overhead. Huge nearby warships shook from the concussion of their massive main batteries. Clouds of cordite smoke enveloped the ships as their weapons fired on targets far inland.

Enemy planes roared by at low level trying to hit the transports and warships, their laboring engines distinct above the noise of the firing. Our carrier aircraft, dodging and weaving, braved the exploding anti-aircraft shells of our ships as they chased the Japanese, machine guns spitting streams of tracers. The screaming sound of the planes, combined with the terrific din of the ships firing and bombs exploding, numbed my senses.

While I looked around at the violent panorama unfolding around us, two bombs straddled our landing craft, exploding close alongside. The enormous waterspouts from the explosions rained down on us, shrapnel splitting the air with a whizzing sound as the craft was lifted bodily out of the water, crashing back down with a sickening thud.

The only casualty was the hull of the landing craft, where patches of light shone through newly-perforated steel. The razor-edged flying steel had sliced the thin sides of the craft like a hot knife through butter. Amazingly, nobody was hit. We all looked at each other with the same "that was too close" look and then proceeded to check our vehicle, gun and equipment for damage.

Slowly drawing nearer to the beach, we noticed that the smoke screen had dissipated. We began to scan the skies for planes. Because of the noise around us earlier, we hadn't heard the Japanese bomber that had nearly gotten us before we had fired a shot. Not that we had the combined firepower to shoot down a fast-moving plane, but at least we might be able to take evasive action if we could see them coming.

Suddenly, our landing craft slid to a halt short of the beach.

We had run aground on a sand bar and were stuck fast. The coxswain tried reversing the engines. Sandy water spewed out from the stern as he tried to free us before we became a target for more Jap bombs or artillery shells from a sharp-eyed Japanese artillery spotter ashore. Short of pushing the truck off the ramp to lighten our load or swimming ashore without our weapons, we were running short of options.

We were unexpectedly delivered from our dilemma by the hair-raising sight of an enormous LST (Landing Ship Tank) bearing down on us from the direction of the convoy. At full speed and many times our size, we were really in a bind now. With no place to go, we shouted at the coxswain to do something—anything—but to get us the hell out of there. Of course, there was nothing he could do, except watch the LST get closer and closer. At the last possible second, it veered to port, striking us a glancing blow, sweeping past at full speed. All of us were thrown off our feet.

Regaining my balance, I stared up at the faces looking down at us from the LST's railing far above, and feebly waved as they continued on their way to the nearby beach. With their shove, we floated off the sand bar and made our way in to the beach.

The ramp lowered and we drove our truck and gun off onto dry land, at last. Looking up the beach about 300 yards, I saw the LST that had side-swiped us take several direct hits from a hidden enemy gun, just after opening its bow doors. Huge explosions ripped its deck and hull as ammunition and gasoline cooked off from direct hits. It was engulfed in flames and burning along its entire length in minutes.

Men jumped over the side, were blown apart by the secondary explosions or were driven off by the flames and shrapnel. I signaled to the driver to move on, as there wasn't anything that we could do to help. We pulled off the beach and headed inland towards our assembly area, San Jacinto.

After driving about 100 yards off the beach area, we were flagged down by the Beach Master. He told me to take half of my squad back to the beach and help the shore parties unload the landing craft. Leaving some of my men with the vehicle, equipment and anti-tank gun, we trudged back to the landing area and joined the long, double daisy-chains of soldiers unloading ammunition and supplies from the waiting DUKWs (water borne trucks), LCMs and other landing craft.

Enormous stacks of equipment, hundreds of trucks, jeeps, wreckers, tanks, bulldozers, cranes, self-propelled M-7s, artillery and weapons of all kinds jammed the beachhead for a thousand yards. We stacked cases of grenades, rations, machine gun, mortar and rifle ammunition, water cans, artillery shells, litters and medical supplies away from the water line, where they could be picked up by the supply units and taken to the front lines just a few miles away.

After several hours, we were told to board a landing craft heading out to an ammunition ship to help the crew load small arms and mortar ammo for a return run to the beach. The line companies were using it at such a terrific rate that it couldn't be unloaded fast enough.

I followed my men onto the LCM; the ramp was raised and we backed away from the beach, swinging slowly against the surging tide. When the coxswain had enough maneuvering room, he steered towards the convoy and proceeded to his assigned position where a Liberty ship swung at anchor.

The seas became much rougher as we approached the anchored ships about two miles from shore. As we pulled alongside the ammunition ship, it was rolling heavily. The ship's captain had anchored parallel to the beach instead of perpendicular to it, causing the vessel to roll from side to side. As the cargo nets were loaded in the hold, they would swing violently, hitting the inside of the hull, endangering everyone in the hold and damaging the cases of ammunition.

The working parties tried to convince the captain of the ship to move it slightly, to reduce the rolling and the danger of injury from the swinging nets of ammunition, but he would hear none of it. The loading continued at a feverish pace, with crews of men working on the swinging nets and the rest scanning the water for Japanese suicide boats.

These small, fast, wooden suicide boats were manned by Japanese armed with pole charges or bombs. They would swing in close to a ship and either strike the hull with a pole charge or blow themselves up with explosives in an attempt to sink the ship before it could be unloaded.

For two hours, my men and I loaded ammunition into the nets in the ship's hold. We were then ordered out on deck, because the swinging nets became too dangerous. I didn't take much notice of a stack of huge hatch covers, each weighing several tons that had been positioned by the ship's crew to one side of the open main cargo hold. As the ammunition was lifted out of the cavernous hold, the steel hatch covers had to be stacked to one side, allowing the crew to use their winches to swing the loaded nets up and over the side of the ship. I didn't notice that they hadn't been secured to the deck, as they should have been.

While I was standing at the railing, watching for suicide boats, the ship rolled heavily causing the top hatch cover to slide off the stack and across the deck toward me. In seconds, it slid into the ship's side, twisting my legs, pinning me against the steel railing. The hatch cover hit the ship's side at a slight angle, slamming into the steel railing brace welded to the deck, bending it in against the hull. Only the brace itself saved my legs from being totally crushed.

In the few seconds it took for the accident to occur, the men near me, having barely jumped clear, rushed forward to help me. They couldn't move the cover without the use of a crane, already being used to swing out another load of shells over the side. As they frantically tried to free me, the ship rolled in the opposite direction, causing the hatch cover to slide away from me, enabling them to quickly pull me to safety. No sooner had they dragged me away, than the ship rolled back again, sending the careening cover smashing into the side of the ship where I had been standing.

I was laid out on the deck while my men checked my legs. They assured me that I was all right. I had lost the feeling in both legs and I could see that my coveralls were torn to pieces, although there wasn't much blood. I tried to stand or at least look at my damaged legs to see for myself what was going on, but they wouldn't let me. I was covered with someone's shirt and then with a blanket brought up from below.

Shortly, another GI was carried over from up forward with his right foot crushed. He was in shock, clenching his hands, his eyes closed. He had been standing at the railing up forward when the same thing happened to him. The difference was that he was standing at a spot with no brace to stop the hatch from sliding into him.

One of my men came back and told me that a corpsman was being sent from a nearby ship to treat us, and we would be sent to a hospital ship. I was handed a pack of sweat-stained, crumpled cigarettes, reassured I would soon be back with my squad, and left alone with my injured companion. I lit a smoke and tried to keep from looking under the blanket at my mangled knee which was had started to bleed and hurt like the devil. The skin had been completely torn off, and the kneecap was partially exposed. The sliding hatch had also twisted and badly bruised both legs from knees to ankles.

After what seemed like hours, a Navy corpsman climbed over the railing near us and ran over, his medical bags slapping against his side. He knelt down beside me, lifted the blanket, his face showing concern, and quickly checked my injuries. He quickly tied a compress bandage around my knee. After wrapping the other GI's foot, the corpsman ran up forward and disappeared around the corner of the superstructure.

A short time later, he returned, gave us both a shot for the pain and re-bandaged both of us. Again, he left for a while, returning with several soldiers carrying Bailey Baskets, (metal litters used to transfer wounded from ships) and blankets. They gently lifted us into the baskets, covered us with blankets and strapped us in so that we couldn't move.

I was told that the corpsman had gone to the captain and asked him to turn the ship so that we could be safely transferred to the launch waiting to take us to the hospital ship. The captain told him to "go to hell." Nobody was going to tell him how to run his ship—especially some lowly corpsman. The corpsman went to the radio room, called the Command ship and talked to them about the situation. The captain of our ship was called to the radio and told in no uncertain terms that he was to "move his goddamned ship or lose it on the spot!"

He moved it.

I was brought to the railing, where long ropes were tied to the Bailey Basket. I was lowered slowly over the side until I was suspended about eight feet above the launch. I felt completely helpless, tied in and unable to save myself if I were dropped into the water. All I could do was watch the anxious faces above me as they waited for the right moment to lower the basket into the launch.

They waited until the roll of the sea and the rise of the launch reached the highest point before starting back down again. When the Bosun's Mate at the ship's railing blew his whistle, the ropes were let loose and I sailed down into the launch, landing squarely on the deck. I was quickly moved forward to the bow while the other injured GI was lowered, to repeat my bone-jarring drop.

The launch pulled away, heading for a distant hospital ship. When we arrived, I waited while more ropes were lowered and tied around me. I was rapidly pulled up, lifted over the side and placed on the deck next to the superstructure. I asked one of the corpsmen to untie me from the Bailey Basket so that I could move around a little, which he did. I was given several packs of cigarettes before he hurried off to care for the more seriously wounded.

Looking around, I could see that the deck was packed with horribly injured men in burned, tattered uniforms, victims of Kamikaze attacks.

They were lying about on blood-stained litters, waiting for their turn in the operating rooms, already filled with sailors from the blasted warships and soldiers from the fighting ashore.

The cries of the wounded mixed with the firing of anti-aircraft guns on passing destroyers as they tried to protect the hospital ship from prowling Jap bombers roaring overhead. The defenseless ship was just another target as far as the Japanese were concerned. The only protection for the wounded on these ships were the vigilant gunners on the destroyers that relentlessly circled them, ready to repel any air attacks.

Because of the large numbers of seriously wounded men, I waited until about two o'clock in the morning before I was taken in for treatment. A doctor cleaned my knee, took X-rays and examined me carefully. All the skin on the kneecap was torn away and the ligaments were ripped. Both legs were swollen and black and blue from my thighs to my ankles.

After snipping away the raw, ragged flesh around the edge of the wound and packing it with sulfa powder, the doctor bandaged it. He said that I would be as good as new in a few months and then told me to "get the hell off his ship" to make room for real casualties.

After all the misery and suffering that I had seen while waiting on deck, I couldn't argue with him. All I wanted to do was get back to my outfit as soon as possible. I picked up my remaining cigarettes, grabbed my shoes and hobbled back outside where I was lowered into the next landing craft headed back to the beach. I was dropped off at the wrong beach, far from where I was supposed to be.

"What a helluva day," I thought. "I'm back on this stinking island without a weapon, equipment, helmet or food and no idea where my men are. What else could possibly happen?"

Keeping an eye peeled for Jap planes, I limped down the beach to find my squad. I had a nasty feeling that this was going to be a long campaign. All Hell was breaking loose over the entire invasion area. A battleship was hit and several cargo vessels and landing craft were burning fiercely.

To make matters worse, I didn't have a goddamned thing to fight with, not even a knife. When I had left to unload the ammunition ship, all of our gear had been left with our company. What a nightmare…alone in the middle of Armageddon and not a pot to spit in.

When I was a little kid, I always thought war would be the most exciting, wonderful and glorious thing a man could experience. Now I just wanted to lie down on the sand, roll up in a ball, and let the war disappear.

Just as I sat down, I thought I heard a voice say: "Trust in me." But there was nobody there. "I've gotten this far…keep going." I said to myself.

I brushed off my coveralls and headed down the beach to rejoin my outfit.

Unable to find anyone who knew where the Anti-tank Company of the 35th Regiment might be, all I knew was that they had landed and moved inland somewhere to the east—almost anywhere. After spending almost a full day on the beach, a jeep pulled up beside me and skidded to a stop. The driver asked if I was going out to a hospital ship. I said that I'd just come back from there, and I was looking for my outfit.

He knew that the 35th had followed the 27th towards San Jacinto where our assembly area was located. He was sure that they had already moved out and were headed east toward the Central Plains. If I wanted a ride, he would take me to his supply outfit, where I could get some chow, clean myself up and see if they could find out exactly where I was supposed to be. I climbed painfully into the overloaded jeep and we left the crowded beach behind us.

When we arrived at the inland distribution point, the driver took me to see his captain. He noticed that I was a sergeant and proceeded to try and get me to stay with his outfit, directing his Filipino laborers as they sorted and distributed supplies to the forward units. I told him in no uncertain terms that I was in a combat outfit, not supply, and I needed to get up to the front and rejoin my squad. He told me that nothing was moving that way for a while because all the bridges had been blown up by the Japanese as they were pulling back. It was going to take quite some time for them to be rebuilt, and I might as well stay with his supply unit.

The captain was called away for a few minutes; that's when I noticed several ten wheelers filled with infantry idling nearby. I hobbled over to the nearest one and asked a sergeant where they were headed.

"We're goin' up to the front," he replied.

"I have to get out of here. Can I hitch a ride?" I asked as I glanced over my shoulder to see if the supply captain was still interested in keeping me there.

"Where's your weapon?" asked the sergeant.

I told him what had happened, and that I didn't have one with me. Overhearing our conversation, the truck driver told me that I could ride shotgun with him in the cab.

"Just grab that M-1 in the boot over there," he said. "We'll get out of here before that captain keeps you here for good."

We drove in the darkness for hours on rough, rutted dirt roads until we began to hear firing nearby. It was then that I discovered that all the soldiers on the trucks were replacements and not regular line troops. Every one of them had just arrived from a transport offshore, and they were destined to be sent to different units in the field. They had not even been assigned to an outfit yet and were completely disoriented. As the trucks came to a halt, the replacements jumped off, were led to a small stand of trees and spread out waiting to be shown to their squads.

The driver suggested that I return to his supply company and stay awhile. I agreed, and we drove back, lights out, in the pitch dark, as fast as the terrible roads would allow, my leg bouncing about as we hit potholes and deep ruts. We pulled in to the supply area after a hair-raising ride, and I wearily climbed down from the dusty cab.

Once again, the supply captain I had talked with earlier walked up to me, told me to stick around for a few days and they would help me find my outfit. I reluctantly agreed, was directed to the aid tent nearby to have my knee checked by a medic and shuffled slowly over to the tent. Sitting down on a battered cot, I removed my slimy, salt encrusted shoes (we still hadn't received real combat boots) from my swollen feet.

The medic tried removing the filthy bandage plastered to my knee with pus and dirt, exclaiming: "Jeeesssus Christ!" his face contorting into a grimace. "Why did they send you back here from the ship with your knee like—*this*? When was the last time this bandage was changed?"

"Yesterday," I replied, looking away from the sticky, disgusting yellowish mess on the remnants of the bandage he was holding.

"The doctor told me it wasn't that bad," I replied weakly.

"Don't you know what will happen if this gets infected?" he admonished, cleaning my knee, applying more sulfa and securely tying a new bandage.

"Try and keep this clean and come back tomorrow for a new bandage, okay?" he said.

I thanked him and walked back to a tent next to the road. I collapsed onto an empty, dust-covered cot and was immediately asleep.

In the morning, I grabbed some chow, asked a lot of questions about the positions of the front line companies and had my bandage changed again by the medic. Once again the captain tried to convince me to stay and help him out with his supply problems. By feigning interest in his idea, I was able to hitch a ride with the captain's driver to another supply point.

On the way, the driver told me that I had better take off or the captain would keep me there and I'd never get back to my unit. They were desperately short of men and the captain would do whatever he must to keep me from leaving.

"Bullshit!" I shouted. "He'll have to shoot me first! Just show me the way to the river and I'll get back to my outfit by myself."

"You can't do that. There aren't any bridges left standing. How will you get across?" he asked.

"That's *my* problem. I'll swim across if I have to. I'll be goddamned if I'm going to sit on my ass in some rear area while my squad is out there fighting Japs," I said.

"The river is about half-a-mile down that way, but this is as far as I can go," he said, pointing across a large field covered with grass and scrub brush.

"You'd better take this, just in case," he said as he handed me a grenade from a box next to his seat.

"Thanks for the help," I replied, as we shook hands.

Waving to him as he drove off in a cloud of dust, I stood alone by the side of the road, my throbbing legs stiff and swollen, armed only with a grenade. I checked the cotter pin to be sure that it was bent over, so that it wouldn't explode by accident, then stuffed it into my pocket.

Shuffling along like an old farmer, I limped the half mile to the river bank without seeing another soul. The only sounds were the continuous flights of aircraft overhead, the distant rumble of artillery and the rushing water of the river. As I walked along the weed-choked bank, a large, water-soaked log floated up and beached itself nearby.

"Maybe I could float across the river on this log," I thought to myself.

I looked at the log, across the swiftly flowing river, then back to the log again. The only other alternative was to walk all the way back to the beach, hope to get a lift to the front and just maybe I would find my outfit in a week or so—if I was lucky. Hoping that I hadn't already used up more than my share of luck in the last few days, I decided to cross the river and hope that my legs would hold out for a while longer.

Wading into the warm, swirling water, I grabbed the slippery log, slid onto it and paddled with my arms, using my good leg to help me steer in the general direction of the opposite bank. The current started to carry me downstream much faster than I had anticipated, causing me to increase my paddling. After paddling and pushing for quite a while, I finally made it to shore, exhausted. I rested for about an hour and then proceeded to hobble towards the front lines.

When I had gone about a mile, a jeep approached and stopped a short distance away. Two MPs jumped out and glared at me suspiciously.

"What are you doing out here?" yelled the sergeant, his hands on his hips.

"I'm trying to…" I started to say before the corporal, his right hand poised to pull his Colt at the slightest provocation, interrupted me.

"Who are you and where's your unit?"

Explaining my predicament was going to be a waste of time, so I made it short and to the point.

"My name is Sergeant Donald Anderson. I'm with the 35th Infantry."

"What are you doin' way the hell out here?" the sergeant shouted.

"I'm trying to get back to my outfit. I just came in from a hospital ship and I swam across the river to get here!" I yelled back in his face.

"I think you took off; that's what I think!" spit out the sergeant.

"I don't give a shit *what* you think! Just call the 35th and ask my company commander who I am," I said as I stepped closer to the sergeant.

The MPs put me in the front seat of the jeep and one sat in the back with his weapon close at hand. We raced back to Corps Headquarters and they took me to the CIC (Intelligence) officer sitting in a large tent surrounded by stacks of crumpled maps, papers and scribbled message slips. He looked up at me and demanded to know who I was. Once again I had to tell what had happened and why I was there.

He stared at me for a time and then said: "Well, this should be easy enough to check. Who is your commanding officer?"

"Colonel Larsen, 35th Infantry. Or call General Dalton. I was his driver at Pearl."

"You stay here and I'll be right back," he said over his shoulder as he left the tent.

When the officer came back, he said that my story checked out but I would have to spend the night there, my outfit would be sending a jeep for me in the morning. I was shown to a tent, placed under guard and given some chow. They were obviously not taking chances around Corps Headquarters.

Early the next morning, a jeep arrived and took me to Division Headquarters. I sat down under a tree and waited to be picked up by my outfit. An hour later, I was met by another jeep and driven up to my company, about ten miles away. As we entered the company area, I saw some of my men standing around our truck and asked the driver to drop me off. My buddies had seen me coming and walked over to greet me.

"Oh Christ, here comes the bad penny!" laughed my gunner.

I was back.

CHAPTER 10

Valley of Shadows

After the reunion with my squad, I discovered that they had divided up all of my belongings because they didn't think I would be coming back. I had received a package in the mail from Mrs. Dalton, with maple sugar candy, canned foods and other tidbits, while I was on the hospital ship. It was received at the company; my squad, thinking that I was gone for good, opened it and divided up the spoils of war.

My captain sent me back to the aid station to have my leg checked before we moved out to our next objective. The doctor examined me thoroughly, cleaned and re-bandaged my knee.

"This knee is in tough shape. I'll have to tag you Quarters," he said as he wrote out a medical tag.

"Quarters? Quarters out there is a foxhole or a mud-filled ditch! We're getting ready to move out in an hour!"

"All right, you can go with your unit, but stay off that leg and make sure you change that bandage when it gets dirty!"

I thought to myself: "Besides living in a muddy hole in the ground, crawling around in the dirt and constant fighting, that shouldn't be a problem."

Slowly shaking my head, I left the aid tent, climbed into the jeep with the driver, and we drove off.

Moving east across the Central Plains, we drove in small convoys, leapfrogging outfits as the advance continued. A line company out in front of us engaged any Japanese that fired on the convoy. While the infantry tied down the enemy with direct fire, the remainder of the convoy sped past and kept driving at full speed until they were engaged by the next group of the enemy. Speed was the key to keeping the Japanese from consolidating their positions and blocking our advance. By keeping them off balance, we prevented them from regrouping in strength.

Our turn came to move to the head of our long column of vehicles and resume taking the point to see if we could draw fire from the Japanese up ahead of us. Our platoon lieutenant, platoon sergeant and their driver were in a jeep in front of us on the highway. We were in line with our truck, and behind us were several jeeps and nine more trucks towing anti-tank guns. We were still functioning as a full company, but not for long.

This was really heart-stopping duty. The roads were usually mined and the sniper fire, constant. We didn't know from one minute to the next if we would get blown up or shot. Our officers were told to stop and engage the Japs only if we met heavy resistance. My truck received many hits from snipers, but luckily no one was wounded.

Our company commander caught up with us at a fork in the road. He ordered our platoon leader and my squad to take the right fork and travel down the road about five miles. We were to stay there until we heard from him.

The CO took off, as we turned and headed down the road, following the jeep. Feeling extremely apprehensive about this abrupt turn of events, we kept looking back at the convoy rapidly fading into the distance.

We drove past many rice paddies with water buffalo that stared back at us. After several miles, we came to a river where women and children were bathing and washing clothes in the sluggish brown water. More water buffalo shuffled along with children riding on their massive, dusty backs.

All smiles, the children started to yell at the top of their lungs; "Hi GI, hi Joe, give me gum, give me chock-a-lot!"

We slowed down, threw them some of our rations, waved, and then continued on our way, as they happily scrambled for the treats.

After another mile, the lieutenant raised his hand. We slowed down, and came to a stop at another fork in the road. Nearby, there were several destroyed buildings: a Cal-Tex gas station, a small open-air market and a tiny bank. The lieutenant told me to stay at the fork while he left to attend a meeting somewhere else. He said that the convoy might be turning around and coming down in our direction, so we needed to keep an eye peeled for it—or anything else.

Anything else? That really made me nervous.

"What happens if they don't come back?" I asked warily.

"Don't worry about it. We won't forget you're here."

My men wanted to go back to the river for a swim and a vitally-needed bath. So did I, but I resisted the temptation. We found an old bench, some wooden boxes and a broken chair. We sat around, eating our rations and telling each other about our home states and boyhood escapades, keeping a sharp lookout for any surprises. Everybody was getting restless, so a few of the men went exploring in the ruins. They wandered off toward the bank and began to rummage around inside the building. I ordered them back and gave them a stern lecture about booby traps.

One of them told me that the bank safe's door was partially open and he could see money bags inside. Now *that* was interesting. I took some men with me over to the bank and walked inside. The interior was partially demolished from shelling, but the safe was still intact. We checked all around for booby traps but didn't find anything.

One of my men from Idaho, who was a cowboy before the war, roped the door handle of the safe and slowly pulled it open at a prudent distance, just in case there was a booby trap inside. The Japs never left anything lying around without rigging it, if they had the time, never mind bags of money. We slowly pulled the door open with the rope far enough to get the money bags out, and dragged them outside.

The bags were packed with bundles of crisp, brand new, uncirculated paper money. The catch was, it was all Japanese invasion money. We thought it wasn't worth the paper it was printed on. At least it gave us a bit of entertainment. Even if it had been American currency, there would be no place for us to spend it. We rarely stopped, never mind searched for distractions. Just for the hell of it, we took the heavy money bags and threw them in the back of our truck. Then we went back to waiting.

Just before dark, the rest of our convoy arrived. We parked the vehicles in a circle, like wagons in the Old West; then we dug foxholes and latrines and posted sentries. When we tried to catch some much needed sleep, we weren't successful. Keeping one eye open was required.

Nights were long, nerve-wracking and dangerous. Relaxing totally for just a moment could get your throat sliced open. The Japanese were experts in night fighting and were almost impossible to detect before they struck. Using the night to their advantage, they would probe our positions and then attack, the darkness shielding their movements. This fact described the primary difference in how we fought: We very rarely left our perimeters at night unless there was a patrol going out. We were always on the alert, even when trying to catch a few winks at night. And whatever moved at night was fair game for a grenade.

The next morning, we packed everything and continued driving up the road. We were fired on at several different barrios, where we had to stop and clean the enemy out of their positions before continuing. It was a dirty, brutal business, but there was no other way.

A barrio could be a small town, but often was a group of closely circled huts, some on stilts. Any hut was exceptionally dangerous to approach without attracting fire from another a few yards away. To rout the enemy, they were set on fire using tracer rounds or phosphorus grenades. The Japs jumped out of the doors and windows as the flames quickly enveloped the tinderbox dwellings. We killed them all as they hit the ground. Dozens of GI's surrounding the huts poured aimed rifle and automatic weapons fire and grenades into the enemy, their bodies piling up in grotesque, smoldering heaps. The soldiers who stayed in the huts burned to death, their ammunition and grenades cooking off, sending burning debris flying in all directions as the flaming huts collapsed around them in enormous explosions of brilliant sparks.

Some of our new men, having never been in combat, still had naive notions about "civilized" warfare. I guess they thought that they could get up and ask the enemy to surrender. They tried to get us to stop firing and take prisoners. We told them that if they wanted to take prisoners, they were welcome to go into the barrio under fire and do so. There were no takers. The new men hadn't seen first-hand what the Japanese were capable of.

They would understand soon enough.

The enemy had dug in and camouflaged everything with their usual masterful techniques. What looked like a harmless, sleepy barrio usually concealed dug-in tanks, anti-tank guns, machine gun positions, mines, booby traps and sniper-infested spider holes. We couldn't take anything for granted. Barrios thought to be cleaned out would be re-occupied by the enemy, innocent looking roads heavily mined and empty fields, lousy with snipers.

Seldom were we out in front of the column. Most of the time we were somewhere near the center. In case of an attack, that positioned us to rush either forward or to the rear without having to drive past the entire strung-out column, often several miles long.

One afternoon, as we moved up the highway, we saw some of our trucks and jeeps burning, with dead men sprawled beside the road and in the adjacent rice paddies.

There were no wounded.

The Japs had killed them all.

Many of the men had been stripped of their clothes, mutilated, shot in the head or bayoneted. They had been victims of an ambush. Unfortunately, we couldn't stop to help. We were under orders to drive as quickly as possible to the front of the column and assist the troops with the reduction of another enemy force.

Farther up the road, our people had trapped the enemy outfit responsible for ambushing our men. When we arrived, the fight was already over. After being surrounded by our men, every single Jap was killed or captured. Normally, there weren't any prisoners taken, but this time there was a reason to do so.

When we began to search the Japanese bodies, we found some wearing GI uniforms. Every single one had personal effects taken from our men, some from as far back as 1942 during the Death March on Bataan: family photographs, rings, cigarette lighters, even their dog tags. More of our men savagely butchered without mercy, it was the recurring nightmare of the 'Canal all over again.

We now knew that the dead Japanese sprawled all around us, as well as the prisoners squatting on their haunches under close guard nearby, were the same soldiers responsible for the execution of American prisoners after they had surrendered earlier in the war. They carried photographs of our soldiers being murdered with sabers, bayonets and pistols. Most of them were executed simply because they were sick and starving and couldn't keep up with their comrades. Many were simply beaten to death or had their heads bashed in with shovels and then hastily buried, some while they were still alive.

The prisoners were being questioned one at a time by a Japanese-speaking GI holding a fistful of photographs. He would hold up the photos and other things just taken from the prisoner and ask him where he had gotten them. Every Japanese soldier acted the same way. They seemed to take for granted that killing defenseless prisoners was the thing to do. Not one of them showed any shred of remorse.

One Japanese officer, captured alive and slightly wounded in the arm was surly and arrogant, answering each question with all the venom and contempt that he possessed. When he was confronted with the crumpled, yellowing photos taken of him beheading our people on Bataan, which he readily admitted, he started laughing and nodding his head while pointing at his victims. He was actually proud of what he had done to those prisoners, their bleeding hands bound behind their backs with wire, kneeling in the dust. He must have thought it was a huge joke.

We moved back to the road, sadly holding the re-captured possessions of the men who had been killed by these same Japs. Our new men were now true believers. We could see it in their eyes. They were beginning to get that "hard" look, just like everyone else. A combination of rage and a determination to do whatever they had to. They had just seen for themselves, a small example of what the enemy would do. From now on, the Japanese were going to discover what we were capable of. As we neared our vehicles, a flurry of shots rang out behind us. We didn't turn around. Climbing into our vehicles, we drove off and didn't look back.

Down the road, we encountered one of our Engineer outfits. We told them about the Japs: who they were and what they had in photos and possessions. They would find them in a field about a mile to the rear. Every trace of that Japanese unit would be bulldozed into the Philippine soil, the same soil as their helpless victims, but now *free* soil. I hoped that our men who had been murdered would rest a little easier.

Losing too many men with direct assaults on the small barrios, we changed our tactics. We probed at several different points at the same time to check resistance. If it was a tiny barrio, we would take out the enemy by leveling every building, every hut and anything else giving cover. Blow it up, burn it, destroy everything in sight. Then we went in, killing any survivors hiding in spider holes or covered trenches.

We finally reached Highway Five, the main road running north and south. Stopping for short periods, we made forays up the highway for about five miles. From here on in, it would literally be an up-hill fight, all the way. From the Plains, the terrain changed from flat paddy land to rolling hills to steep mountains studded with caves. The Japanese occupied the high ground in front of us, looking right down our throats and watching every move we made.

It seemed impossible to have even one light moment in the face of what lay ahead of us, but you never knew when one might pop up. As we were stopped by the side of the road one day, about a hundred refugees came down the road in front of us trying to escape the fighting they knew was coming. They were a sorry sight, carrying the few pitiful possessions they had left after the Japanese got through taking what they wanted. Many had only a few filthy bundles, some scrawny chickens and an old, fire-blackened cooking pot. As they drew abreast of us, my men and I looked at each other and then started throwing the money we had "liberated" from the bank, over the side of the truck into the crowd.

The refugees went wild with joy, scooping up stacks of bills and stuffing them into their clothes and baskets. They must have figured it was manna from heaven. They could exchange it later for pesos and use the money to buy food or rebuild their destroyed homes. They looked at us with tears in their eyes as they joyfully packed away their new found fortunes. We felt a little like Robin Hood.

Battalion told us to get ready to move out with as much ammo as we could jam into our vehicles. The area ahead of us on the San Leon road was being scouted on the ground by Recon Teams and in the air by observers in light observation planes, nicknamed "grasshoppers." The pilots of these "low and slow" unarmed aircraft were known for their exploits in spotting for the field artillery: locating enemy convoys and gun positions by flying at or below tree top level.

Moving out in small convoys, our trucks straining from the loads of shells for our 37s, small arms and pedestal mounted fifty-caliber machine guns, we bounced and rattled our way down the dusty roads, fingers on triggers. Even though the roads were reported clear, we knew that if there were Japs around, they would wait for the Recon Teams to pass, then plant mines in the road behind them—and in front of us. They almost always planted them in the road itself, so we always drove on the shoulders of the road wherever possible. It was rough going, but a hell of a lot safer.

Every bridge was blown and had to be bypassed, a ford found or a new bridge built by the Engineers. The advance had to be maintained, no matter what the obstacle. Our orders were to keep moving. Blast it, bridge it; go over it, around it or through it. Whatever it took to just keep going was seldom that simple.

Culverts lay on the sides of the roads, about six feet deep or more. At night, we manhandled the 37s into the bottom of them and set up the guns facing the direction we expected the Japs to come from. We had stocked as many canister shells as we could for just such a situation.

We knew that every night the enemy would attempt to compromise our positions by silently using the culverts to bypass our front line and attack in our rear. Experts at stealth and infiltration, they'd leave their grisly handiwork for us to find in the morning: GI's were killed with knives and left. The Japanese crept back out again, undetected. We had done the same thing to them several times on the 'Canal.

If we thought we were being observed (we probably were), the guns would be set up on the road's surface at dusk. The enemy would get a good look at us setting the guns up and pass the word to the patrols and ambush teams setting out on their nocturnal missions. After it got dark, we moved the guns down into the culverts, one on each side of the road, loaded with canister. Then we waited, sitting in the bottom of a ditch or culvert, soaked by the water running down from the hills, cold and miserable, unable to sleep or even get comfortable. We waited. No smoking, talking or noise of any kind, every sense we possessed strained to detect the approach of men, whose only intention was to kill us any way they could.

During the night, we'd hear a faint rustling or shuffling sound, the enemy crawling or stealthily walking straight at us through the darkness. We could literally smell them coming; the sour odor that was peculiar to their rations carried to us on the still night air. The hair on my arms and the back of my neck would stand on end as they got close. The Japs couldn't climb out of the culvert or they would be spotted by the infantry on the road. They had to come down the culverts where we were waiting. We hoped they didn't know we were there. If the enemy hadn't seen us move our guns after dark, we usually had them cold. There would be a canister round loaded and ready. Grenades were arranged with the pins already straightened, ready to throw, although most of the time the enemy were much too close to use them. Weapons were ready. Several men usually carried shotguns for close fighting. Canister rounds were stacked right at hand.

And we'd wait.

Straining our eyes to catch a glimpse of nearly invisible, moving shadows of approaching killers was intolerable. The smallest sound might be the key to opening fire at the right moment, saving your life and the lives of your buddies—or losing them all. The night discipline of the enemy was uncanny. We usually didn't hear them coming until they were right on top of us, too close for anything except small arms or knives.

We knew when we had them cold. As they closed in, the loader knelt in the water, waiting with another round, slowly turning its cool metal casing in his calloused hands, staring into the blackness. Time slowed to an interminable crawl as the slight noises grew closer. They were only yards away. The Japs entered the killing zone, padding almost imperceptibly in their split-toed shoes. A quick tap on the gunner's helmet signaled him to open fire.

BANG!

The gun jumped as the round spiraled down the barrel.

As the canister left the muzzle, it opened out, like a giant shotgun shell. Possibly, the first Japanese saw the muzzle flash before he died. The men behind him would be killed a split second later, shredded by hundreds of small, resin-packed steel pellets, propelled out in a deadly cone of fire that transformed men into riddled corpses in an instant.

Already, a second shell was rammed home and fired before the mangled enemy bodies had fallen to the bottom of the culvert. Several more rounds fired, scouring the sides of the culvert, and then silence.

The smell of warm blood and cool water, running over our shoes, hung around us all night.

At first light, the gruesome results would be clearly visible. The Japanese were torn apart by the force of the blasts: limbs ripped off, the culvert red with gore and littered with shredded, bloody equipment. The enemy would have been only about ten or fifteen yards away at the most when the gun was fired. Swarms of scavenging flies had already begun their sickening work on the tangled mass of eviscerated bodies, soon bursting with thousands of fat, wriggling maggots.

After checking the bodies for documents, the guns were manhandled back up on the road and hitched to the trucks; we drove to the next barrio. It was a dangerous, monotonous grind. We would drive for a few miles and stop, then wait on the side of the road while tanks, jeeps, SP guns and all manner of vehicles passed by, churning up rolling, choking clouds of dust that settled over everything. We had to keep the guns covered to keep the dust and dirt out of their mechanisms. If we had handkerchiefs or pieces of cloth, we tied them over our faces. Long, unending lines of filthy, exhausted infantry trudged along both shoulders of the road while the vehicles passed between them, chewing up the hot, cracking roadbeds and engulfing the men in thick dust and nauseating exhaust fumes.

After a few hours, our tiny column would start up again, drive up the road for a mile or so and then stop. Occasionally we deployed in the fields beside the road for security but usually kept starting and stopping until we hit the enemy—or they hit us.

Tank shells, mortar rounds or small arms fire would erupt from a stand of woods or a small barrio. All our firepower would be directed at the suspected position. Occasionally, we had the support of our planes, called in by forward observers traveling with our column. The aircraft would paste the target with bombs and bullets. Their heavy machine gun rounds ricocheted in all directions when they hit a hidden tank or anti-tank gun inside the barrio.

The huts were quickly torn apart by the volume of fire brought to bear by our column. The huts would start to burn, the tremendous heat incinerating everything in its path in a matter of minutes. Many of the Japanese were reduced to smoking ash before we even entered the barrio. Fire had been enlisted to save the lives of our people.

After we had killed all the Japanese in the barrio, we checked our weapons and climbed back into our vehicles to continue our drive up the road. We didn't have the time or the inclination to bury the bodies. Our only job was to kill the enemy. It was somebody else's job to follow behind us and police the area.

A mass grave was the preferred method of disposing of remains, always a health hazard in that climate. By the time the rear echelon arrived to sanitize the battlefield, the stinking, fly-infested piles of blackened, bursting corpses had already been torn apart and partially devoured by roaming packs of dogs or swarmed by vicious, starving rats—the size of house cats. They defended the decaying bodies against all comers, as they gorged themselves with slimy flesh, rotting in the intense heat. Baring their sharp teeth, slick with blood, maggots and shreds of reeking skin, they would fight each other to the death over a rope of intestines or the contents of a smashed skull. They didn't scurry away when our men approached to start their gruesome work—they attacked. Every rat would have to be shot before the bulldozers could get close enough to bury everything. The terrible, unmistakable stench fouled the air for miles. Several pilots of the observation planes complained that the smell was so bad they couldn't fly low over the battlefield without retching.

We pulled into a barrio one morning and parked our vehicles on the side of the road. We had two jeeps and six trucks towing our anti-tank guns. Our people climbed down to stretch out the kinks from the jarring, bone-rattling drive from the last barrio. Here we observed ramshackle huts and a few shops with paddies surrounding them.

It seemed that most of the inhabitants were milling around the center of the place, yelling and waving their arms. There was wild commotion, which we couldn't see, in the middle of them. We walked over with our weapons at the ready to find a savage cock-fight going on, and fists full of pesos waving in the air around it—a wild version of a busy floor at the New York Stock Exchange. The squawking of the birds was almost drowned out by the enthusiastic betting of the Filipino onlookers.

Flecks of blood splattered the ground from the combatants; the air was thick with dust from the frenzied fighting and the constant jockeying of the people trying to get a better view of the action. Dozens of emaciated dogs, their ribs sticking out from their dusty hides, prowled around the barrio looking for some tiny morsel to steal. The smell of the place was revolting—a combination of unwashed bodies, moldy paddy water and years of human and animal excrement baked into the soil.

We looked at each other and walked back to our vehicles.

As we waited our turn to continue our push up the Highway, a brawl erupted in the midst of the cock-fight. Several men were knocked to the ground and decided to retreat to their huts before it got any worse. The situation was rapidly "going south." We climbed back in our vehicles and started to move slowly into the crawling traffic of M-7s, supply trucks and tanks.

Just as we were pulling out, two men separated from the milling crowd and proceeded to beat the hell out of each other a few yards away from our vehicle. One man repeatedly punched the other in the face five or six times, knocking him to the ground. As he bent over to hit him again, the bleeding Filipino pulled a knife like a flash and thrust it into his assailant's chest. The victim keeled over, dropped to the ground, holding his chest. He writhed for a few seconds and then lay still. A pool of blood slowly spread from under him, as the other man simply wiped the knife off and rejoined the crowd. Seemingly, nobody took any notice of the murder. They just kept on betting on the cock-fight.

Later that same afternoon, we drove back to Battalion to pick up ammo, rations, water and mail. We passed by the same barrio where the fight had broken out and noticed that most of the people had left or were going about their normal routines: fetching water, cooking, working the paddies, little children playing in the dirt. The dead man was still lying in the same spot, bloated and covered with flies. Other Filipinos were walking around him, going about their business, taking absolutely no notice of him at all.

We spent several hours at Battalion, loaded our supplies and mail, and headed back up the Highway to our forward positions. We once again passed by the barrio, and much to our disgust, the murdered Filipino was still in the same place. Worse, the starving dogs running through the barrio had begun to feed on him. We thought that the populace would at least bury him. But I guess after living in the primitive squalor of the barrios for their whole lives, they probably didn't even notice the smell.

While we advanced down the mined San Leon road, word came down that we were to be ready to go in against the next town, Umingan. Division fully expected enemy tanks and infantry to block our advance in force. The main outfits of the Regiment were sent in to help destroy the Japs in the town, while we circled around to the other side. We headed towards Lupao, a dirty little place, hardly deserving a mark on our maps.

Nobody had ever heard of it.

Those of us who fought there, will never forget it.

We were told that the Recon Troop had driven through the place on the only road and had seen no sign of Japs. Reaching the northern outskirts of the town, they turned around and barreled back through to report that the place was undefended. Meanwhile, the well-entrenched enemy simply held their fire, in order to ambush the larger main force they knew was coming. With large numbers of dug-in, camouflaged tanks, machine guns, mortars and anti-tank guns, the enemy simply sat back and waited.

For whatever reason, foot patrols were never sent in to check the town itself, before the main force arrived on the 2nd of February. The first outfit that advanced on the town through the fields was decimated. Seemingly empty huts and harmless stacks of debris were, in fact, tanks turned into steel pillboxes, buried in the ground up to their turrets. They could be knocked out only by a direct hit. Our heavy artillery couldn't be used effectively because of the proximity of our own troops to the enemy. Every avenue of approach was covered by a withering storm of fire and the road had been heavily mined after the Recon Troop had returned to report that the place was empty.

Our casualties quickly mounted from the sweep of bullets and shells coming from the barrio and the surrounding woods and fields. As enemy tank rounds found their mark, vehicles exploded in flames, men running for what little cover they could find in the flat, open fields. Mortar blasts sprayed the area with jagged shrapnel as the infantry pulled back, dragging the screaming wounded to relative safety. Machine guns swept the area with pinpoint accuracy, covering every inch of the deadly fields.

In order to get into position around Lupao, bulldozers from the 65th Engineers were used to cut rough roads through the fields and paddies. Large steel plates were welded on the dozer blades to protect the exposed drivers from sniper fire. Heavily armed GI's riding shotgun and infantry support were necessary just to enable us to move against the town's outer perimeter. We met heavy resistance from dug-in tanks, mortars, artillery and small arms fire on our approach.

It was decided to make an end-run around Lupao and attack from several different points at once to divide the enemy's fire. Our job was to circle the town, blocking the enemy's avenue of retreat in a hammer-and-anvil movement.

We were the anvil.

The Japs had no intention of going anywhere; they were too well entrenched and had a very strong position. Their job was to kill as many of us as possible before they were all killed. The enemy was astride the only road. We couldn't bypass the town and leave them to threaten our rear as we advanced to the next objective. They would have to be wiped out.

The Third Platoon drove in a column through the fields around the town, taking heavy fire all the way. Our bouncing truck, with our anti-tank gun in tow, was the last vehicle in line as we snaked our way through the open fields, bullets whining and cracking all around us. As we slowed to keep from running into the truck in front of us, one of our men, Sergeant Jackson from Florida, sitting on the back of that truck, was shot through the leg. Our two vehicles stopped.

My gunner jumped behind the mounted fifty-caliber machine gun and started raking the trees, swearing at the top of his voice. The hot, expended cartridge casings cascaded into the truck bed as he blasted the enemy positions. The deafening blast of the "fifty" just above our heads was so loud that we had to yell at each other to be heard.

Our lieutenant pulled up in his jeep and jumped out. His faded, filthy uniform was covered with white sweat stains and layers of dust from the explosions of nearby shells.

"What the hell are you stopping here for?" he yelled over the din of the still chattering fifty.

"Cease fire!...Cease fire!...CEASE FIRE...GODDAMN IT!" I yelled at the swearing gunner. He stopped firing, looked down at us, looked back at the barrio, and then spit over the side of the truck.

"Shouldn't we throw a few shells in there with the thirty-seven, lieutenant? Maybe we can knock out some of those goddamned Jap guns."

"You'll risk losing men if you don't keep moving with this column. We can't see where the fire is coming from anyway. Get this gun the hell out of here! We have to get into position before the attack starts!" he exclaimed, motioning toward the column.

We caught up with the advancing vehicles and reached our new position. We were forming a block across the road leading out of the town. Unhitching our gun, my squad quickly pushed it behind some bushes to use as cover. The other two guns positioned themselves on the opposite side of the road, the second gun behind some brush and the third near the corner of a weather-worn warehouse building farther back.

Just as it was getting dark, I was called by our ex-company commander. He had been transferred to Battalion Headquarters and working from a massive underground bunker, built out in a field behind us. It was the first time that I had seen him since we had been on the beach. I entered the bunker and walked over to a small table covered with maps. He was standing there looking at a message slip. I stood there waiting for him to finish reading. The place stank of damp earth, stale sweat, cigarette smoke and the warm, metallic heat from the bank of humming radio equipment, a few feet away. I wondered why the Brass had spent so much time constructing this log-reinforced bunker, when we would, in all likelihood, be moving out of here in a day or two anyway. We were always short of men on the line and couldn't get replacements when our people were wounded and evacuated. And now the Brass had a company of GI's back here digging this big-ass hole in the ground.

I knew better than to voice my opinion.

"Sergeant Anderson reporting, Sir."

"Sergeant, load up your squad and take your gun up the road to support the line company north of us. Make sure you take plenty of ammunition and dig in when you get there."

I stood there for a few seconds trying to comprehend what he was saying. We never moved our vehicles at night, especially when we were so close to the Japanese. We knew they had direct observation of the area and had the road zeroed in with artillery and mortars. The noise of the vehicles moving would be enough to bring a shit-storm of shells down on us. We always moved our guns into position just before dark and stayed there until it was light.

Nobody moved around at night—it just wasn't done.

"*Sir!* It's already dark. We have orders not to move at night. It's too dangerous to try and get a vehicle up the road. We could get knocked off by our *own guys,* never *mind* the goddamned Japs. They *know* that nothing of ours moves after dark."

"I didn't ask for your opinion, *Sergeant!* Move your gun up that road, now!"

"How am I supposed to know where to stop, Sir?"

"A lieutenant with the line company is already up there. He'll whistle when you get to his position."

"He'll *whistle?* Whistle what? *Dixie?*" I asked incredulously. "Sir, I could lose my whole squad *and* my gun! That road is *fucking zeroed.* We lost *four* vehicles on that same goddamned stretch from Jap artillery, just a few hours ago!"

"This is a direct order, Sergeant! Get your goddamned squad on your vehicle and get the hell out on that road!"

I walked out of the bunker into the darkness. I stood there for a minute trying to clear my mind and calm myself.

"This is insane," I thought. That line outfit had been up there for hours. Why hadn't anybody thought of sending us up there before it got dark? Somebody had really missed the boat on this job.

I gripped my Tommy gun and walked back to my outfit. I gathered my squad to give them the bad news. My gunner was the first to vent his spleen.

"Are you shittin' me? We were told never to move after dark! This is fucking *suicide!*"

They all looked at me with a mixture of anger, disbelief and fear.

"Well' I ain't *goin'* goddamnit!"

"They can kiss my *ass!* I ain't goin' either!"

"Damn straight! *They* can go up that fuckin' road! *I* ain't!"

"Look." I said. "We don't have any choice. It's a direct order. If we don't go, we get shot! Anybody that doesn't want to go *still* goes. *Got it?*"

I stared into the eyes of each man in turn.

They knew we had no choice but to do as we were told.

"Now load up."

We manhandled our gun out onto the road, hooked it to the truck and loaded our ammo and gear in the back. Four men climbed in with the gear, and I sat in the cab with the driver. The windshield had been taken down and covered with canvas to prevent the light from reflecting off the glass during the day. We couldn't use the headlights and had to drive up the road in the dark. We could barely see the outline of the road because of the lighter color of the dirt it was made from. The driver was looking ahead of the vehicle, trying to brace himself for the dash up the road.

I tapped him on the shoulder to get his attention.

"As soon as you *start* this bitch, I want you to floor it and drive as fast as you can. The quicker we get up there, the less time the Japs will have to hit us—right?"

He nodded.

The four men in the back were bracing themselves by hanging onto the sides of the truck and the pedestal-mounted machine gun bolted to the truck bed. Cases of ammunition and grenades were stacked around their feet.

I turned back to the driver and nodded to him.

"Okay, let's go."

I steadied my Tommy gun with one hand and the dusty metal of the truck body with the other. I felt cold sweat crawling down my back, seeping through my coveralls. The driver looked at me fearfully, started the vehicle and gripped the steering wheel.

He gunned the engine and we drove off into the unknown.

We sped into the night without lights, straining to pick out any signs of Japanese infiltrators laying mines or ambushes. Speed was basically our only defense in the near-total blackness. The fastest way between the two points was, in this case, a straight line—the pitted dirt roadway. The whining roar of the straining engine was deafening in the still night air.

I thought, "How the hell could the Japs miss hearing this damned thing. They'll nail us for sure." Every nerve in my body felt like a hot wire coursing through me. This was *nuts!*

All of a sudden, the night shattered into thunderous, clattering noise seemingly all around us. I instinctively brought up my Tommy gun and whipped my head around to see what the hell the terrifying sounds were. The men in the back had done the same, their heads swiveling around the vehicle in a full arc, weapons at the ready. Then, they saw what had caused the racket, as they looked out over the gun behind the truck: a large piece of corrugated metal from a damaged warehouse lay squarely in the road, and we had run over it.

Jesus Christ!

We drove on for a short distance when I barely heard somebody whistle.

"Stop! Stop!" I whispered to the driver as loudly as I dared.

The driver hit the brakes and we rolled to halt. I still couldn't see anything.

"Back up."

I looked at the driver, his eyes wide.

I turned around and peered into the darkness as we slowly moved back down the road. In the rear of the truck, my men covered both sides of the vehicle with their weapons, ready to open fire at the slightest signal.

The tires loudly crunched and crackled on the dirt.

There was no place to turn the vehicle around, the road wasn't wide enough. The shoulders of the road were slightly raised with small berms, the ground sloping down on both sides, swallowed by the blackness. The driver continued slowly to keep the gun we towed from skewing off the rutted surface and flipping over.

I jumped off the vehicle, scanning the ground for any sign of our new position. I couldn't see a damned thing. I whispered to the driver, and the vehicle rolled to a stop, the hot engine ticking over—my men still at the ready.

"Over here! Over here!" came a faint whisper from out of the gloom to my right.

I crab-walked over to a small cluster of foxholes just off the road. A lieutenant was kneeling on the ground cradling his rifle, his head turning slowly first right, then left.

"Where do we dig in?" I asked him softly.

"You're not going to dig in. The road's too hard. Just set up your gun."

"Which way do we face the gun? Give me a *hand* here! Where the hell are the *Japs?*"

"Set it up over there." He pointed over the road to the other side. "And keep the noise down. I'm amazed the fucking Nips haven't dropped anything in here as it is."

My squad jumped down from the truck and quickly unhitched the gun and moved it to the side of the road. We stacked cases of ammo in the dirt as fast as we could unload them. Our bazooka was carefully laid next to the ammo, out of the dirt.

The driver still couldn't turn around because of the danger of hitting a mine (the road hadn't been cleared as far as we knew), or running into a ditch and getting stuck. He had to back all the way down the road, looking to the rear, struggling to see the road and still steer a straight line to keep from wrecking the vehicle. We watched as the truck disappeared from view within seconds. We could still hear it winding up in reverse. Miraculously, the Japanese still hadn't fired on him.

We turned our attention back to the problems at hand.

Opening the trails on the gun, we began to set it up. I still couldn't see much of anything around us. The men of the line company, dug in nearby, began to whisper desperate warnings to us.

"Get the fuck off the road!"

"For Christ's sake, get the hell out of here!"

"We *can't*, we've got the gun." I explained softly to another disembodied voice.

"Well, get the fuckin' gun off the fuckin' road!"

"Sonofabitch! Where are we going to move it?" I said to my gunner, who was nervously looking around, his rifle at the ready. He just shrugged and gripped his weapon more tightly.

Just then, a shadowy figure appeared from out of the dark and knelt beside me. It was the lieutenant from the line company carrying a sweat-slicked Tommy gun.

"You'd better get this fucking gun off the road before the Nips *nail* you guys. After hearing your truck, they'll be sweeping this whole area with fire. You're going to bring a world of *shit* down on us."

"I would, but I can't see where to set up the gun," I explained.

"It doesn't matter. Just get it the fuck *off* the road."

"Where the hell am I supposed to *aim* it, for *Christ's sake?* That's why we're here. I have to aim it to fire on tanks coming down the road!"

"Okay, I'll get a couple of guys to help you move it."

"No! My guys will move it. Your men don't know what they're doing and I don't want anybody getting hurt. Just tell me where to put it. We'll take it from there."

"Take it down that bank—there's a flat spot next to the road. You should be able to sight down the road from there." He swept his arm up, indicating the invisible road in the distance.

"Where *is* everybody? I need to know where everybody is in case I have to fire tonight."

He stabbed his hand into the darkness, explaining where the positions were.

"They're over here—there and over there—there's a line of holes over there—"

I interrupted him, "So, in other words, the only safe place for us to fire is down the road, right?"

"Yeah. That's right. Unless an attack comes across the field," he added, almost as an afterthought.

My mind raced: *Oh, shit! What field?*

"Well, what's over there to the left?" I asked.

"We don't know."

"Is it our own men?"

"I don't know that. All I know is that you can fire down the road. If you have to fire anywhere else, you're on your own."

"Okay," I said. "Let's get ready."

The lieutenant scrambled across the road and vanished from sight. We positioned the gun to fire down the road, spread the trails out and stacked our ammo, the bazooka team was just behind us, their small rockets placed on a piece of canvas. I checked to be sure everything was ready in case we were hit during the night.

"Here's how we're going to set up. Hicks and I will take the first watch. In two hours we'll wake the bazooka team. After two hours, they will turn over the watch to the next two. Got it?"

Nobody was going to sleep anyway, but at least the roster was straight. We had all been in combat long enough to know, that even if you were off watch, most guys stayed awake out of sheer instinct. The mind stayed active even when the body was screaming like a banshee for sleep.

It was a typical night, with just enough moonlight to see shadows above us on the road's surface. It remained fairly quiet until about one o'clock in the morning. As I lay on the hard ground, trying to pick up any signs of enemy infiltration, there was a quiet whispering from out in front of us.

It kept repeating and getting closer.

What in God's name *was* that?

Whoever it was, they were coming right down the road. I touched my gunner on the shoulder and pointed down the road. Then, I pointed at my ear and cocked my head to signal him to listen. The strange, chanting whisper became louder, but I still couldn't tell what it was. It sounded like Japanese to me, though I didn't speak the language.

As quietly as possible, we loaded a round in the gun and prepared to fire. I could see shadows moving against the night sky. There were four, trotting by twos at a crouch, carrying something between them. Two more men were trotting along just behind them.

It looked exactly like the set-up the Japanese machine gun teams used. Two men would carry one leg of the gun cradle in one hand and a weapon in the other hand. The gunners were usually accompanied by teams of bearers carrying boxes of ammunition for the machine gun.

They moved together at the same loping gait.

Goddamnit, they must not know we're here, I thought. They're trying to bring up a gun to fire behind us or set up an ambush near the road to knock off some of our vehicles.

My gunner looked at me nervously and then back up the road.

"Is that a canister in the chamber?"

"Yeah—but don't fire until I tell you to. I've got a funny feeling about this," I whispered.

The chattering from down the road was getting closer and closer.

My gunner was turning another canister round in his hands, ready to load it as soon as we fired the first one. It was a habit of his, to keep himself focused, when the strain became too much. I could barely hear the faint rustling of the metal turning in his hands.

"Hold your fire. Don't fire."

"For Christ's sake, they're almost on top of us!" he pleaded.

"I want to hear what they're saying," I said.

"Goddamnit! You can't speak Japanese," he groaned.

"If I tap you on the shoulder, fire. Otherwise, don't."

At the last second, I heard what the whispering really was. A wounded GI was being taken to the rear after dark. The men were whispering; *"Medics...medics...litter bearers...litter bearers..."* repeating it every few seconds to warn us that they were coming.

"Don't fire! Don't fire! They're medics!"

They passed right by us, still whispering, and disappeared into the night.

The litter was being carried by four bearers, each one holding a corner with one hand. They were followed by two medics trotting along behind the litter. In the near-total blackness, their shadowy silhouettes gave the exact appearance of a Jap machine gun team trotting down the middle of the road.

I broke out in a cold sweat when I realized what had almost happened. If we had opened up, every one of those seven men would have been killed. Of course, we should have been told that we had positions out to our front, so we would know what to expect. "Friendly fire" incidents happened all the time. Men were killed by accident, bad judgment, inexperience or just plain stupidity. This had been too close. The worst part was, the next time it might be you—hesitating to fire—costing everyone dearly.

Better to forget it and move on.

When it started to get light, I heard a... *PING!*

Right near my head.

I was lying flat on the ground behind the gun, with my face next to a tire. The rounds were coming from behind us and off to the left.

"Holy shit! Somebody's firing on us!" I exclaimed.

There was another—PIIINNNGGG—as a bullet bounced off our gun shield. Then two more—*PING—PING!* The rounds weren't coming from down the road. I immediately suspected it was friendly fire from behind us.

"Hold your fire, you goddamned idiots!" I yelled.

PING...PING...BRRAAAAAAPP...PING...PING!

The men in the line company began firing in the opposite direction. We were pinned down and couldn't turn the gun around. The Japs obviously had positions on our open flank to our left and a clear field of fire on us. I was so damned mad at the line company guys for having us set up right out in the open, on the wrong side of the road, that I began yelling at them as loudly as I could.

"You stupid sonsofbitches! Why didn't you tell us to set up on the other side of the road?"

"We didn't know the fuckin' Japs were over there!" A sergeant yelled back.

The line company GI's had stopped firing and were just sitting in their holes looking around. Japanese rounds were whistling through the area and bouncing off our shield and chewing up the road next to us.

The sergeant yelled over to me after several minutes.

"Why don't you just fire your gun at 'em?"

"We can't move the gun, goddamnit...we're pinned down! Why don't you guys open up for Christ's sake?"

"Okay! We'll drop everything we have on 'em and you turn your gun around!"

The entire line opened fire with every weapon they had, trying to keep the enemy pinned down while we moved our gun. The din was terrific as rounds ripped by overhead. We struggled to push the gun around to face the enemy, a few inches at a time, not daring to raise our heads above the flimsy gun shield.

We fired a canister shell into a stand of trees about forty yards away and the incoming fire immediately slackened. After several more rounds were fired into the same spot, we traversed, covering a wider area with canister, to discourage any diehards from repeating their comrades' actions. The firing ceased.

Our ammo bearers were feverishly stacking different types of shells. Armor-piercing (basically useless in stopping Jap tanks), canister (antipersonnel) and H.E. (high explosive), were stacked next to the gun where they could be easily reached when we were attacked. Bazooka teams were spread out behind cover near the three guns, ready to take on any enemy tanks attempting to break through. In addition, each squad leader was armed with rifle grenades.

The rest of our platoon feverishly dug in around their positions. The lieutenant told us to manhandle our gun out onto the road.

"You can get a clear shot at the Nips from there," he said over his shoulder as he crab-walked past us to check on the other squads.

"No *shit!* And they can get a nice clear shot at us, too!" I replied, disgustedly.

We discovered there was nothing in front of us but flat ground and a whole town full of heavily-armed Japanese, supported by tanks. The infantry dug in between us and the town had been ordered to pull back because of the threat of an imminent tank assault.

We could clearly hear Jap medium tanks roaring to life nearby, the drivers revving their engines. My gunner slammed an armor-piercing round into the breech of our tiny thirty-seven, looked over the top of the gun shield and spit.

Time was running out.

CHAPTER 11

In the Midst of Lions

Directly in front of us, about 50 or 60 yards away, were piles of debris and low scrub brush. The land itself was as flat as a billiard table with stands of trees and buildings scattered about the town as if randomly dropped there by a myopic giant. We knew there were GI's on the other side of the town, but we couldn't see much from where we were on the outskirts. If the Japs wanted to get out, we were on our own.

A tank engine coughed to life in front of us and it was—close!

Suddenly a large pile of debris heaved, off to my right. Wooden beams, corrugated sheet metal, trash and dirt flew in every direction. A Japanese tank emerged from its camouflaged hiding place under the junk pile, engine roaring and gears grinding. A thin cloud of dirty blue smoke poured from its exhaust. Surging up sharply from the hole where it had been dug-in, the tank swerved directly toward us, shedding loose dirt from the hull like a flimsy skirt.

Before we could aim, the tank fired its main gun at us. The shell exploded directly in front of our gun, spraying our two ammo bearers with dirt and metal splinters. The tank's ungreased treads and bogie wheels screeched horribly as they ripped and crushed metal sheeting on the ground. The turret slowly traversed toward us again as the driver locked his right tread, the ugly smoke-blackened muzzle of the gun barrel slowly lining up for a killing shot.

"Got 'em!" yelled our gunner.

BANG!

The Jap tank was only twenty yards away when our tiny gun barked, the recoil forcing the gun trails to jump on the road. As the report echoed from our barrel, the round struck the tank between the turret and driver's hatch, bouncing off at an angle, its screaming whine signifying that it had not penetrated their armor plate. As soon as the round was fired, another was loaded and the breech slammed shut. It wasn't quick enough...the Jap was on us.

A bazooka round exploded on the tank with a shower of brilliant sparks, but didn't stop it. It was still coming on. The tank's cannon was pointed right at me. I was staring right down the barrel. The next shell, nestled in that length of rifled Japanese steel, had my name written all over it.

Then a blinding, mind-numbing flash!

I was thrown backwards and slammed to the ground. With the tank only twenty yards away, it had suddenly exploded! The tremendous blast blew off the turret, sending it twisting high in the air, tracing spinning, smoke-curled circles as it tumbled back to earth with a metallic, fluttering cry.

We were so close to the explosion, I expected the burning, tumbling wreckage to crush us. The sizzling turret smashed heavily into the ground close by, twisted and blackened, partially burying itself, warped and smoking. The concussion had knocked down my whole crew, sending us flying in all directions. Two were slightly wounded and the rest of us were dazed. We tried to clear our heads; the tank continued to burn fiercely as thick gouts of oily, black smoke, tinged with red, spewed from the engine compartment and the stripped, cratered hull, where the turret and crew had been.

I lay on my side, stunned, watching in a fog. The titanic explosion had literally torn the tank apart. Had the Jap been hit by a round from one of the bazookas? Was it a lucky shot from one of the 37s? Did they run over an undiscovered mine or was it a bomb dropped from one of our planes? All of us were dazed from the concussion and couldn't tell what had happened. It was a miracle. We were lying on the road, completely out in the open, defenseless.

Jap tank rounds continued to crack past our gun, sitting askew on the side of the road, unused shells strewn around it on the ground. As we slowly regained our senses, there was a revving of a large engine behind us. An M-7 self-propelled gun emerged from inside the metal-sided warehouse to our rear, backing up for all it was worth.

It came to a rocking stop, turned and headed for us, the crew firing at the enemy with everything they had. So that's what had knocked out the tank! They had waited with the warehouse doors open about three feet… just enough for them to see out, but not enough to be spotted by the Japs. As soon as the enemy tank left its hole, the M-7 tracked it until they had a perfect shot. The heavy shell screamed directly over us and nailed the tank with a direct hit, squarely between the hull and turret. The round had evidently gone right through the armor and a fraction of a second later, detonated inside the turret. The simultaneous explosions of the shell, fuel and stored ammunition, created a volcanic eruption that had blown the entire turret, both fuel tanks, and most of the interior, straight up into the air. It rained down all over the area.

The M-7 surged past us, the driver locking his right track, swerving to the right and coming to a creaking halt in a blinding cloud of dust. They pulled in front of us as protection from enemy fire while we pulled our gun back to a better position. We manhandled our gun, its trails damaged from the blast and shrapnel, down the road about thirty yards and started to dig in before the next attack.

While we dug our new gun position, the fighting continued, unabated. More Jap tanks shed their cover and attacked. Their terrible squealing and rumbling could be heard even above the noise of the battle. Advancing over the flat ground, the Japs continuously fired at us until they were destroyed. Tank rounds streaked by us—going both ways and machine gun bullets zipped over our gun shield.

A second enemy tank was knocked out at close range after one of its treads was damaged and unraveled by a near miss. It swung around in a massive shower of dirt and stones, dragging the severed track like an enormous snake shedding its old skin, the damaged bogies chewing into the ground, giving a bazooka team a chance for a killing shot. The careening tank suddenly jerked to a stop amid streams of colored sparks spitting from severed wiring in the engine compartment. Thick, oily-black smoke erupted from the rear deck and a second later, searing blow-torch flames licked at its fractured fuel tanks. As the crew frantically pushed open the hatches, the tank blew up with an ear-splitting roar, spewing burning fuel, red-hot metal and sizzling flesh skyward.

Closing from a different direction, the third tank tried to advance after being damaged by several direct, small-caliber hits, but was stopped for good by a courageous GI. Armed only with a steel bar, a few grenades and a Colt .45, he leaped out of a shell hole.

Climbing up onto the hot rear deck, he stood up in full view of the Japanese infantry and pulled open the traversing turret's unlocked hatch. Balancing himself in a half-crouch, keeping his head below the turret-hatch, he jammed the Colt into the turret. Squeezing the trigger as fast as he could, he emptied a full clip into the interior. He set the pistol down on the deck and grabbed a grenade. He pulled the pin and threw it into the turret. The hatch cover slammed back down on the turret roof as he grabbed his pistol and jumped from the tank, rolling into a nearby shell hole. The confined explosion of the grenade must have pasted the vehicle's crew to the interior.

The tank stopped only after it ran into a large shell hole and overturned, its engine still running.

A direct hit from an M-7 finished off the last tank before it had traveled more than a few yards, the heavy shell blowing the dirt-covered turret completely off the hull and incinerating those inside. The sides of the vehicle bulged out like a giant, overheated can. Enormous flames scoured the wrecked interior, spewing from the twisted, blackened hatches. The remainder of the hull disintegrated as blast-furnace heat ignited the ammunition.

Finishing off our gun position, we proceeded to dig individual foxholes on both sides of the road. The M-7 backed up near our position and shut down its engine. They would either have to pull out and go back to get more gas and ammunition or sit tight until after dark, when more would be brought up. They decided to stay. The crew reloaded their weapons and stared alertly at the town in the rapidly waning daylight. Darkness settled quickly over the battlefield. Streams of tracers streaked through the night, ricocheting at fantastic speeds and angles. Small arms fire cracked and snapped overhead.

Explosions suddenly lit up a smoking Jap tank about 20 yards away. A badly-charred crewman, burned black from the intense heat of an explosion, hung backwards out of the turret. His arms, split wide open, reached out to the heavens, claw-hands frozen in mid-air. His jaw had been blown off and his seared, white skull shone through the stiff, cracking flesh. Thin wisps of blue-white smoke curled up from the still-smoldering interior, streaming slowly into the night.

Flares popped overhead, sparking and blossoming white and red, twisting in the light wind, producing fantastic shadows that leapt and jumped, expanding and shrinking at fantastic speed, all around us. As a flare drifted down behind us or into the center of the town, another immediately took its place, spitting and popping, swinging gently through the suffocating night like the glowing lantern of an old, slowly-shuffling night watchman making his rounds: back and forth, back and forth, back and forth—

The metallic smell of smoke, cordite, fuel-scorched tanks and freshly-churned dirt, mixed with the sickly, inescapable stench of death. Dismembered bodies sat in their knocked-out vehicles, unable to be buried. The winds bore the unbearable smell and the horrible humming of millions of flies that crawled on the corpses.

We crouched fearfully in our holes, weapons at the ready. The squat shape of an M-7 sat nearby, immobile in the cool, graveyard mist barely moving along the ground. We fought to stay alert.

In my exhaustion, I imagined that dead Japanese were moving all around us: grim shattered forms watching, waiting or gliding through the thin mist—dark shadows vaguely caressed by the light from the ceaseless procession of drifting, sparking flares. Machine gun and rifle fire shrieked overhead, ripping the night like enormous claws scraping rough stone.

We heard more screaming and shouting on the other side of the town and spent the terrifying hours of dark waiting for the Japanese to attack.

Philippine Clipper, Hawaii, 1941. Flying boats flew regular passenger runs between the West Coast and Pacific Islands: Hawaii, Wake Island and the Philippines. (Author photograph)

The author with a 37mm anti-tank gun. Oahu, Hawaii, 1941. These small guns were more effective when loaded with canister shells against infantry than they were when firing armor-piercing rounds against Japanese tanks. (Photographer unknown)

Aloha Tower, 1940. Honolulu. Oahu, Hawaii. (Author photograph)

"God of Happiness." On Guadalcanal, its fingers and toes were clipped off by enemy bullets scant inches from the author's head. (D. E. Anderson Jr. photograph)

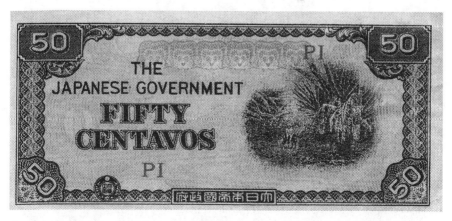

Japanese Government occupation money, Philippine Islands, 1942-1945. (D. E. Anderson Jr. photograph)

U.S. Army Transport *Leonard Wood*, 1940. Large illuminated American flags were painted on both sides of the hull amidships as a warning to German U-boats of the ship's nationality as it sailed from the East Coast to the Panama Canal. (Author photograph)

Back row, l to r: Sergeant Meklos, Corporal Arnold, Sergeant Van Sant, Sergeant Ranucci, the author, Sergeant Higgerson. Front row, l to r: Corporal Hill, Sergeant Jackson, Corporal Craig, Sergeant Shadrick, Sergeant Black. (Photographer unknown)

The author at Alert Call, Schofield Barracks, Oahu, Hawaii. October, 1940. Note the WWI style helmet in use until 1942. (Photographer unknown)

Searchlights blazing over the naval base at Pearl Harbor, Oahu, Hawaii.
July, 1941. (Author photograph)

Native Grass Shacks, Oahu, Hawaii. 1940. (Author photograph)

Field Inspection. Oahu, Hawaii. 1941. Two man pup tent and two sets of equipment ready for inspection with bolt-action Springfield rifles. (Author photograph)

The 35th Regimental Motor Pool at Schofield Barracks, Oahu, Hawaii. 1941. Trucks on the left were used for towing anti-tank guns. Command Cars on the right were reconnaissance and communication vehicles. On the morning of December 7, the vehicles were lined up as they are here. (Author photograph)

Tank shed at Schofield Barracks, Oahu, Hawaii. 1941. Light tanks were equipped with a 37mm main gun and a hull machine gun. (Author photograph)

The author with number 18 at Schofield Barracks Motor Pool. Oahu, Hawaii, 1941. These trucks towed 37mm anti-tank guns. When the 35th Regiment departed Hawaii, they were equipped with newer vehicles. (Photographer unknown)

Firing Range. Hawaii, 1941. (Author photograph)

Pack mule in the mountains. Hawaii, 1941. The gun carriage here is loaded with supplies. 37mm mountain guns, broken down into three sections, were also hauled by mules. Ammunition was normally packed on special frames strapped to their backs. (Author photograph)

Small unit maneuvers with infantry column. Mules and wagon are hauling supplies and ammunition. Note the use of pre-war wide-brimmed "campaign hats" instead of helmets. Hawaii. 1941. (Author photograph)

Deserted Lever Brothers plantation near the coast damaged by shell-fire and bombing during the fighting on Guadalcanal, 1943. (Author photograph)

The steep approaches to Mount Austen through the heavy jungle. All supplies had to be carried by native bearers or infantry to keep the line companies operating. Supply trails are visible in the distance. Guadalcanal, January, 1943. (Author photograph)

Henderson Field. Expanded runways and new aircraft revetments under construction. P-39 fighter-bomber is visible, right of center. Guadalcanal, 1943. (Author photograph)

An amphibious tractor lies half-submerged and abandoned next to the jungle-covered banks of the Tenaru River near the beach following a typhoon. Guadalcanal, 1943. (Author photograph)

"Wildcat" fighter. Henderson Field, Guadalcanal, 1943. (Author photograph)

A battle-damaged P-38 Lightning being stripped in the bone-yard at Henderson Field. Usable parts kept other planes flying. Guadalcanal, 1943. (Author photograph)

A line of shark-mouthed P-40s, sit ready for take-off at Henderson Field's dirt fighter strip. Guadalcanal, 1943 (Author photograph)

37mm anti-tank gun with captured Japanese flag draped on the gun shield. Author standing, far right. Luzon, Philippines. February, 1945. (Unknown photographer)

CHAPTER 12

Blood and Steel

Darkness dissolved over the death-blackened town. Tiny spotter planes were already weaving about overhead like giant dragonflies, the pilots clearly visible as they plied their trade slightly above the trees. We sat in our foxholes amidst the smoldering junkyard of battlefield as the mist and smoke grudgingly twisted into a morning sky.

Scattered burned-out tanks bore mute testimony to the ferocity of the fighting. The fears of the long, sleepless night were replaced by the horrors of daylight: bloated corpses already crawled with maggots. We knew the enemy was still firmly entrenched in the town. They weren't about to leave just because we had knocked out a few tanks.

A warning came down to us from a spotter plane overhead. He could see enemy tanks moving in the town but, he didn't know how many. Then heavy ground fire forced him to swing away to the west to avoid being shot down.

I thought, "How many of those bastards are in there?"

If they tried to break out we could get a shot at them. It would be a miracle to knock out more than one or two with our tiny thirty-sevens even with three guns on the line. What would we do if they all came out at once?

I looked over at the steel bulk of the M-7. I thanked the Good Lord for delivering us from the previous day's battle. It had been a very close call; two men were wounded but no one killed. The bravery of the M-7s crew, the bazooka men, the lone GI and all the others around us had saved our lives. The men near me were all filthy, faces and hands blackened and smeared with gunpowder, dirt, dust and sweat; some wore seeping, blood-stained bandages. They stared back at me through tense, red-rimmed eyes, unbearably strained from too many sleepless days and nights of fear, close combat and violent death.

Some were carefully cleaning their weapons, a few were poking at their congealing rations, a handful smoking and staring out at the town that before yesterday, nobody had even heard of. We all knew that if the enemy didn't attack us, we would have to go in and dig them out, an all-too-familiar pattern.

At 0700 our questions were answered when explosions began to dot the town, sparsely at first, then with increasing intensity. Sweeping clouds of acrid smoke blew across our positions masking our view. The deadly bursts were from our heavy mortars, brought up during the night. Their detonations threw up dirty, red-tinged fingers of flying debris every few seconds. Razor-edged shards of hot steel shrieked through the town.

While the mortar shells blasted the enemy, we heard our attack start on the other side of the town. The Japs opened up, pouring fire on our men as they tried to advance (lack of ammunition was obviously not a problem for them). The din of battle increased to a deafening roar as tanks, M-7s and everything else, short of heavy artillery, opened fire to knock out the enemy's positions.

Anything short of a direct hit wouldn't knock out a tank buried in the ground as a stationary pillbox. Because of the superb job they did in camouflaging their tanks, they were very hard to detect until they fired in your face. Once the pressure became too great on the other side of the town, the enemy would hit us again. There was no doubt about that. We blocked the exit, the only way out. They knew it as well as we did. We didn't have long to wait.

The squealing and grinding of Japanese tanks on the move reached us before we could see them coming. The nerve-stripping noise stiffened the hair on the back of my neck. It sounded like a whole damned company coming through the town right at us. The worst part was waiting for them to show themselves. The vehicles were moving around behind the huts and in the trees off to our left, but they were still out of sight. The screeching and rumbling sounds they made, as if the air itself was being torn apart, swirled around us, louder and louder. They were getting too damned close. Loose dirt piled around my foxhole began to collapse, dribbling into the hole from the heavy vibrations in the ground.

The crew of the M-7 had already loaded their main gun. Their mounted fifty-caliber machine gun was slowly traversing on a small arc, back and forth, the gunner waiting patiently for a target to appear. What was it we said, "Let them come out so we could get a shot at them"?

Several enemy medium tanks suddenly charged into view, their turrets swinging slowly, searching for targets. They moved toward us, picking up speed, sweeping through small stands of trees and around the few rickety buildings to their left.

I grabbed a rifle grenade from the bag in my foxhole and loaded it on my Garand. I jammed the stock into the ground to absorb the recoil, judging the distance by eye. A split second before pulling the trigger, I stopped cold. In the rush of the moment, I had forgotten to remove the live round from the chamber. It should have been removed and replaced with a blank round used to propel the rifle grenade to its target. If I had squeezed the trigger—

Fumbling for the right cartridge, I watched the first tank getting closer, the black muzzle of its cannon swinging toward me. With one eye on the tank, I ejected the live round and loaded a blank.

Again, I placed the weapon's stock on the ground and squeezed the trigger. The recoil jammed the stock into the dirt, as the armed grenade sailed in a graceful, curving arc right over the advancing tank. We all watched incredulously as it came back to earth and exploded with a roar— right on top of an outhouse. The tiny building disintegrated, pieces flying everywhere, raining down behind the tank. Even with the Jap rapidly approaching, my gun crew looked at me in amazement and started to laugh like hell.

"*Holy shit!*" My gunner exclaimed.

In the meantime, bazooka teams managed to knock out the tank with three direct hits. It swerved to the right and smashed into a tiny school house, where it stalled, the building collapsing around it.

A second tank disappeared behind one of the buildings though we could still hear it maneuvering off to our right. The remainder of the Japanese armor was still hidden from view, waiting to sucker us into their sights. They knew we would attack soon, if they didn't attack us. They would sacrifice a few tanks so that they could see where our positions were, then blast us when we moved.

After a short wait, we were ordered to attack across the open ground toward the town. We grabbed our grenades and ammunition, then scrambled from our holes and started moving cautiously into no-man's land, using fire-and-movement. A few men would advance at a crouch while they were covered by GI's behind them. The first team would then cover the second team as they moved up. The M-7 slowly moved forward with us, its engine roaring and straining. The machine gunner on the vehicle was raking the area with his "fifty."

Suddenly, the M-7 received a direct hit from a Japanese gun, decapitating the driver and killing the entire crew. The massive vehicle, with a full load of shells and fuel aboard, sat there idling, a defenseless target. A lieutenant and his squad from a line company had been defending the M-7 against enemy infantry when it was hit. Without hesitation, he leaped aboard the smoking, blood-spattered vehicle with several of his men, to try and back it out of the way before it was hit again and destroyed.

Before they could move it, the M-7 was hit once more, this time wounding the lieutenant and his men. With both hands and feet blown off and his stomach torn apart, the dying lieutenant screamed, "*Save my men! Save my men! Get my men out!"* Another member of the squad climbed up, removed the mangled body of the driver, and backed the vehicle out of the line of fire.

After it stopped, medics rushed to help the young officer but he had already bled to death. The rest of the wounded were sent back to the aid station for treatment. The dead were laid out in a field and covered with shelter halves.

Our platoon leader told us to hold where we were and dig in as mortars from the Chemical Company were being brought up to hit the area in front of us. We scraped out shallow foxholes as quickly as we could and waited for them to get into position down the road behind us. Mortars were also being set up opposite our positions on the other side of town to fire on the enemy at the same time, squeezing them in an explosive vise.

The mortars began firing on the Japanese using "Willie Peter," (WP) white phosphorus rounds, which burned at extremely high temperatures and couldn't be extinguished with water. Rounds started falling in our position, killing and horribly wounding our own men. We were sustaining casualties to friendly fire faster than we were to the enemy.

As men were hit with the WP, they ran screaming in agony, the white-hot chemical searing through their bubbling flesh, to be killed or wounded by shell fragments sweeping through our tiny area. Through the storm of fire that enveloped us, partly Japanese and our own mortars, we could only lie there in our shallow holes and pray that the fire would lift before we were all killed or wounded. There were no communications lines between our positions and the mortars that continued to blast us unmercifully.

Above the explosions I could hear the terrible screams of burned, wounded and shell-shocked men all around me, their pitiful, pleading cries for help unanswered. It would have been suicide to try and move until the shelling stopped. Finally, someone noticed what was happening to us and relayed a message to the mortars to cease fire.

As the clouds of dust, steel and flying debris subsided, I raised myself up and saw near-total destruction. There were burning, smoking shell holes everywhere. Shattered weapons, equipment and ammunition lay all around us. The stench of explosives hung heavily in the air. Men sprawled on the ground, their bodies smoking from the phosphorus that had struck them down. Others writhed in unbearable agony, the "WP" still burning them after they had been hit.

We stumbled out of our holes and tried to help evacuate the wounded as quickly as possible. Virtually all of us were in shock from the barrage.

Some men walked around muttering and holding their ears. Some were bleeding from their noses, ears and eyes. It was all too obvious that the attack for this day was over. They pulled us back and we dug-in for the night to re-group for the next push, first thing in the morning.

Bracing ourselves for the terrors of another sleepless night, we busied ourselves—resupplied and readied our weapons for a new assault. There were still many more enemy tanks and only one road for them to leave on. More M-7s and Sherman tanks had moved up behind us to bolster our thinning ranks. There would be tank shells firing over our heads in both directions again.

We were thankful because of the support we received from our Sherman tanks directly behind us, but we hated to be so close to them because they drew heavy fire from the enemy as they tried to knock out the armor with artillery or anti-tank guns. We were in the middle with both sides banging away at one another with everything they had.

Soon the night swallowed us up. Nobody moved from his hole. Horrors of the previous night played out; nightmares continued. The suffocating stench of the battlefield settled in around us, seeping into our holes, saturating our coveralls and clinging to everything. Smoke burned my eyes and throat, causing me to retch. The tepid water in my canteen didn't help much, tasting like dirty metal mixed with pond scum. I swirled some around in my mouth and spit into the bottom of my hole. I settled down with my weapons and waited.

Out of the night, came the nerve-stabbing sound of tanks starting up again, the rough rasping coughs of heavy engines washing over us. I dreaded what I knew would happen next: the Japanese tankers would rev their engines, echoing all around us. We'd glance back at our own tanks—then scan the barely discernible outlines of the shattered trees and buildings in the town.

My mouth tasting like dirt and steel wool, guts tightening. The familiar sounds of heavy machine gun bolts cocking, resounding all along the line. Men just behind us, swearing and slamming home a round in an M-7, with a dull, sliding, metallic... CLAAANG! Wiping the cold sweat from my eyes and raising my Garand.

They were coming.

"Flares!"

With a clattering roar, the Jap tanks began their attempt to break out, the bone-shaking noise, terrifying. Rounds began to fall in the town as our heavy mortar crews attempted to track the tanks by sound. Maybe the shells would hit the infantry riding or following the vehicles before they got too close. Firing ripped up and down our line, building rapidly.

A Japanese medium was getting closer but hadn't fired yet, hoping to use the darkness as cover for as long as he could. Close to the ground, we could barely see his outline.

"Bazookas!"

The calls echoed down the line, section by section.

The tank's stinking exhaust flared briefly in the darkness, a bright firefly hovering above the engine deck. At forty yards, everything opened up. Smaller shells and tracers ricocheted into the night, streaking the battlefield with glowing sparks. The noise was unbearable as every weapon fired over and around us.

A heavy shell struck the tank solidly directly under the turret. There was an instantaneous, tiny red glow where the round hit and then an explosion split the hull wide open. Creaking to a stop, smoke and flames reaching up through the open turret hatch like a furnace, a screaming human torch tried to blindly climb up out of the flames roaring through the hatch but was immediately shot, his bullet-riddled, blazing body slumping over the turret's rim.

More enemy tanks were taken under fire as they approached. M-7s, Sherman tanks, bazookas, 37s, mortars, machine guns and rifle grenades all concentrated on their annihilation. The accompanying Japanese infantry were cut down on all sides. An avalanche of shells poured into the enemy, the sheer volume of the noise deafening; men held their ears and cried out in pain from the waves of concussion.

Another Jap medium was hit many times and exploded, its turret lifting clear of the hull and igniting the fuel tanks at the same instant. The sides of the hull seemed to bulge out for a split second as a bright, flashing glow burst from within. The explosion ripped the tank completely apart in an eye-searing blast, lighting up the entire area as if it were mid-day.

I threw my arms in front of my eyes against the unexpected brilliance of detonating fuel and ammunition. The fireball carried a volcano of burning debris: shredded pieces of fenders, bogie wheels, exhaust pipes, engine parts, seats, shell casings and mangled flesh. The wreckage smashed to earth all around us as we crouched under our helmets. Smoking, red-hot steel shards protruded from the dirt, spitting, sizzling and crackling.

A flare appeared overhead, but it misfired with a pathetic *pop* and immediately fizzled, swinging in the light breeze as it drooled a sickly stream of pale smoke and sparks. It slowly drifted behind us, a massive sputtering firecracker.

The night filled with a tremendous rain of explosions. The Japs opened up to give their tanks support, tracers and shells ripping the air like the tearing of an enormous piece of burning cloth. Some of the shells plowed into their own vehicles from behind, as they fired into the uneven flare-light. Tank cannons and machine guns fired as fast as they could be loaded. Both sides were expending ammunition at an unbelievable rate.

Dancing outlines of nearby buildings shone briefly in the shadows caused by floating flares and grenade detonations. Knee mortars, fired from behind some neighboring trees, split the night with their popping explosions spraying thousands of pieces of shrapnel over the area. Screams rang out as men were hit, the cries of *"Medic! Medic!"* Signaling another desperate run under murderous direct fire by a courageous aid man.

After fighting most of the night, the last two Jap tanks in the attack were destroyed. A GI climbed up onto the glacis plate of an enemy tank as it rumbled by his foxhole. Holding on to the cannon barrel with one hand, he waited for it to fire, hanging on for dear life as it bounced along the shell-torn ground. After it fired its main gun, and the Japs opened the breech to extract the expended shell, he jammed the barrel of his Tommy gun into the cannon's muzzle and emptied a full clip into the tank's interior, the heavy forty-five-caliber slugs ricocheting through the vehicle, evidently killing the crew. The soldier leaped clear as the tank, steered by lifeless hands, slowly nosed into a large crater, its treads continuing to churn the loose dirt for a few seconds until the engine died.

Another tank blew up off to our left. A member of my squad said that he thought a GI had crawled under it while it was still moving and attached a satchel charge to it. As the tank continued on, the GI was able to roll away into a shell hole to escape before it blew up. It was a desperate, all-night battle.

Before we realized it, dawn was upon us, the sun's pale rays a most welcome sight. Once again, the entire battlefield had been violently transformed during the night. The smoking wrecks of more Japanese vehicles littered the town, silently squatting in the swirling gray mist where they had been knocked out, like the discarded victims of some grisly big-game hunt. Their fire-blackened carcasses creaked and popped as fires died down and tortured metal cooled in the early morning chill. Melted wire harnesses and severed pipes, dripping dirty oil, hung limply from the engine compartments like twisted, black, glistening guts.

The torn, swelling bodies of the tank crews remained where they had died, stiffening in their scorched metal coffins. They were already blanketed with flies and maggots. We were so close, we had to watch them crawling in and out of the corpses' eyes, ears, noses and mouths—so many of them that the bodies seemed to move. The stink had already begun to draw the rats, as they burrowed into the slippery bodies to gorge themselves, gnawing their way through the gaseous, dripping flesh.

The overpowering stench of gunpowder, burning rubber and death made us retch. We cut pieces from our coveralls and tied them around our noses and mouths in a vain attempt to block out the terrible smell. It seeped through everything. Men vomited in their holes, unable to control the bitter bile rising from their stomachs. Most of our rations went untouched. Nobody was hungry. When somebody did try to eat, his food was instantly swarmed by the wet, glistening flies, which seconds before, had been crawling and laying eggs inside the dead Japanese. Nobody could keep anything down.

We were literally captives in a charnel pit from Hell and there was no escaping it. We were exhausted and almost out on our feet. Nobody had slept for over four days. A few minutes at a time was all anyone could manage, since closing your eyes could get you killed.

I blinked through the drifting smoke and mist trying to see what was happening in the town. It was fairly quiet compared to the tremendous firing during the night. A machine gun would open up and small arms fire would break out, swell for a few minutes and then die down. An occasional scream or shout and grenade explosion was heard, but for the most part, it was relatively calm. It was a good time to re-supply with ammo. Water was brought up, but it was hot, scummy and tasted like burnt, oily metal. Predictably, it acted on the bowels within minutes of drinking.

We prepared to move out for the final assault on Lupao. Our numbers had dwindled even more since the previous day, with the wounded being sent to the aid station about a hundred yards on the other side of the town.

The dead were laid out in long lines, side by side, and tagged for the Graves Registration teams. Walking past those lines of men, their dirty shoes and bare feet grimly sticking out from the bloody pieces of shelter halves covering them, was more than I could bear. The sight of dead and mangled Japanese had long since ceased to bother me. We had been hardened to the sight of the enemy in death. I was overcome by the sight of our comrades' shoes lying in pairs by the road—men we had fought side by side with, forever silenced.

After returning to our holes, we carefully cleaned and reloaded our weapons. No one said a word. All of us were seething with rage after seeing our friends killed and maimed. All we wanted was to kill every Jap we could find. If they suffered before dying for their Emperor, so be it. They had started this war, but we were determined to finish it. Too many men had died already for this tiny patch of dirt, way the hell out in the middle of nowhere. We still had scores to settle.

As we finished cleaning and loading our weapons, I heard a loud rumbling behind us. Two Sherman tanks clanked up the road toward us. The sergeant in the turret of the first tank had his goggles perched on his helmet and dirty smudges on his face where they had been protecting his eyes. The entire vehicle was covered with a thick coating of dirt, dust and grease stains.

As the first tank clattered by, its tracks squealing and rattling, the sergeant peered down at me and yelled over the tremendous noise of his vehicle.

"You guys can get out of your holes, now. This will all be over in a few minutes!"

He laughed and waved to us, then turned back to watch the town.

Jesus Christ!

I thought. "What did he think this was, a goddamned football game?"

The two tanks bravely rumbled slowly down the road towards the Japanese as though they were invincible. The turrets slowly turned from side to side seeking a target for their cannon and machine guns. My gunner and I watched in amazement at the tiny "Charge of the Light Brigade," its modern equivalent of the attack in the Crimea, reminder of a bygone era.

Straight up the middle.

Cannon to the right of them...cannon to the left of them.

Into the valley of death...

A tremendous, clanging explosion mushroomed from the first Sherman, setting it on fire. As flames began licking the engine compartment, the hatches popped open and the crew emerged like so many "jacks-in-the-box" from the smoking, creaking hull. Japanese machine gunners raked the burning tank, trying to kill the men leaping from the flames. Bullets clanged and sparked all over the vehicle, but not a single man was hit as they scrambled madly for cover behind the second tank. The burning Sherman was hit again (probably by an anti-tank gun), and blew up spraying burning fuel over a wide area.

The second tank fired blindly to the left where they believed the shots had come from. The hull machine gun chattered in short bursts, ripping up trees and buildings on the edge of the town. Its main gun fired twice, the shells exploding near several large mounds of debris, judged to be concealing the deadly Jap gun. The tank couldn't go forward because the burning vehicle in front of it was blocking the road. The crew wouldn't turn off the road for fear of hitting mines. Before it could back up, the crewmen hiding behind it had to make a dash for the dubious safety of our foxholes.

We opened up on the town, trying to lay down some covering fire for the "orphaned" tank crew. They ran like the devil, flat out, as fast as they could. They reached us safely, out of breath, soaked with sweat and eyes wide with fear.

The commander of the first Sherman made a diving slide for my gun pit, as if trying to beat the throw to home plate to score the winning run of the World Series. He tumbled into our hole in a dusty heap; swearing a blue streak. He looked back at his fiercely burning vehicle, turned and stared at me with a wild expression. I looked him straight in the eye and slowly grinned. After his pompous attitude a few minutes before, I couldn't help myself.

"I guess we'll have to wait a little bit longer before we get out of our holes!"

Then the second tank began backing up through the smoke roiling from its now-gutted sister. Traveling only a few yards, it too was hit by a heavy shell and knocked out. The Japanese gun crew had evidently waited for the vehicle to back away from the first victim until they had a clear shot and then nailed it through the side. Two men ran back under heavy small-arms fire, one man rolling on the ground to extinguish the flames devouring his heavy coveralls as he scrambled towards a nearby gun pit.

The rest of the crew didn't get out.

The thoroughly cowed tank sergeant looked to our rear, then back at the burning vehicles and to our rear again. He was evidently weighing his chances of making a break for it. He clawed his way out of our hole, leaped up and took off like a scalded rabbit. His crew took off at the same time, running like Olympic sprinters. The Japs instantly opened fire, raking the area. Puffs of dust spurted from the ground all around us, clanging off the gun shield. The tankers made it back safely, undoubtedly blessing their lucky stars.

"I guess they won't try *that* again!" My gunner muttered to no one in particular as he stared at the burning tanks over the lip of the hole. Then he slid back down and lit a crumpled cigarette, puffing contentedly. I looked at him and said; "Yeah. I guess not. That's a hell of a way to learn a lesson, though."

He simply nodded, as the two tanks continued to burn.

The last push through the town began well enough. My squad and I moved up on the line, weapons at the ready, loaded down with mule-loads of ammunition and grenades. We advanced slowly, using what pathetically meager cover we could find, squeezing the enemy into a smaller and smaller area. It was ominously quiet after the action of the last two days—too quiet.

Hundreds of bodies lay scattered everywhere. Most of them had been repeatedly chewed up by mortar and tank fire. I thought that maybe the Japs were all dead. Maybe they had gotten past us during the night and pulled out already. "Maybe they're just waiting to draw us in and then—"

With each step the tension became worse. We walked on at a crouch, leapfrogging ahead, listening to the firing that had started at the other side of town. We tried to avoid crawling through the larger pieces of bodies, if we could. Our coveralls were slimy with decomposing flesh. When we got up to advance, sticky maggots tumbled from our coveralls.

"Jesus Christ! Where the hell are they?" I asked.

Then we were hit by heavy machine gun, tank and small arms fire.

Luckily, the first bursts were high, giving everyone a chance to dive for whatever cover they could find: a shell hole, piece of corrugated roofing or an oozing corpse. Crazed rats scampered around in circles or leaped into the air, arching their backs and baring their teeth as they were rattled by concussion, scrambling over us as we returned fire. We couldn't pinpoint the emplacements where rounds were coming from.

There wasn't much natural cover where we had been forced to hit the dirt. It had been blasted, smashed and blown up many times in the past few days by artillery, scattering shards everywhere. We were basically out in the open, hugging the ground, firing at invisible targets. It was like crawling on a pool table covered with razor-sharp pieces of metal.

"Move to the right! Move to the right! Get moving, goddamnit!"

Covering fire was laid down as we moved, loaded down with ammunition and equipment, rolling and crawling to positions off to our right, looking like a pack of filthy, bearded, hunchbacked trolls.

A wooden fence ran somewhat parallel to our advance, its bullet-pocked posts and rails still standing, one of the few structures that hadn't been flattened by tanks or artillery. The rails were low to the ground, without enough room to crawl under them—and they were too strong to push over. We couldn't blow it up because of the proximity of our own people. The only way to tie in with the outfit in the field on the other side was to stand up and climb over. The only problem was the incredible amount of lead screaming by all around us.

"Oh…shit," I thought as I jumped up and began climbing over the fence. I felt like I was ten feet in the air, though it was probably closer to four. Japanese mortar shells were exploding everywhere, as if giant hands were scooping up dirt and tossing it high into the air. Swarms of bullets whizzed by my head, snapping by my ears.

Suddenly, I was engulfed by a sharp, blinding *CRRRAAAACK!*

A rush of hot air and a thick shower of dirt, stones and steel fragments slammed into my face as a mortar round hit the ground right next to me. A piece of shrapnel hit me like a blow from a sledge hammer. The jagged, red-hot metal ripped open my cheek, passed through my mouth, which erupted in a spray of blood, sliced my tongue and then exited without hitting my teeth; a bullet carved a ragged, bloody furrow down my arm, blowing the watch off my left wrist, the impact hurling me sideways to the ground. I landed heavily on my right side, on top of my rifle, stunned and bleeding. A buddy from my squad ran to the fence, scrambled over and knelt beside me. He turned me over and started to check me for wounds. I still didn't realize what had happened.

"Oh God, you're hit!" he exclaimed.

"What? What happened?" I mumbled slowly.

My mouth wouldn't work properly and my face was wet and sticky.

"You're covered with blood, where are you hit?"

"My mouth hurts…" I stammered as he checked my cheek. Blood streamed from my face and mouth. It covered my face, chin and arm, mixing with dirt to form a red paste on my coveralls. My buddy thought I had been shot in the head and kept talking to keep me from going into shock. He quickly wrapped bandages around my face and arm, then helped me back to the medics, all the while under enemy fire. It was a miracle that we weren't hit or killed crossing the battlefield with both sides firing past us the whole time.

After seeing that I was all right, he headed back to the battle, running in a crouch.

A medic decided to send me back to the Battalion Aid Station in a litter jeep. They put me in the back of the next jeep, sitting next to a badly wounded GI on a stretcher. He was tied to the litter, his chest swathed in bloody bandages. His pooling blood ran off the end of the litter in little scarlet streams as we took off. The terrible condition of the road made the trip a nightmare for him. The driver had to go like a bat-out-of-hell because of the danger of snipers, who had no compunction whatsoever about shooting medics or our wounded.

When we arrived at the aid station, I was directed to a tent and examined by a medic. After a short wait, I was taken in to the hospital tent where they removed my tattered coveralls. The smell from my unwashed, filthy body was awful. They cleaned me up as best they could from a large bowl of warm water and proceeded to examine my wounds. A doctor applied antiseptic to my arm, then bandaged it. Then he trimmed and bandaged the hole in my right cheek. He managed to slow the bleeding to a trickle.

He told me how lucky I was not to have been hit when my mouth was closed. The shrapnel could have torn out my teeth or been deflected down into my throat or up through my brain. My damaged knee, injured on the ship, was next. The infected, partially healed wound was a sticky, disgusting mess. Filthy clumps of pus-clotted bandage and God-knows-what-else had been ground into it from crawling in dirt and rotting corpses. The bone was scored by shrapnel.

"What happened here?" he asked as he probed my knee with a metal instrument.

"I hurt it on an ammunition ship."

He proceeded to clean my knee with torture devices that must have been devised during the Spanish Inquisition. The pain was excruciating. No anesthetic, he said; they had to save it for the worst cases—not for scrapes.

When the doctor was finished cleaning the wound as best he could, he applied sulfa and re-bandaged it. I was told to keep the bandages clean and come back each day to get them changed.

"What do you think we do on the line? Play cards and drink coffee all day?" I asked him.

Predictably, he was not amused.

After several hours, I was driven back to my outfit and took command of my squad back from my gunner.

The first thing I did when I got back, was rub dirt on my bandages to keep the Japs from using all that stark white gauze for targets. Infection, be damned. I wasn't about to walk around setting myself up for snipers.

The fighting had slowed down. More Japanese tanks had been knocked out, gun emplacements destroyed and most of the Emperor's infantry killed. Some of their tanks had eluded us and escaped the trap. One drove into a mine field and blew up. Several more were knocked out by roadblocks farther up the road. Only a few Jap infantrymen were taken alive, all seriously wounded or unconscious, for our Intelligence people to try and "obtain information essential to our operations" as they were always telling us.

They knew as well as we did, that the ordinary Japanese soldier knew little more of what was happening than the average GI. We were told to go to a certain place on a map and tried to get there without getting killed in the process. Rarely were we told about the reasons for these moves or their relationship to an overall plan. It really didn't matter to us. We were there to kill Japanese soldiers. It was as basic as that.

Slowly, the firing died down to occasional shots or brief, fierce fire-fights followed by several explosions, signaling the end of another pocket of resistance. By mid-day, the town was almost totally cleared. The enemy's last stand in the town held us up for four days. An American flag, hidden in the town by the inhabitants since the Japanese occupied the town in 1942, was brought out and raised on a rickety pole in the center of the wrecked town.

The main force moved in to begin the massive job of clearing away the mountains of debris caused by the fighting. Many of the buildings were either heavily damaged or totally destroyed. Some were completely gone, pulverized by heavy shelling. Few had escaped serious damage; their bullet and shell-riddled skeletons smoking and creaking in the light breeze. As we stood there scanning the destruction, several corrugated metal structures slowly collapsed with loud screeching groans, spewing clouds of thick, choking dust.

More than thirty enemy tanks sat burned, blasted and motionless, scattered all over the town. The putrefying remains of over eight hundred dead Japanese caused a health hazard for our troops. The vicious rats, as usual, had to be shot to enable troops to drag away what remained of the bodies. The blasted remains of the battle fouled what was left of the town, now reduced to a sprawling dump. We had destroyed the last remaining units of the Japanese Second Armored Division. They had ceased to exist, except for scattered survivors who had somehow escaped the battle.

Hundreds of our vehicles were already moving north. The road was once again open for the traffic waiting to move up as soon as the battle was over. Our advance continued even as the debris was being pushed off the road. General Yamashita and his troops were slowly withdrawing into the mountains. But they weren't running, not by any means. They were staging a clever, fighting withdrawal, making us pay in blood for every mile we advanced. And that meant plenty of mines and snipers.

Snipers were an omnipresent hazard—to everyone. The Japanese would leave men behind in spider holes, trees or caves as they pulled back. Sometimes they'd wait for days before opening fire. By then, the area would have been considered "safe." GI's would fall, the crack of a Jap's rifle signaling a wild scramble for cover. A few soldiers would take off into the bush to hunt him down. The fusillade of shots or a grenade explosion brought the episode to a close.

CHAPTER 13

Victory at the Quarter-Moon

After fighting for Lupao, we were able to pull some much needed maintenance on our weapons, vehicles and ourselves, in that order. Supplies and ammunition were brought up and stockpiled in designated areas of the town, cleared by bulldozers. Our outfit sent people down to pick up ammo, water, rations and mail, if it had caught up with us.

After being in combat and awake for days, everyone was dead tired, but it was SOP to resupply before anybody rested. We had learned long ago, that the Japanese always hit us when we weren't ready—low on ammo or too tired to stay awake.

Our squad truck arrived from the rear to pick up our thirty-seven for repair at the maintenance depot, set up down the road. The gun's trails had been damaged by near misses and needed to be repaired before going back into action. The vehicle pulled up and we hitched the gun on. I pulled myself up into the passenger's seat and placed my rifle next to me. Someone called to me, and as I stepped out of the truck, I collapsed onto the road. My right leg had given out unexpectedly. My buddies rushed over and helped me up.

"Are you okay?" asked my gunner.

"Yeah, just tired, I guess," I replied.

I rubbed my sore leg and walked over to talk with a member of my squad. After a few minutes, we mounted up, drove back to the rear area and dropped the gun off.

Returning to the forward area, we pulled up to our bivouac, our truck skidding to a stop. As I stepped out, once again my leg gave out, and I went down like a load of bricks. My buddies rushed over and helped me to my feet. This time, my leg was really hurting. I was helped over to a small stack of crates and sat down.

"What's wrong? Are you all right?" asked one of my buddies.

"Jesus, I don't know. My leg just gave out on me," I replied, rubbing it.

"I'll go get Doc," said my gunner, as he walked off toward our medic, who was standing near the supply area.

The medic returned with my gunner and proceeded to remove my shoe. It was difficult to take off not only because was it plastered on with dirt, sweat and putrid water, but my whole leg was swollen and tender. The medic had me pull down my coveralls and then examined my leg. There were dozens of puffy, red puncture holes all over my calf, covered with dried blood.

"Didn't you know you were hit?" asked the incredulous medic.

"I didn't feel anything hit me there," I told him, looking at the puncture wounds. They didn't appear to be serious. My leg was black and blue—just a little shrapnel. With so many tears and holes in my coveralls, so smeared with dried blood, I hadn't notice the "new" holes.

"Well, they are going to have to get those pieces out, or you'll wind up losing that leg. I'm sending you back to the Battalion Aid Station. They can check out your other wounds at the same time." He mumbled continuously as he filled out a crumpled white tag, which he tied to my coveralls. I put them back on and grabbed my gear.

"Here we go again," I muttered.

The medic flagged down a beat-up litter jeep and I climbed painfully into the back next to the litter. For once it was empty. The driver took off like a shot and gave me another hair-raising ride to the Battalion Aid Station. I didn't know which was more dangerous, being in combat with the Japanese or riding with these crazy "evac" drivers.

I was dropped off at the aid tent and the driver took off again, after being loaded up with medical supplies. I walked over and sat down on a rickety old litter near the tent's entrance. Leaning my weapon against a bullet-scarred tree, I watched the bustle of activity in front of the tent.

Jeeps arrived continuously with wounded on litters, a few with walking wounded. Several men suffering from shock or concussion (commonly called war neurosis, psycho-neurosis or simply shell-shock) were gently led from a nearby tent to a jeep going farther back to Division. They stared vacantly, straight ahead, and sat limply in the jeep. A medic climbed in the back and gently held onto the man in the front seat so that he wouldn't fall out. The casualty seemed completely unaware of his surroundings. The driver slowly turned left and disappeared down the road.

I was taken into the aid tent where after removing my coveralls and shoes, medics cleaned my leg and examined it closely. There were dozens of metal fragments lodged in my calf, which was still swelling.

I sat there for a short time until the doctor was ready for me. They X-rayed my leg and decided that they didn't want to operate on it but would try and get the fragments out using a powerful magnet. The doctor was able to remove most of them, dropping them into a metal pan with bloody water in it. *Clink—clink—clink—* A few were too deep, but would supposedly find their way out.

While the medics were working on my calf, another medic removed the bandages from my face and wrist, cleaned and re-bandaged the wounds. After my calf was finished, a doctor treated my knee. I listened to the familiar comments about keeping it clean and dry, then put my coveralls and moldy, stinking shoes back on, grabbed my weapon, and hitched another wild ride back to my outfit in a supply jeep.

I climbed stiffly out of the jeep and shuffled over to our foxholes. I was sore all over and felt like twenty miles of bad road. I propped up my weapon against my pack and stood for a few minutes looking around at the buildup that had begun since we had taken Lupao.

A steady stream of vehicles was moving north, bumper-to-bumper, raising stifling clouds of dust as they drove by. Weary, bearded, dirt-covered infantry shuffled along on both sides of the single road snaking through town. The exhausted line companies were moving back up to the next spot on the map. Spotter planes buzzed impatiently overhead, sharp-eyed pilots keeping a close watch over the advance.

"Well, well, well…if it isn't the Ghost." A voice behind me exclaimed. "You keep disappearing and re-appearing every time we turn around. When you do come back, you're always wrapped up like a mummy."

It was my gunner again, trying to make me feel at home.

"Don't go to sleep yet, Sarge. There's something you have to inspect first," he grinned.

We walked over to the 37, which had been returned from the repair shop. My gunner strolled around to the front of the gun and stood there with his hands behind his back, rocking back on his heels, a big grin on his dirty face.

As I stood between the trails, I thought, "Yeah, it's been fixed, I'm going to get some sleep." I turned to walk back to my hole. The gun looked all right to me. I was exhausted and just wanted to collapse for a while before we moved out again.

"No, no, no!" he chided. "You'll have to check out the change we made."

Oh great. They came through with another modification while the gun was in the rear and now we get to see if it works, while staring down the length of a goddamned Jap tank cannon. No thanks. I'd seen enough of that to last me the rest of my life.

I walked around to the front of the gun and looked at the shield.

There it was, on the bullet-scarred metal, as clear as day, for everyone to see.

A Victory silhouette had been painted there by my crew.

It was a large outhouse with a quarter-moon painted on the door.

A direct hit on a Japanese crapper.

Everyone in the squad began laughing like hell, tears rolling down their faces.

That story won't make the hometown newspapers. At least not on the front page!

CHAPTER 14

Whirlwind

Leaving the shattered remains of Lupao, we headed north up Highway Five toward the Caraballo Mountains.

As a unit, our Anti-tank Company never stayed in our Battalion for long but was usually divided into three platoons. Some of the time, we were all assigned to one battalion, at other times we were separated and fought as a single platoon, roaming wherever we were needed.

After traveling up Highway Five for several miles, we halted. We were supposed to wait until we were told which outfit to support in the drive north. While we waited, I was told by my platoon sergeant to take two men and accompany a K9 team on a patrol of a nearby area that was supposedly cleared of the enemy.

The dogs were specially trained to detect the presence of Japanese soldiers by their scent. (Unfortunately, the Filipinos and Japanese soldiers, their diets apparently being somewhat similar, sometimes confused the dogs as to who was the enemy.) Each dog had two handlers, one moving out with the patrol and the other back at the company CP. If the handler on patrol with the dog ran into trouble, he wrote a message and tucked it firmly under the dog's collar. He then ordered the animal to go back to his other handler in the rear—often many miles away.

I was sent to observe how the K9 team worked in the field. Picking two of my newest men, we joined up with the dog and his handler, and a sergeant and two men from one of the line companies. They told us to ditch our steel helmets and wear our soft fatigue hats to minimize noise in the bush. There would be no smoking and an absolute minimum of talking. We were to make sure our dog tags were taped together so they wouldn't rattle and our canteens were full so that they wouldn't slosh as we walked.

We knew all these things already, having gone on countless patrols, but since they didn't know us from Adam, they weren't taking any chances with any unknowns.

This patrol was to be a simple training exercise for both us and the K9 team. We had to learn how to work with the dogs and their handlers once we started to advance into the mountains.

Each man had his personal weapon, (a rifle or Tommy gun), ammo and a few grenades. One line company man was assigned as point, followed by the dog and his handler, the sergeant and his other man, followed by me and my two men, all in Indian file.

We set off and circled a small barrio, passing large rice paddies with roaming water buffalo. After covering about five miles, we came to a wooded area with a small trail running through it. Keeping our eyes peeled for any sign of Japanese, we entered the forest and cautiously followed the narrow trail. The dog had shown no sign that he had sensed anything out of the ordinary. So far, it was just a walk in the woods.

Approaching a tiny clearing, the dog suddenly gave his handler a signal that brought us to an abrupt halt. The handler knelt down, put his face close to the dog's ear and gently talked to him. The hair on the dog's back was standing straight up, and he was growling softly as he stared straight ahead, shaking slightly.

The point man came back at the same moment and told us a patrol of about 30 Japanese was heading right for us. The dog had saved us from running into them. There was only one trail with all of us on it.

A fast conference decided to send the dog back by himself. Then we would haul ass back through the woods and take cover behind the paddy dikes. No way could we hold off that many Japanese with the small amount of ammo that we carried. The forest wasn't thick enough to conceal us that close to the trail. We could ambush the enemy, killing as many as possible, but we didn't have any automatic weapons, except for one Tommy gun with a few clips. It wasn't very accurate for more than a very short distance and it chewed up ammunition at a horrendous rate. The ammo was heavy and usually not carried in bulk on long patrols. We had no BAR (Browning Automatic Rifle) for the same reason. The likelihood of killing the entire Jap patrol before we ran out of ammo was slim to none.

We had been told not to engage the enemy unless absolutely necessary. The dog would alert the handler at the CP and hopefully bring help. The only chance we had.

The handler spoke softly to the dog, patted his head, tucked a tiny message slip under his collar and tapped him sharply on the rump. The dog took off like a flash and was gone. I hoped that he remembered his way back to the CP. We had covered a lot of ground since we left that morning.

We ran back down the trail through the woods as fast as we could, jumping over fallen trees, dodging limbs, branches whipping our faces and slicing our hands. We had to put as much distance between ourselves and the Japanese as quickly as possible, in order to give us a minute or so to camouflage ourselves with the slime from the paddies.

Once out of the woods, we raced single file, traveling parallel on the dikes away from the trail, four of us to the right and three to the left. The paddies were flooded with filthy, black water, the dikes only several feet above the surface. We slid down into the slimy muck and lay down flat with only our eyes and noses exposed. We barely made it before the first Japanese walked out of the tree line, chattering loudly, leisurely carrying their weapons on their shoulders or by their sides. They obviously weren't expecting to meet any Americans.

Just as the Japanese reached the first paddy, the water buffalo began moving toward us, slowly shuffling through the stinking water, snorting and shaking their massive heads. We were faced with the possibility of either being trampled by buffalo or shot by the enemy if we moved. We had smeared our heads and hands with the thick, black mud, (a mix of dirt, scum, filthy water, excrement (buffalo and human), to blend in with the paddy dike. I prayed it would work.

None of us dared to look up over the top of the dike or even move. We would have been quickly spotted by the Japs as they sauntered by, talking and gesturing, their equipment clinking softly. Most of them were carrying Arisaka rifles. Each man had three or four grenades, a pack and each carried a long bayonet. Their faded uniforms looked as badly worn as ours did. We had to wait for them to pass.

By some miracle, they didn't see us even though they walked right past us only a few feet away. Not one of them looked into the paddy where we were hiding. Fortunately, the curious buffalo decided not to investigate we intruders in their paddy more closely. The animals watched as we slowly rose from the muddy water and cautiously peeked over the dike to see where the Japs had gone.

After waiting several minutes, we climbed out and crouched on the dike, dripping weapons at the ready, stinking slop draining from our coveralls and shoes. The patrol didn't return.

We would rather have tried hiding in the woods, but if we had run into wild boars, we would have had to shoot them to protect ourselves, alerting the enemy to our presence. There was also the danger of flushing birds into flight, also a dead giveaway to the enemy. As it turned out, we only got soaking wet.

The dog made it back safely to the CP, alerting our troops to be on the lookout for us. When we arrived back, covered from head to toe with black mud and smelling like an open sewer, nobody would come near us. We were so ripe that even the dog whined and backed away. No offense taken.

Several days later, we moved out with our 37s to support a line company mopping up an area about five miles to the northeast of us. There had been reports of large Japanese troop movements heading north. Our job was to be the stopper in the bottleneck that the enemy had to travel through to reach their forces in the mountains. We drove in a tiny column up to the front with our guns in tow and met our infantry. They had dug their foxholes in a large circle for an all-around defense.

As we arrived, we met our two friends from the K9 team. It was nearly dark, so we checked in with the line company and were shown where to dig in. While positioning the guns, we stacked shells next to them and surveyed the area for fields of fire. The ground in front of us was totally flat, ideal for using canister rounds. Fortunately, we had begged, borrowed and finagled a fairly large stock for defensive use.

The artillery battery near our old area was called to fire a few rounds to register their impact in case we ran into trouble during the night. The K9 handler dug in next to my foxhole. Next to him the radio operator and a lieutenant from the line company shared a "command" hole.

I took out my grenades, straightened the pins and laid them on the edge of my hole. I checked and wiped down my rifle and re-checked my clips, then took out my knife and stuck it into the lip of my foxhole. We double checked our shells stacked near the gun and settled in our holes for another long night of fitful dozing. As I scanned the holes around me, I noticed there was a much higher percentage of automatic weapons being used by the line company. There were many more BARs and machine guns in the perimeter. Quite a few men were carrying pump shotguns; most had the stocks cut off with only a small pistol grip remaining.

I was shaken awake at two in the morning to take my shift on guard. Everything was dead quiet. The dog was lying on the ground, right up close to his dozing handler. After about a half hour, the dog began to fidget and whine nervously. His handler whispered something to him, turned to me and quietly said he thought we were about to have company. The dog was giving him signals that there were a lot of Japs out there... not very far out.

I told him to wake the lieutenant, and I would alert the men on my side. I passed the word down the line to get ready to be hit. Our anti-tank guns were already loaded with canister and ready to fire.

The lieutenant whispered that he was going to send up a flare. It burst overhead in a brilliant cascade, illuminating a large number of Japanese as they sprang up from the ground and charged.

Everything opened up as the Japanese ran straight in, waving sabers and firing rifles from the hip. Enemy soldiers stopped for a moment, took a grenade, tapped it against their helmet to arm it and then threw it into our foxhole line. Many were immediately riddled, their dropped grenades exploding among their own men.

Anti-tank guns, machine guns, shotguns, rifles and BARs poured fire into the enemy. As fast as they were cut down, more took their place. Our hoard of grenades was gone in only a few minutes as we threw them out to our front as quickly as we could yank the pins. Concentrations of artillery were called in, but the enemy kept on coming even though bodies were piling up in front of our gun emplacements. Some of the machine guns quit firing because there were bodies and wounded stacked too high to fire over.

A line company sergeant climbed out of his hole just to the right of me, yelling and cursing the Japanese while firing his pump shotgun into them as they tried to climb over the bloody mounds to get at us with their bayonets. He ran out of shells, pulled his forty-five and emptied that at point blank range. Grabbing his Bowie knife, he killed three soldiers with it before we could cover him. Splattered with blood, he calmly reloaded his shotgun with some of his buddy's shells and resumed firing. His Bowie knife remained rammed to the hilt in the chest of the last man he had killed with it.

Our 37s fired as quickly as they could be loaded, the canister shredding the enemy so close to the barrels that their helmets and weapons flew into our holes when they were hit. Dozens fell at a time from the scything shrapnel of exploding artillery shells. Bodies flew apart in mid-air.

The radioman was frantically pleading with the artillery to pull their fire in on our positions. The Japanese were among us now, and the artillery wasn't close enough.

"I repeat! Drop fifty! Drop fifty!"!

He yelled into the radio, struggling to be heard over the roar of the battle. The artillery radioman was undoubtedly yelling back at him; "Negative, negative…!" telling him that they couldn't fire any closer for fear of hitting us. It was understandable from their point of view, but they weren't the ones being overrun.

"I say again! I say again! Bring it in closer, for Christ's sake!"

The shells were still too far out, and they weren't adjusting their fire.

"We're overrun you stupid bastard—drop those rounds or I'll come down there and blow your fucking brains out! Drop fifty!"

The heavy shells screaming in, sounding like incoming freight trains, engulfed our positions. We crouched in our holes as shrapnel tore through the air. The violent concussion from the shells collapsed the sides of our holes and made our anti-tank guns jump and shake. The noise was deafening as artillery plowed up the area all around us. The storm of dirt, shrapnel, stones and chunks of bloody flesh flew in all directions, slamming against the gun shields like hail. The only way to stop the enemy from totally overrunning us was to keep dropping our shells right on top of our own positions until they were all killed. If we stayed in our holes, we would be relatively safe, unless we were unlucky enough to suffer a direct hit. The attacking Japanese, out in the open, didn't stand a chance. After saturating the area with hundreds of shells, they stopped coming. There weren't any left.

The artillery was called to cease fire, and the attack tapered off to sporadic grenade explosions and small arms fire. The screams and moans of wounded Japanese were answered with grenades, canister or rifle shots. The noise dropped off until there was only an occasional moan or whimper from the tangled mounds of Japanese in front of us. The piles of mangled bodies were dragged away from the smoking guns, clearing the muzzles.

We spent the rest of the night staring into the darkness, listening for any telltale sound.

In the morning, the remains of hundreds of Japanese covered the field in front of us. Most of them had been torn to pieces by the barrage of heavy shells. We couldn't tell for sure how many. There were parts of bodies strewn everywhere, splattered over our gun's shield, barrel and tires. The flies already covered everything: the moonscape of shell holes, torn equipment, shattered rifles and Japanese soldiers.

Because we had stayed in our holes, our casualties were light.

The dog and his handler, (and the artillery), had once again "saved our bacon." They stayed with us on the line for two more days. Never were two GI's more welcome. If the dog hadn't been there to alert us to the presence of the enemy, we would have been completely overrun—without a doubt. We never heard anything from the artillery about our radioman threatening to shoot people during the height of the barrage. I guess they figured it was his call, after all.

After patrols were sent out and the area declared clear, we rejoined our outfit.

Several days of "rest and refit" enabled our platoon to square away our weapons and vehicles so we could start out again. We had three of our 37s, three bazookas and a heavy restock of ammo. Our new orders were to drive five miles out and set up a road block. Ordinarily, a line company moved with us to provide security, but everybody was moving and regrouping, so this time, we would be reinforced by Filipino guerrillas. We never knew what to expect when we met up with them.

They often came into our lines swinging the severed heads of enemy soldiers by their bloody helmet straps to trade them for tobacco, the price on their heads as far as the Filipinos were concerned. The going rate was one pouch of tobacco for each head brought in. In some areas, we discovered large numbers of decapitated Japanese bodies strewn about, stripped of anything usable, obviously victims of chance meetings with Filipinos on the hunt for more weapons and equipment or simply revenge.

We met groups of tough Filipino men with hair reaching down their backs. They told us that they had taken a solemn vow in 1942 not to cut their hair again until the Japanese had been driven out of the Philippines. They had been constantly fighting in the mountains and jungles for almost four years. Now that the end was in sight (for them anyway), their merciless ferocity in battle and revenge knew no bounds.

We had taken vows of our own.

Several times, while holding our nightly jungle positions before entering a Japanese-occupied barrio in the morning, we had plainly heard the screams, pleading cries and horrible sounds of the retreating Japanese torturing and murdering every man, woman and child in cold blood. We were forbidden from entering the barrio before daylight, to avoid hitting our own men. Crouching there in the pitch black jungle, helplessly listening to innocent people being systematically butchered was the toughest thing all of us had to do in the entire war.

We were as close to mutiny as we could get. We knew damned well that the morning would be too late to save them. Why wouldn't they take the chance on casualties and let us go in? What about all those poor little children? The Japanese used the night to their advantage; we could too, if our officers would just turn us loose. But; after dire threats to shoot the first men who pulled out of the line to help the civilians down in the barrio, we had to sit there with barely-controlled hatred of the Japanese gnawing at our guts.

We finally entered the barrio in the morning, the Japanese having already pulled out as we knew they had. The only sounds were the soft clinking of our equipment, the awful hum and buzz of swarming flies and the sobbing and cursing of our men as they finally saw what the enemy had done. Not one person had been spared. Even babies had been hacked apart with swords, bayoneted or bashed against trees, their tiny bodies left in the dirt for the rats. We swore at that moment, to avenge those defenseless children and their families. The Japanese would pay dearly for their horrible atrocities. Tough, grizzled, battle-hardened men wept openly, tears streaming down their faces, as they tenderly carried the lifeless, mutilated people to the jungle's edge. We dug their graves and buried each one in the shade beneath the trees.

We would now be the last men to stand in the way of the Filipinos who exacted revenge for the unspeakable acts against their own people. They didn't give a damn whether the captured Japanese gave up useful information or not. However much they cooperated during their "questioning," their fate was already sealed. Only the methods differed. And the Filipinos were very inventive people. It was no worse than what the Japanese had done to the population over the years. Evidently, the Japanese had found the horrific remains of many of the guerrillas' victims and taken their fury out on the inhabitants of the surrounding barrios. Such barbarity didn't deter the guerrillas one bit; it seemed that they lived for nothing more than both killing as many Japanese as they could and also fighting their political rivals.

I, for one, was glad the Filipinos were on our side. We knew about their bravery in battle, especially the legendary Philippine Scouts. But the guerrillas were usually an unknown quantity. We always tried to keep one eye peeled while they were around us with weapons at the ready. Though we were very heavily-armed, they even made us nervous.

We never knew which group we were dealing with or where their sympathies lay. Whether they were communists or local guerrilla bands fighting against each other, anti-Japanese didn't always mean pro-anybody. Often, they obtained weapons and ammunition wherever and whenever they could—at gunpoint, if need be. From other guerillas, why not? They obviously believed that the end justified the means. After all, there was a war going on. We had our orders; they had their motives.

We drove to a crossroads where we were supposed to meet the guerrillas, way out in the boondocks. According to our map overlay, the spot didn't even exist. The Filipinos were nowhere in sight. We sat in our vehicles for several minutes to see if the rendezvous would be kept, or if this was going to be another wild goose chase like several before. We never learned whether they'd detoured or been killed. Especially because they had special fates reserved for them by the Japanese.

Suddenly, a foliage-camouflaged jeep shot out of the woods and skidded up to us.

Holy shit!

Where had they come from?

The Filipinos jumped out before the jeep even stopped rolling and strode over to us. They looked like gangsters, dressed in a motley combination of weapons and equipment, civilian and military clothing, both American and Japanese, some sporting bullet holes and bloodstains. Most of them had faded ammo belts wrapped across their chests, "bandit style." It was no wonder the Japanese were petrified of being captured by them. This was a fierce looking bunch.

The guerrillas walked over to our vehicle.

"Hey, Joe!" they shouted. "MacArthur! MacArthur!"

"Yeah, MacArthur," I replied as I took out my map, spreading it out on the jeep's hood, and pointed to the spot where I thought we were. Surprisingly, one of the Filipinos pulled his map overlay from inside his shirt and placed it on our map. Pointing enthusiastically, he said, "We go here, Joe!" He was all smiles. But where in hell was the rest of his outfit? We looked around and then asked him where his men were.

He just continued smiling and said, "Oh, they here, Joe!"

As he waved his arms, camouflaged jeeps, filled with guerrillas, emerged from every direction and pulled up to our tiny column.

Sonofabitch!

They had been all around us the whole time and we hadn't even seen them. The widely-grinning Filipino leader jumped back into his jeep and motioned for us to follow. Then he took off like a bat-out-of-hell. Shaking our heads from the suddenness of the strange meeting, we raced after them, pedal to the floor.

Our guide had told us that we were just south of a town named Rizal. Large numbers of "Japnees" were in the vicinity. An enemy armored unit was to the north "somewhere." We were to set up a road block to keep them from attacking south and hitting our people from the rear. In a matter of a few hours, the place could be crawling with Japanese, including tanks. The only thing we knew for certain was that they had to come down the road we were on. It was the only one in the area.

We drove at break-neck speed along a twisting, deeply-rutted dirt road until the jeep in front of us skidded sideways to a sudden stop. A tiny bridge lay just in front of us. We dug in our guns on the south side. One 37 was placed on each side of the road and the third was sited farther down the road behind us to give covering fire if we needed it. Individual foxholes were dug and ready ammunition was stacked around the guns. A tiny perimeter defense was set up for the night.

In the meantime, the guerrillas walked around trying to talk us out of weapons, ammunition and food, but we told them we only had enough for two days and couldn't spare any. Our officers had told us not to give them anything because they were being supplied through different channels. There being many political factions in the guerrilla organizations, they enthusiastically used their weapons on each other as often as they did on the Japs. As long as they kept on killing them, we couldn't care less about their political affiliations.

The guerillas moved off into the woods as night fell, leaving us to our own devices. We were pretty nervous about being stuck way out in the middle of nowhere with just thirty men, a few puny 37s, individual weapons and several bazookas. At least we had the support of the Filipinos if we were attacked. We spent a long, sleepless night, wondering what the enemy was up to. We could expect patrols, infiltration, Banzai attacks, artillery, mortars or tanks.

Dawn brought a disturbing revelation. As we looked around our positions, there wasn't a single guerrilla to be seen anywhere.

What the hell?

A member of the third gun crew down the road told us that the Filipinos had silently pushed their jeeps down the road just before dawn, and left without so much as a by-your-leave. Now we were *really* up the proverbial creek without a paddle. Thirty GI's against a few thousand Japanese infantry with tanks. Well, we had orders to hold until relieved, so that was that. We couldn't pull out and leave the bridge unguarded as a gift for the Japs. All we could do now was trust the Creator to pull us out of our bind when the time came.

Later in the morning, an olive-drab Army spotter plane flew over us at low level and dropped a weighted message. At least somebody knew we were there. I had privately begun to have my doubts. The message told us to maintain our position. The main column had been delayed and would not be able to reach us for five more hours at least.

This was not good.

Our only reinforcements were stalled. We had no resupply available for ammo. The Filipinos had lit-out on us. The last part of the message, hand-scribbled by the pilot, noted matter-of-factly that a large column of Jap tanks and trucks towing field guns and packed with infantry was approaching our position from the north. The fat was in the fire.

We made frantic preparations for immediate action as I anxiously scanned the distance with my field glasses for signs of the approaching column. How many tanks constituted a large column? How many trucks, guns and troops? It would only take a single round to blow a whole crew right out of existence. Never mind an entire Japanese battalion!

Armor-piercing rounds were loaded in the guns. Continuous rooster-tails of dirt flew from our holes like geysers as we rapidly dug them deeper. Everyone checked and rechecked their weapons and ammo for the tenth time. Clips were cleaned and tapped on the helmet to seat the rounds. Grenades were arranged around the rims of foxholes and everyone nervously settled down to see what would happen next. We sat around our guns, profusely sweating under a sweltering, deep blue, cloudless sky. I began to informally talk to the Creator again, as I often did when I was in a jam. These talks happened more often these days.

"What I wouldn't give for the company of a single M-7. Anything you can arrange for us. A small miracle would be nice—not a big one. Just enough to get us past today. Tomorrow will take care of itself. Just this one day. Thanks, Lord."

I pulled out my God of Happiness from my pack and slowly rubbed his polished belly for several minutes for luck. It didn't hurt to cover all the bases. I'm sure there were a lot of crossed fingers in the squad at the same time. We weren't just sweating from the broiling, mid-day sun.

After an interminable hour had passed, the faint but distinctive sound of trucks, heavy vehicles and tanks caught our attention. It became louder and louder as the Japanese slowly advanced on our pitiful postage-stamp of a road block. The unmistakable screeching, grinding noise of tank treads sent a chill down my spine. It sure as hell wasn't our relief column. We could see mushrooming clouds of gray dust in the distance, thrown up by the Jap column, heading straight for us.

It sure looked as if this was going to be our last stand.

I thought to myself, "This is how Custer felt."

We might be able to hold them off for a short time, if we were extremely lucky, but it wouldn't be for very long. Our 37s didn't have much impact on Japanese armor and to fire a bazooka effectively you had to expose yourself to enemy fire. There wasn't much future in that. What we needed was heavy artillery, a few M-7s or a company of Sherman tanks.

Or a genuine miracle.

Seconds later, a plane screamed over us, at about 100 feet.

Nobody heard it coming.

All of a sudden, it was just—there!

It scared the living daylights out of all of us. Everybody dove head-first for their holes as it came around again. The pilot banked to show us his markings. I could see him looking down at us through his gleaming, spotless canopy.

Thank Christ!

It was ours. Here was our miracle.

And, not a moment too soon.

I yelled to my men to spread out the orange air recognition panels in the middle of the road. They had to be weighted down with shells from our 37 to keep them from blowing away. Every time the plane came down over us at low-level, the wind from its passage caused small dust storms to swirl around our positions. Everyone jumped back into their holes like burrowing prairie dogs before the action started.

No sooner had we put out the flapping panels, than a procession of fighter planes shrieked over at tree top level and started their firing runs on the advance units of the Jap armored force. Our aircraft were flying at less than 100 feet as they made their passes, machine guns and cannon winking along their wings, hanging bombs and rockets.

They opened up way behind us, the flat trajectory carrying the ordnance over our heads and into the enemy, who were jammed into their trucks. As the planes thundered over, hundreds of empty shell casings from their machine guns rained down on us, bouncing off the guns and the road. We hunkered down under our steel pots and watched the show with our fingers crossed. If the planes didn't stop the Japanese, the shit was really going to hit the fan.

The first wave was a formation of P-51 Mustangs. Their highly-polished aluminum skins sparkled in the sunlight as they roared by, their heavy fifty-caliber shells ripping into the trucks. The fuel tanks on vehicle after vehicle caught fire from the tracers clawing through their thin skins and exploded in monstrous fire-balls, blowing soldiers high in the air, incinerated by flaming gasoline.

The Mustangs flashed by, one after the other, their wing guns blinking and streaming tracers. They were so low we could see the pilots' faces clearly as they streaked past. Some of the planes had colorful names or cartoon characters painted on the nose. Several came dangerously close to clipping the trees around our position as they made their runs.

These men *definitely* knew their business.

Next, a flight of F-4U Corsairs, easily recognizable by their gull wings and massive engines, roared overhead. We could see why the Japanese called them "Whistling Death." The Corsairs screamed down one after another pouring fire into the enemy. The eerie, spine-tingling howl from their shallow dives was music to our ears, as they raked the Jap column with their machine guns and rockets from one end to the other. Passing over the enemy, braving ground fire at extremely low level, they pulled up sharply, banking around for pass after pass. We watched in awe as the pilots kept flying into the teeth of heavy ground fire, time after time. We didn't see how they survived without being repeatedly hit or shot down. After all, by now, they were flying at about 100 feet or less off the ground.

After the Corsairs had expended their ordnance, the third wave, consisting of A-20s and B-26s, dropped tons of bombs into the burning column, making repeated passes, strafing the survivors. The Japanese were so close, we could feel the pressure waves from the concussion of the explosions washing over us and tugging at our coveralls. We kept our mouths open to equalize the pressure and avoid damage to our ear drums.

Splashes of brilliant-orange fire spewed into the air as each vehicle was hit.

Towering clouds of thick, oily smoke rose from the decimated enemy formations as tanks and trucks by the score were hit, their exploding fuel tanks adding to a widening funeral pyre that had minutes before been a complete armored unit. Burning ammunition trucks and fuel drums exploded high into the air, twisted wreckage slowly falling back to earth, trailing pieces of metal and smoking, burning bodies tumbling end over end, before smashing into the ground.

The planes had proved to be our genuine miracle.

As soon as the air strikes ended, a lone Mustang flew over us waggling his wings, pulled up slowly, performing several victory rolls through the boiling columns of smoke, the burning remains of the Jap armored unit. Then he was gone.

We sat there, stunned, watching the smoke from the still-exploding vehicles curl into the sky and counted our blessings on both hands. The Creator had done it. I closed my eyes and thanked Him for delivering us, yet again.

The spotter plane returned and dropped us another scribbled message It told us to pack up and move out to meet our outfit at Rizal, about 20 miles away from the carnage that had come so close to us.

Our tiny band hooked up our guns and we drove off to Rizal. We were constantly peppered by snipers the whole way, but nobody was hit. Our vehicles sported new bullet holes, but the wisdom of keeping the column moving at top speed paid off.

A bottleneck slowed traffic at Rizal because everyone was heading through the town to continue the advance north into the foothills. Because of the huge number of vehicles using the road, bulldozers from the Engineers had to widen the small trails bypassing the town. We started off cross-country to engage the retreating Japanese.

We headed east, widely circled to the north, and then cut back to Highway Five to get behind the enemy before they could slip away from our tightening noose. Units of the 161st and 27th Regiments attacked the Japanese farther south to keep them from escaping. They "grabbed them by the nose" and kept them pinned until we were in place. Once we were in position, the reduction of the pocket could take place. Reduction meant killing Japanese as quickly as we could.

We pushed up to Carranglan, then headed southeast to Digdig. We were sent in on foot to carry out the wounded from the line units fighting ahead of us because there was no road to the nearest aid station, about three miles away.

It was a brutal trip.

The terrain was up and down steep, rocky hills and across swiftly-flowing streams. The slippery, uneven footing was very treacherous, making it extremely difficult to keep the casualties from falling off the litters onto the rocky ground. Many of the litter bearers became casualties themselves from sprained or broken knees, ankles or wrists. Recurring bouts of malaria claimed some. Exhaustion and snipers also took their toll. Some simply collapsed from the strain. Every man had his breaking point. Some could rest for a few days in the rear and return. A few reached the point where they were no good to themselves or their outfit any longer. They had gone beyond the point of no return and didn't come back.

We had to keep resting because the heat and humidity constantly drained our energy. Flying insects and dust got into our eyes and mouths. Rivers of sweat soaked our stinking coveralls and the stony ground tore up what was left of our dilapidated shoes.

The futility of trying to get severely wounded men to the aid station, when it took hours to manhandle the litters down from the fighting, was especially tough. Some of them may have been saved by the presence of a single jeep and a bulldozer path. But the fighting had advanced into the hills too quickly and there wasn't any other way to get men out.

The jolting of the litters was unbearable for the casualties, but couldn't be helped. Many of those poor guys didn't survive the ordeal. I couldn't escape thinking that the trails were being stained with the blood of kids that should have been at home in school, flirting with their girlfriends. Now, they were bleeding to death on some god-forsaken hillside on the other side of the world. And for what? Because the Japanese wanted to rule the Pacific?

Now that the Nazis had been ground into the dust and the misguided Italians defeated along with them by the very nations they had derided and attacked years before, the Japanese would be next. If they wanted to fight without mercy, so be it. They should have expected no less from us.

CHAPTER 15

Attrition

After several days, our platoon leader told us to assemble our men and get back to the bulldozer road, where our trucks would be waiting for us. We were to go back to Rizal, pick up our 37s, and load up with arms, ammunition, and enough rations for seven days. No one knew any more than that. We knew that it wasn't for a picnic or a rest.

It took us all day to get back down to Rizal. We pulled in just as it got dark. An officer led us over to a mobile command van parked by the side of the road. Squad leaders and our platoon leader were hustled inside where an officer from G-2 proceeded to fill us in on our next assignment.

"Everything you need is in six piles outside, stacked where you just pulled in. The thirty-sevens are out front, along with an extra jeep and a half-ton truck for the ammo and rations."

So far, so good.

Then, he pointed to a map on the table and began to trace a route with his finger.

"You will load up immediately, then rest for four hours exactly. You will leave here at 6 o'clock and proceed southwest onto Highway Five, twelve and a half miles from this point. Then, another eight and a half miles south. You will be met by MPs and directed to your objective, which is a field hospital. Once there, you will become part of the defense perimeter. There have been large groups of Japs moving north, and this unit could be in trouble if the enemy stumbles on them. Your thirty-sevens, with canister, should fit in perfectly there. Make *damned* sure you dig in."

He looked at each of us in turn and asked if we understood.

We all nodded.

"There is a line company from another regiment already dug in there, but you people will have your own sector to take care of. Any questions?"

There were none.

We went back to our men, filled them in and loaded our equipment and ammunition on the vehicles. Lookouts were posted and we all tried to grab what passed for a few hours of rest. Then it was time to get up and haul ass down to our new adventure. It felt strange to be heading away from all the action. Some of the guys thought that it would be a great chance to relax and kick off our shoes. But we squad leaders discouraged that kind of thinking. It usually got people killed.

Late that afternoon, we met the MPs and they took us to our new position. It was on a flat plateau, adjacent to the Talavera River running through a large gully. There was a thick, tangled maze of undergrowth between our location and the river. We were about 100 yards from the hospital, which was just a few large tents and some smaller ones nearby.

Our fields of fire were cleared. We set up our guns in pits and dug foxholes and a latrine trench. Grenade traps were set out, thirty yards in front of our foxholes. All the vehicles except for one jeep were sent back to the motor pool. The guard roster was finished just as darkness set in. Everyone else fell into fitful, exhausted cat naps.

Without the sounds of battle around me, I kept waking up and looking around. In the distance, our heavy stuff was banging away at something, but nothing close. I spent the whole night waking up every few minutes and scanning the darkness. The following morning, we distributed rations and ammo to each crew. Some of the men wanted to go down to the river to wash and swim but the lieutenant said; "No way! No one was to leave the area at any time. No exceptions."

It was too dangerous.

One of our trucks brought up five gallon Jerry cans of water. As we unloaded them, I was talking to one of my crewmen, telling him that I didn't like the set-up, because there were no patrols being sent out. The Japs could be on top of us before we could detect them. The only way to know where they were, was to send out small patrols and thoroughly recon the area. Otherwise, it was an invitation to disaster.

"Aw, you've been over here too long." he replied. "You're always worrying about something. Why don't you just relax?"

"Well, that's my job. And if you relax, somebody will wind up dead," I said, scanning the area in front of us.

I didn't like it.

Not one bit.

Heavy brush grew all over the place. The Japanese could have hidden a few companies in there with no problem at all. The banks of the river were heavily overgrown, providing perfect hiding places for the enemy heading north, right past us.

The next morning, all of my fears came true. Two other squad leaders and I were shooting the breeze when we heard several loud explosions down at the river.

"What in the hell was that? Man the guns!" I shouted.

Before we could disperse to our positions, one of the men nearby yelled that a few guys were down at the river fishing with grenades—it was nothing to worry about, was it?

Then we heard a lot of rifle fire and I knew then, we were in trouble. One of our men who had been foolishly fishing with grenades, came running up, unarmed, panicky and white as a ghost. He was stammering something about Japanese being down at the river.

"They're killing our guys!" he shouted hysterically.

I was so mad that I wanted to shoot the sonofabitch right then and there. They had no business being outside the perimeter, and now they were in real trouble. The three of us decided that we had to act fast.

We grabbed our weapons and two men from each squad headed for the river. Sergeant Higgerson told me to take two men to cover the rear and the right flank. He and my best friend, Shadrick, with their four men would move down to the river and check things out. We rushed into a position with some low cover and readied our weapons.

After several minutes, we heard heavy firing: two Garand rifles and the heavy, stuttering of a BAR mixing with the popping sounds of Japanese Arisaka rifles, a grenade explosion and then an ominous silence.

I started to move forward to help, when Sergeant Higgerson came out of the heavy brush and said that Sergeant Shadrick had been killed. Two others were badly wounded. I told one of my men to go back to the field hospital and get a medic, litters and bearers. A lieutenant came down and told me to keep watching the right flank.

He and Higgerson went back down to the river.

The lieutenant came back up carrying one of the casualties on his back. His coveralls were wet with blood. Staggering under the weight, he came over to us and we gently lowered the wounded man to the ground. Then he headed back to the river.

We did what we could for the kid, only nineteen years old. He had no combat experience. The Japs had shot him from close range and he was bleeding badly. There were two small bullet holes about three inches apart in his chest. His face was ashen and his breathing labored and irregular. Blood bubbled out of his mouth and slowly dribbled down his neck to the ground. He just stared at me, eyes wide with fear and pain. The man next to me was tightly holding the kid's left hand and talking to keep him from going into shock. One man stood guard with a raised BAR while we attended to the casualty.

After applying compresses to the bullet wounds to try and stop the bleeding, we kept watching the underbrush for any attacking Japanese trying to get through from the river.

"Where are those goddamned litters?" I yelled.

Suddenly, there was more heavy firing and a lot of yelling. I told my other man to get on the radio and tell them to get a mortar crew down to us, now!

The lieutenant and Higgerson came back carrying another wounded man, also with several bullet wounds, evidently hit with several .25 caliber rifle bullets.

Soldiers arrived with litters and took the two wounded kids out, both barely alive.

Shells from our mortars started landing near the river, but too late. The Japanese were long gone. The irony was that they must have known we were there, but were only interested in moving along the river to join up with their comrades for a last stand. They didn't want to start a fight but had stumbled upon our men at the river, opening up on them as they ran past.

If our men had obeyed orders and stayed in the perimeter, six of our men wouldn't have died needlessly. Sergeant Shadrick was one of my closest friends, a caring and heroic soldier. Men went in after we left to go north again and recovered his body. I never got the chance to say goodbye to him.

A few days later, we were ordered to move up to the front lines at Carranglan, almost to Balete Pass. While we were getting everything together to move out in the morning, we were to go out and disarm our booby traps. Sergeant Higgerson had finished his and went to help Sergeant Van Sant, our platoon leader, with his. Higgerson inadvertently tripped one that Sergeant Van Sant had missed. The explosion seriously wounded him, and he was evacuated soon after. The medics didn't think that he was going to make it back to the aid station.

Another squad leader and my last close friend was gone. I was now the only one left from our original group stationed in Hawaii, back in 1940. I started to come apart, crying and shaking uncontrollably, cursing the Japanese, the Army and everything else I could think of. I was all alone, no friends left, at the end of my rope.

The war had been going on for three and a half years with no end in sight. Everybody I had served with was either maimed for life or dead. I had seen so much violent death and destruction that my nerves were ruined. I had been wounded four times, had malaria and yellow jaundice thirteen times—and was still in the line. What else had to happen to me before I was sent home? Even if I survived this battle, there was still the looming specter of invading the Japanese mainland. What were the odds of surviving that? It was too much to take. What was the use?

I had given up.

Then I remembered something a young, eighteen-year-old girl named June had written in her first letter to me only a few weeks before. My name had been given to her by my mother, who was working for a local committee sending packages to servicemen overseas. June volunteered to write to me, even though we had never met.

She didn't write silly things, just funny, light stuff. She said that she had two brothers in the Army somewhere overseas. She was praying for me, was sure that God would protect me and I would get home safely. I realized then that I couldn't let such a wonderful girl down. It was as if someone had thrown me a lifeline. I just had to hang on and get back to meet her.

I stood up in my foxhole, grabbed my pack and rifle and rejoined my squad determined to get through and make it home.

CHAPTER 16

Unsung

We drove all day with snipers, as usual shooting at us most of the way. Several ten-wheelers passed us coming down from the fighting in the mountains, streams of congealing blood spilling down the sides and out the back. We could trace the path of the vehicles by following the spattered blood trails they left in the dust. They were loaded with dead GI's, stacked on one another like cordwood. Their feet were hanging out the back, worn, muddy shoes bouncing limply as the vehicles drove past. It was a terribly depressing sight.

We rejoined our Regiment at Carranglan, northeast of Digdig and started on another advance to eliminate more Japanese soldiers. Then we were to link up with the 27th Regiment at Putcan. After it was light, we hitched up the guns and headed north. Using the bulldozer road, we drove up and down ridges, across rivers and streams, bouncing through fields and around shell holes. Throughout the trip, we watched for snipers and possible ambush sites. Weapons were kept at the ready, locked and loaded.

Late one day, after following the Carranglan River about six miles north of a barrio, we moved up to a flat plateau. It was decided to stay there and dig in for the night.

After settling down, I took two men out to see what was over the next rise, roughly 150 yards north. It was almost dusk, and we couldn't stay out very long. We had to get back to our perimeter before dark or risk getting shot by our own men.

As we reached the top of the rise and looked over, we saw open, fairly flat terrain. White parachutes were scattered over the area. One of my new men started to move toward them, saying that he thought the Air Corps had dropped us supplies and we ought to go check it out. I snarled at him and told him to get back before he got us all killed. We had to get back and radio Battalion to check this out and we never, ever went out into an open area without checking our flanks first. It had ambush written all over it.

When we arrived back and radioed Battalion, they told us to "wait one." By then, it was totally dark. They came back on the radio and told us that the Air Corps had indeed dropped those 'chutes. But they weren't supplies. They were small antipersonnel bombs.

Evidently, there were Japs in the area and the bombs were meant for them. But they must have been dropped in the wrong place or the Japs high-tailed it up to the next ridge, which was more likely. Headquarters recommended that we pull back from the area at least 500 yards.

Tomorrow, when we pulled out, we should detour around the area at least 100 yards.

Nobody knew when, or if, the bombs would go off.

Our officers decided it would be too dangerous to try and relocate in the pitch darkness. We were at least 150 yards from the nearest chute. Everyone was ordered not to move from his hole until daylight. Nobody argued.

We "guarded" the bombs all night long, waiting for them to go off. Not one of them did. They managed to fray a lot of nerves by morning.

Our bulldozer moved to the left a few hundred yards and plowed a new path for us to bypass the field dotted with explosives.

To continue our end-around tactics, we were forced to use the river beds as roadways. Highway Five was under direct observation by Japanese artillery spotters. Every time our columns tried to move up the road, the Japs would pound the hell out of them with heavy artillery pieces mounted in caves in the hills. We needed to get around those positions and attack them from the rear. There were no other roads. With the invaluable help from the Engineers, we advanced by carving our own roads through the hills.

Using the dry river beds prevented us from being silhouetted against the ridge lines and becoming targets for enemy artillery.

We continued our drive into the mountains.

The next day it started to rain. It was really coming down in buckets. We were at about two thousand feet elevation, most of the time in the clouds and fog, totally socked in, reducing visibility to a few feet. The weather had deteriorated so quickly that we had no chance to notify anyone of our predicament. It had been begun raining higher up in the mountains and had thoroughly saturated the rocky soil in a matter of hours. With no place to go, the runoff rapidly began following the low spots and streamed faster and faster downhill until it hit the river beds—then it started down the mountain.

A bulldozer was cutting a path through the river bank, when all of a sudden, a Filipino scout ran out of the rain like a phantom, yelling at us as loudly as he could.

"Get out! Get out! Water is coming! Get out!" He screamed the warning, running down the column as fast as he could, frantically waving at everyone to get out of the river bed.

Fortunately, the bulldozer had finished building a dirt ramp to the top of the embankment and moved out of the way. Most of the trucks and jeeps made it out—the last few were abandoned, the drivers jumping out and madly scrambling up the riverbank to safety—not a moment too soon.

The air and ground shook with a thundering roar like an approaching express train as a massive, roiling wall of muddy water crashed past us, sweeping trees and boulders, the size of trucks, through the river bed we had just scrambled from. The vehicles abandoned in the river bed were swept away like so many toys.

Unfortunately, they were loaded with most of our supplies and were now long gone. We had extra ammunition but few rations, and no gasoline or diesel fuel. Because of the mountainous terrain, our radios wouldn't work, so we couldn't call for an air drop. In the rotten weather, planes wouldn't be able to fly anyway. We were literally up the proverbial creek.

With no way to go back, we dug-in as well as we could. We couldn't use the vehicles because there wasn't enough fuel and would just have to sit there until we were resupplied when the weather cleared. Cases of ammunition and grenades in one of our trucks would serve for "emergencies." But that wouldn't last very long in a prolonged firefight.

We all hunkered down, wondering who would get to us first, our relief or the Japs.

Sitting in our water-filled holes in the torrential downpour, we waited. Numbing cold typhoon winds lashed us with relentless fury. We couldn't see three feet. No one was to fire his weapon unless there was a full-scale attack. If there were probing attacks, the enemy was to be killed with knives, machetes or axes—silently.

Why we had to be silent with the screaming wind and deafening downpours engulfing us wasn't explained. We hadn't put a listening post out in front of us because the weather was so foul that they wouldn't have heard or seen the Japanese coming, even within five feet of them. We relied on the storm to hide us from view.

About an hour later, the enemy attacked out of the slashing rain and thick fog. There was no artillery "prep" or mortars used. They simply appeared as ghosts, charging us with bayonets fixed and hurling grenades.

We opened up at point blank range on the first wave. We had been told not to fire unless it was a major attack. The shock of seeing those Japanese emerge from the swirling mist right in front of us without a sound was too much. We weren't about to jump up and fight bayoneted rifles unless all our ammo was already gone.

Spare bullets wouldn't do much good if you were dead.

The first 15 or 20 Japanese were cut down within yards of our foxholes. There was none of their usual screaming and yelling during the attack.

They just ran at us and were killed.

This was something new and unnerving. We couldn't shoot them if we couldn't see or hear them. And this was no silent infiltration at night with knives. It was a daylight assault with full equipment and grenades. They had been able to approach within ten yards of us before they charged. What the hell was going to happen when night came? We had no flares, couldn't call for artillery or air support and didn't have any mortars. We had our 37s but not enough canister rounds to last very long—especially if they attacked from two directions at once. The worst part was, the ground was so rocky, we could barely scrape our holes deep enough to protect us against exploding shells. If the Japs had mortars, we were in deep trouble.

When it was dark, they came again.

Once more, they were able to get right up on us before they attacked. A few managed to get in our holes but were quickly killed. The bodies were pushed aside and we checked our weapons for the next attack.

There were two men to each overflowing foxhole and a reduced squad with each anti-tank gun. Nobody slept. There were three more attacks during the night. We were fortunate to have only a few men wounded. There were dead Japanese scattered in front of our positions from one side to the other. The ground was laced with streams of pink, bloody water, running into our holes.

We had been lucky so far, but how long could we last?

We still had no communications with anyone. The weather was still terrible, and we had used up a good portion of our ammunition. Everyone had made each bullet count, not firing unless there was a definite target. Knives, machetes, axes and helmets were used for "close work." We were conserving our grenades as much as possible. Usually, the Japs were too close to us to use them. Because of the downpour, we couldn't hear them coming soon enough to give us adequate warning.

The coming of daylight didn't give us any respite. The weather was the same. Our situation wasn't about to get any better and only bound to get worse.

The enemy hit us again, every few hours, all day. They were still attacking with a few squads at a time from only one direction. The Japanese had a habit of repeating their rigid tactics over and over again, even when they failed. If they had hit us with everything at once, they might have wiped us out. Instead, they used their men in "penny packet" assaults. We assumed that the only reason they didn't send all their forces against us was that they didn't really know how many men we had. The weather that everyone had been cursing about had probably been saving us all along. The enemy couldn't see our positions. We couldn't even see our own men from six feet away. We were, for all intents and purposes, alone. We relied on the rest of our people to cover our backs, as we covered theirs, but each foxhole was visually isolated from most of the others around it.

Before dawn, my platoon leader came to my hole.

"I need you to take three men and do a recon. Don't take any chances. Just take a look around and get your ass back here," he whispered.

"Right," I said, looking past him, out into the mist.

I tapped three men and motioned for them to follow me. We knelt in the runny mud, in the middle of the perimeter, while I told them what I wanted them to do. There was to be no firing, if at all possible. If we met any Japs, we would use knives. We would go out as far as I deemed necessary, make a short sweep, and come back.

Word was quickly passed down the line.

"Patrol going out..."

We slowly went out through the perimeter, the ground thick with the decaying Japanese dead, picking our way, carefully watching for any movement in the bodies. The Japs often booby-trapped themselves before attacking so that even if they were killed, they could still inflict casualties on the enemy attempting to move the body.

We moved ahead, stepping around the foul-smelling, ballooning corpses.

The heavy downpour drowned out the sounds of the muck sucking on our shoes. Raindrops formed millions of tiny explosions as they impacted the water running over the ground, sounding like a fire hose hitting a flat rock. The cold slop washed around our ankles as it ran downhill into the perimeter behind us.

After about 10 yards, the dead bodies thinned out until they were only a few scattered about like fat, soaked, stinking bundles of discarded clothing. I tried to see through the swirling fog, but it was hopeless.

Using my compass, we headed out to the northeast. There were a few water-filled craters from artillery shells but nothing else. We went out about 75 yards and stopped. We knelt down in a small circle, weapons pointed out, listening for any sound we could pick out from the rain.

After waiting for a few minutes, we moved out another 25 yards and listened some more.

I signaled with my hand to move west on an arc to cover more ground before we started back. The ground became even more rocky and less muddy. It was definitely rising higher as we pushed farther to the northwest. No surprises there. The Japanese were always up higher than we were. The land was definitely favoring the defenders.

We still hadn't heard anything.

Opening and closing my hand three times, I signaled that we would stay out for another fifteen minutes and then head back.

We headed slightly more north and slowly picked our way over the rough ground. We had to be extremely careful not to trip or knock any rocks loose, giving away our presence to the enemy. We also had to watch for Japanese patrols out doing the same thing we were.

Suddenly, I stopped dead in my tracks.

The hair on the back of my neck and hands stiffened and a twinge shot through me.

An all-too-familiar, sour stink wafted toward us through the fog.

Dried fish, moldy rice, wet leather and human sweat.

Japs!

I silently dropped to the ground.

Instantly, my men did the same.

I looked back at the next man in line and motioned slowly to my front. He nodded and did the same thing to the other two behind him. He looked back at me and pointed to his nose. Then he pointed ahead into the fog to the right. He slowly waved his hand and pointed back the way we had come.

I motioned for him to wait, while we listened for any sounds.

We lay there on the rocks, cold water running through our soaked, muddy coveralls, gripping our weapons, every nerve jangling. My whole body tingled. It was a defensive mechanism telling the brain it was time to get the body up and get the hell out before something bad happened to it.

Fight or flight.

There! Off to the right...a cough!

The Japanese seemed to be out to the north of us about 10 yards or so. Discretion being the better part of valor, there was no need to get any closer. They might find us at any second. We were much closer than we thought. We had probably been crossing their front for the last five minutes. It was time to go.

We started back as quietly as we could. The heavy rain had masked our approach and was the only reason we had been able to get as close as we did without being spotted.

After slithering and crab-peddling our way for about 50 yards, we stopped to get our bearings with the compass.

"We should check over to the west, too," I barely whispered.

"The whole fucking Imperial *Army* could be out there and we wouldn't even see 'em!" whispered one of my men, as the driving rain painfully lashed our faces.

"Let's get the hell out of here and go back!" said another.

The third man simply squatted in the rain, eyes wide, water pouring off his drenched fatigue hat like a miniature waterfall.

"What the hell. Let's go. We got what we came for," I said.

We slid and stumbled back using the compass, because we seriously couldn't see where we were going. The fog had closed over everything with an impenetrable gray wall.

As we approached where we hoped our perimeter was, I whispered the password as loudly as I dared.

Nothing!

We went ahead another ten yards and stopped.

Again, I stage whispered the password.

"Luscious—" We always used a password with *"ells"* in them because the Japanese had trouble pronouncing them.

Still nothing!

I checked the compass and we moved over about 20 yards to the left. The men were holding on to each other's cartridge belt so we wouldn't lose anyone in the thick fog.

I licked my lips and mentally crossed my fingers as I stared into the rain.

"Luscious—"

"Lola!" answered from just ahead.

We made it.

Scrambling back through the perimeter, I reported the rough positions we had mapped out. We received a "well-done" from the platoon leader and went back to our water-pits.

Our officers decided to send a four-man detail out to contact the other battalion moving up the Old Spanish Trail, north of Carranglan. The tiny patrol was sent out with instructions for our relief, and they disappeared into the deepening gloom. The next day, another patrol reported that a large number of Japs were bivouacked only a few hundred yards away over the next ridge to the east.

They hit us again during the night.

By the fifth day, everyone was a physical wreck. The Japanese had been assaulting us on and off, day and night, the entire time. Nobody slept, except for short catnaps. The combination of exhaustion, little food and horrendous conditions had taken their toll. There were only ten rounds of canister left for the guns. Each man had a few pouches of thirty-caliber rifle ammo left and a grenade or two for each foxhole. We had no idea where any of our outfits were. There were still no communications with the outside. I thought it was high time we folded our cards, cut our losses, and got the hell out of Dodge.

We huddled around our lieutenant as he gave us "the word." We were going to make a break for it before we ran out of ammunition. The rations were gone and we were still unable to use our radios. We had no idea if the patrol we had sent out had successfully made it back or not. They could have gotten lost or been killed by the Japanese. We couldn't wait much longer. It had to be now or never.

At 0500 the next morning, we would blow up our guns, burn our vehicles and then it would be every man for himself. It was going to be too dangerous to attempt movement by the entire outfit at one time. A squad would take off every few minutes, breaking up as necessary and making their own way back to the foothills. There was less risk of the Japanese getting all of us if we were spread out and travelling fast.

We spent a miserable night waiting for them to attack us from out of the howling, rain-swept storm. Everybody was on alert for the entire night. The Japanese tried infiltrating in different points in the perimeter. Not a shot was fired. Every enemy soldier was killed with bare hands and knives. As the time neared for us to begin our pull-out, we packed our gear and held a hurried last meeting.

Someone had decided to pack the barrels of the guns with dirt and fire a shell to wreck the barrels. The Japanese weren't going to get a present of our weapons. We dispersed to our holes and made final preparations for our departure.

At the last minute, as several crews were stuffing dirt down the barrels of their thirty-sevens, the plan was changed. We would take out the breech blocks and remove the firing pins. The weapons would be useless to the enemy and they would still be recoverable by our own people in the future. The drivers of the trucks removed the coils rendering them unusable.

Then it happened.

Low and behold, the rain suddenly stopped, and the leaden skies began to clear. The fog dissipated and the clouds were swept away as if by magic. The sun appeared for the first time in almost a week.

We stood there gawking at the miracle, condemned men unexpectedly given a reprieve.

Then the Army Air Corps arrived. Transport planes flew up through the Pass. As they approached, the planes banked on one wing, their cargo doors off. The crewmen were hanging half-out of the fuselage, held only by long harness straps. As the planes thundered over us, the crews kicked out the supplies, without parachutes. It began raining supplies. We jumped back in our holes to keep from getting mashed by the falling bundles.

Two of our men were killed when they were hit by falling 5-gallon water cans and crates of ammunition.

The second plane flew over, dropping ration boxes by parachute. There was a mad scramble to unpack the ammunition from the air drop. We figured that the Japanese would hit us with everything they had once they saw the parachutes dropping into our perimeter.

Quite a few of our supplies floated overhead and landed inside the Japanese positions. We bitched mightily about parachutes carrying *our* food over to them. It was bad enough that we had to fight the enemy day and night but did we have to *feed* them *too*?

As it turned out, the Japs thought better of it, pulled out of their positions and moved higher into the mountains.

Our mission was still to meet up with our outfit near Highway Five. In order to do that, we had to leave our bulldozer and vehicles behind (with still no fuel), pack our supplies on our backs and hoof it to the rendezvous point. We would reorganize and then continue the arduous journey toward Puncan. We walked down the river banks heading east, loaded down with all the rations and ammo we could physically carry. The rest was buried near the disabled vehicles.

As we walked down from the hills after so many days without contact with anybody, the GI's of the 27th Infantry, whose positions we were approaching, were suspicious about our identity. They had not been notified to expect us or anybody else coming down from the hills. Evidently, our four man patrol had been discovered and killed by the Japanese; they were never seen again. Nervous trigger-fingers would need to relax as we approached to within hailing distance. The enemy had been known to strip our dead of their uniforms and then approach our positions until they got close enough to throw grenades or satchel charges. The GI's obviously thought that this might be the case, for everyone kept us covered with machine guns until they confirmed who we were.

After several days, the Engineers had laboriously cleared the river bed of most of the debris left there by the raging flash floods. Our columns could once again utilize their successful tactics of circling in behind the enemy and relieving some of the pressure from the 27th Infantry.

As the 27th moved straight up Highway Five, the 161st and the 35th Regiments flanked the advance on both sides. They came under fire from Japanese gun positions dug in above the road. The 27th was being hit from reinforced dugouts and enemy mountain guns blocking the advance. Aircraft and artillery were needed to blast the gun positions before they could continue.

The Japanese used caves more frequently now, each cave a mini-fortress. Neutralized one by one, utilizing a combination of firepower and guts, eventually they were assaulted by infantry outfits and cleaned out with flame throwers, satchel charges, grenades and bullets. In the end, it usually came down to the GI carrying a rifle to clean out the enemy from his fortified positions.

The terrain had, in many cases, negated the use of much of our superior firepower. The caves were constructed with anterooms that absorbed the blast effect of explosives from pole charges or direct fire from tanks. Consequently, the Japs had to be cleared from these positions using hand weapons.

Our units entered the next valley from the east, above the barrio of Puncan, where there was a short, sharp battle. It was a small place, with one road running through it, a few huts and a church, all damaged by artillery and tank fire. It was ringed by stagnant paddies and low hills affording little cover.

Thick smoke smeared the sky as the line companies pushed through the place and killed the remaining Japanese as we continued our end-around drive into the hills. Our observation planes constantly buzzed the area at low level, checking the supply road being carved out by bulldozers of the 65th Engineers, which wound around the countryside like an undulating serpent, along ridges, through streams and around paddies. The pilots radioed coordinates to the artillery as they spotted targets ahead of us.

Difficulty arose when Japanese snipers and infantry started firing on the heavy equipment operators following behind our people walking point. The operators couldn't fire back because they had their hands full of bulldozer controls. The only protection they had was the blade in front of them, when it was in the raised position. A few of the bulldozers had steel plates welded around the cab, but most didn't. The operators were sitting ducks, way up in the driver's seat with a GI riding shotgun, both prime targets for shrapnel, bullets and everything lethal flying around.

Often the bulldozer drivers, taking fire from caves or bunkers, raised the blade to deflect the bullets while our people followed right behind them. As the infantry pinned down the Japanese with direct fire, the operator would quickly drop the blade, scoop out a pile of dirt and ram it right into the cave mouth or bunker aperture.

Then, it was back to work on the river beds.

Days were spent fighting the rough terrain with the help of bulldozers. The operators braved the dangers of mines or rolling the machine off the top of a ridge. Pulling mired vehicles out of the mud and burying piles of stinking enemy corpses in mass graves had to be done. They endured terrible heat and humidity, made worse by the heat from the engine, insects, dust and constant vibration and jerking of the machine as it scraped a rough path of dirt, grass and stones for the advancing columns. Several hours were spent each night pulling maintenance and refueling, followed by nights of pouring rain, deadly infiltrators, Jap infantry attacks, artillery fire, snipers and lack of sleep.

Every day, it started all over again.

Our Regiment marched right through Puncan without stopping and continued the push. After leaving the barrio, we headed west to Digdig.

Once again, the 27th started up Highway Five, flanked by its sister regiments, the 161st to the west and the 35th to the east. Digdig was important only because several roads intersected there, the junction leading off in several directions.

By March 2, 1945, the Second Battalion, 35th Infantry, had fought its way into position to protect our flank. We were part of the Third Battalion's direct assault advancing on Digdig on the afternoon of March 3rd. The place itself wasn't even what we would call a town. It was basically a few huts on stilts amid sun-baked fields that stretched out on both sides of the main road.

The enemy had dug-in tanks and guns in the town, along with light weapons, mortars and infantry. There were several Japanese supply and ammunition dumps in the area. The main ammo dump was set alight and detonated with a thunderous roar, spewing exploding, burning munitions over the area. The scattered dumps were either destroyed or captured intact. The enemy tanks, guns and infantry were wiped out after a coordinated attack by our combined arms. It was a now familiar scenario. Air strikes, artillery, tanks and infantry, followed by bulldozers plowing piles of enemy corpses into pits and clearing the road for the waiting columns of vehicles. After a stiff fight, we moved into the smoldering, blasted remains of the town and joined the advance once again.

CHAPTER 17

The Siege of Balete Pass

The number of cave emplacements and pillboxes increased even more as we moved north to Putlan. The Japanese had mounted heavy artillery pieces on tracks inside many of the caves. The guns would be rolled out to fire a few rounds and then pushed back in to avoid detection. These positions were tough to spot.

One day, we watched as our aircraft tried to destroy a series of caves on a hillside in front of us. We were being held in place by several mountain guns that rained shells on us every time we attempted to move up. The steep slopes were sparsely covered with scrub brush and small trees. Artillery couldn't hit the positions, and tanks weren't able to maneuver close enough to get a clear shot.

As the planes came in, they were forced to weave around the hills, trying to plant their bombs in the cave entrances. Only a near miss above a cave's entrance would have any effect by causing a landslide of dirt and rocks, sealing the Japanese inside. At the last second, the planes pulled up to avoid slamming into the surrounding hills. It was a nerve-wracking display.

One plane came in so low that we thought he would pile right into the slope he was targeting. The pilot dropped his 500 pound bomb directly into the cave's mouth but was hit a split-second later by heavy ground fire from the surrounding heights. As the cave blew up with an earth-shattering roar, a large puff of smoke blew back from the plane's engine and it immediately caught fire.

The pilot pulled his plane up into a steep climb, trying to gain some altitude, long tongues of orange flame licking his cockpit. His coughing engine laboring under the strain, he pushed back his canopy. Thick entrails of smoke smudging the sky, the aircraft flipped over on its back and the pilot dropped free. The plane continued for a short distance and then, burning like a torch, plowed upside down into a ridge. The pilot's parachute had opened just after clearing the aircraft and he wasn't very high when he bailed out. It only took a short time before he disappeared from view drifting down into a ravine less than a mile away.

Someone immediately radioed headquarters about the incident. After learning of the pilot's plight, they sent word down to send out a patrol to rescue and return him to our lines. Unfortunately, we were pinned down and stalemated. There was no way to reach him. We couldn't move forward. We radioed back our reply and that was it.

Happily, we learned later that after several days of cleverly evading the enemy, the courageous pilot walked back through our lines on his own, hungry and dirty, suffering only from a wrenched back when he hit the ground and superficial burns from the engine fire.

The Japanese still had the upper hand as we fought our way closer to the mountains. The bridge at Putlan had been thoroughly demolished as they pulled back and was under intermittent artillery fire to keep our Engineers from rebuilding it. Fire from the brooding heights of Balete Pass rained down whenever our columns of vehicles advanced up the road. The Japs had a perfect view of everything that moved. They were able to drop shells on us with pinpoint accuracy.

Our artillery spotter planes crisscrossed the valley and the dominating hills during daylight, often through unbelievably heavy ground fire. Several were damaged and flew low over us, heading south, their wings and fuselages riddled by bullets.

Unfortunately, by this time, the supply of shells for our big guns to our rear was insufficient to allow saturation of the areas with explosives. We called in for artillery support, only to be told that the "heavies" were limited to a certain number of rounds for that day. They wouldn't authorize any fire mission unless we were in danger of being overrun; and even then, we were only allowed five or ten rounds per gun, if that. There would be few, if any, "recon by fire" missions approved. This involved sweeping a suspected enemy area with artillery or air strikes before sending in the infantry to clear it out. There was no doubt that the lack of artillery support cost many GI's their lives.

The remainder of March was spent attempting to clear the fanatical Japanese from areas leading to Balete Pass. We fought our way up into the mountains through hot, punishing days and interminable fear-filled, sleepless nights, painfully pushing the enemy back into his prepared emplacements. They still had excellent observation points and used them to their best advantage. Every time we took a hill or ridge, the enemy still saw what we were doing. They would bring down accurate artillery fire on us, but we couldn't see them because they were using heavily camouflaged gun positions farther up in the mountains.

We felt like fat flies on a wall, and the Japanese were holding the swatters.

We spent day after day, week after week, climbing and fighting in the hills leading up to the Pass. Every lousy hillside, ridge, ravine, tiny fold of ground, every spider hole and sniper's nest had to be cleared.

Men were wounded, fell to the ground and tumbled back down the steep hillsides. Some were killed instantly or were hit and fell into ravines.

Others, hit and pulled to cover quickly enough, were treated and evacuated before the ever-present Japanese snipers could shoot them. Casualties had to be carried out on litters along steep, slippery paths worn into the hillsides by the constant foot traffic. In most places, we had to carry out our wounded on hills so steep that the front men on the litter were supporting it on their shoulders and the rear team held it near their ankles, slipping and sliding, trying to keep the casualty from falling down rock-studded slopes.

All of our ammunition, rations and supplies were manhandled up the slopes on the backs of exhausted infantry.

I thought back to the days before the war on Hawaii, when we toiled high up in the mountains with the mule trains. We vehemently cursed and complained about the evil-tempered, foul-smelling beasts, who liked nothing better than to sneak up behind us and clamp down on a shoulder or arm. They would throw back their enormous heads, lips drawn back over their thick, yellow teeth and loudly bray at us, as if to say, *"Take that! Now who's the boss?"*

Loaded down with supplies, ammunition and dismantled mountain guns, they had performed an important role but they were cranky as hell. Now, I knew how they must have felt, as we hauled back-breaking loads up through the steep mountains of Luzon. I would have gladly kissed each one on its ugly, bristling mug, if they had they only been allowed to come with us. It wasn't meant to be. We continued to be the mules.

The entire area was strewn with the pathetic waste of war. Crumbling foxholes by the thousands were littered with ripped helmets, splintered grenade cases, crushed ration boxes, stinking, dripping bandages, destroyed equipment, shell casings, broken rifles, loose ammunition, blackened grass and the hated, liquefying Japanese dead. Gaseous latrine trenches, stagnant, slime-filled shell holes and bomb craters, carpeted with razor-sharp shrapnel, fouled the landscape. Burned, shattered trees, their bark and leaves destroyed by the vicious fighting, dotted the slopes like tortured, hopeless old men, their crooked limbs stiffly reaching out from their naked trunks for a tiny bit of the dignity that had been denied them in their final moments.

Patrols were constantly sent out. Sometimes they left and never returned. Intelligence gathered on the area was often completely wrong or unusable. Nobody knew what resistance was up ahead until we smacked right into it.

The point man usually went down first, unless the Japs let him go by, and then opened up on the men following. A few GI's wounded and a few enemy killed, if we were lucky. Somebody else would take point and we moved on.

Balete Pass was a confusing maze of steep hills, razor-back ridges, deep valleys, thick woods, jungle-like foliage—and no roads. The area was infested with heavily fortified caves, spider holes, mines, snipers, booby traps, knee mortars and pre-registered artillery traps—a man-killing nightmare.

It was so formidable that we were halted so that heavy 90mm anti-aircraft guns could be brought up to fire on the caves studding the adjacent slopes. Aircraft were limited by the surrounding heights and the jumbled terrain features. It had taken us weeks of bloody fighting to advance less than a mile. Once again, it fell to the "Queen of Battle," the infantry, to go in and dig the Japanese out of their caves that had been laboriously carved out of solid rock.

With only a small entrance, the interior might be several stories deep, equipped with electric lights, ammunition storage, water, food and underground hospitals. Caves were connected by tunnels, stairways, ladders and crawl spaces with blast-absorbing ante-rooms built into them. Fighting eventually became hand-to-hand inside these caves, when conventional methods failed to destroy the soldiers inside. Some were burned out by dumping in huge amounts of gasoline or flame-thrower fuel and then igniting it with grenades or satchel charges swung into the caves on ropes.

These defensive fortifications had been built with the labor of American and Filipino POWs when the Japanese realized that the Americans were going to come back to Luzon. The elaborate layout of the whole area was proof of the amount of time and effort that the enemy had invested in this one place. If the rest of the island was defended like this, we would be here for years. That was exactly what the Japanese had planned for. Hold us up for as long as possible. One man with a machine gun or a knee mortar in terrain like that could hold up a company for days.

The Engineers were called upon to build artillery positions that would enable the big nineties to fire without fear of counter-battery fire from the enemy. The steep slopes of the mountains before Balete were totally impassable to vehicles. The only way to get massive guns up to the crests of the ridges was to winch them up using thick steel cables and bulldozers. A path was cleared up the side of the hill away from direct enemy fire. A bulldozer would connect large cables to the gun and laboriously winch it up the hill, foot by foot.

At the crest of the hill, a large hole was scooped out, open on two sides. One faced the enemy, permitting the gun to fire on a fixed traverse. The open rear of the position enabled the loading and servicing of the weapon and allowed sufficient room for the recoil as it fired. Two sides were heavily reinforced with sand bags and trees, cut down and driven into the ground in vertical layers to form a massive blast wall, offering protection against counter-battery artillery fire. The roof of the position was built by placing more layers of trees over the top, reinforced with dirt and more sand bags. These positions were very solidly built in order to stand up to the vibration of the recoil and muzzle blast of the weapon, as well as to protect against any incoming enemy artillery.

The 90mm gun was normally used for anti-aircraft defense. It weighed well over a ton and needed a solid footing while firing. The shells traveled at high velocity and were especially effective against aircraft when using proximity fuses. Using the weapon for ground attack support took careful coordination and control. The shells had an unbelievable blast pattern when they exploded.

While the guns were being set up, we carried supplies and shells, stockpiling them in the new position. Everything had to be hand-carried from the bulldozer road at the base of the hill, all the way up to the forward positions, up and down, up and down, up and down, day after day. Sections of the hill were so steep we had to laboriously pull ourselves up, supporting our weight with one hand, balancing a heavy shell or grenade case on our shoulder with the other. I could have used a third hand to keep my steel pot from constantly sliding down over my eyes while climbing.

The trail was a muddy, glutinous mess—at times, almost impassable. Each man could carry only one shell at a time, sliding back one step for every two taken. Sapped by the exertion of constant climbing and the terrible, enervating heat, we stacked our shells on the crest and then slipped and slid back down to pick up another one from the ammo dump at the base of the hill. Everyone was drenched with sweat after just a few minutes and stayed that way until it cooled off at night.

After stockpiling enough shells, we returned to our outfit back on Highway Five. It was going to take quite a while to get ready for the coming attack. At this point, we had been trying to knock out the caves for weeks without success.

Sherman tanks were brought up over a period of several days, lining the muddy shoulders of the road like massive circus elephants waiting for the next show to begin. Many were equipped with bulldozer blades, and all had sun-bleached tarps stretched over open hatches, rear decks piled high with filthy bed rolls, cases of rations, tools, rust-encrusted tow cables, ammunition boxes and heavily-dented Jerry cans of water or fuel. Fifty-caliber machine guns perched on dirty turrets, draped with jackets or ragged pieces of canvas to keep out the rain.

Once again, it was "hurry up and wait."

Every morning, weather permitting, unarmed twin-engine, twin-tail P-38 photo-reconnaissance planes flew up the valley and through the Pass to photograph enemy gun positions and cave locations in the surrounding mountains. We could see them coming up through the morning mist, twisting and turning at low level. We were up so high that when the planes flew into the Pass, they were actually below us. We could hear the droning of the engines echoing through the valley.

Suddenly, it would pop up out of the clouds like a giant silver dragonfly, moisture streaming from its wings in gray, twisting tendrils, banking and side-slipping between the cloud-shrouded heights. Sparkling mist and water streamed back from the propellers in glistening corkscrew-rings as the plane shouldered aside the saturated air.

Several mornings, when a P-38 started through the Pass, we waited until he was almost even with us and waved to the pilot as he flashed by. He pulled up a little and did a barrel roll to let us know that he saw us. It was quite a thrill to see those courageous pilots threading their way at high speed through the Pass, following the jagged contours, jinking and banking first one way and then another, right between the mountains.

As the day for the main attack drew closer, Intelligence tried to draw fire from the hidden enemy emplacements. They must have concluded that the Japs wouldn't be able to resist firing if our armor exposed itself to their artillery. Then the emplacements could be marked for destruction. At the same time, all of our tanks started up and maneuvered up Highway Five. Sirens blaring and engines racing, the armor bravely paraded up the road, completely out in the open, in a thunderous, deafening display. It was a huge failure. The Japanese knew well what we were doing. Why would they waste precious ammunition on tanks that couldn't bother them in their caves? For us—it was seemed a waste of gasoline but it was still a damned good parade.

One day, we started to receive heavy, accurate mortar and artillery fire. Shells were plowing up the area all around us every few seconds. At first we thought that these were "short" rounds from our own guns. We called back over the radio to tell our batteries to cease fire. The artillery told us that they weren't "short" rounds but Jap guns to our rear.

What the hell did that mean?

Evidently, the Japanese positioned weapons caches just behind our lines in remote areas. They buried mortars, machine guns, small arms and sometimes, artillery, along with large amounts of ammunition, before they pulled back. Their gun crews either hid in small caves or in the underbrush and allowed our units to bypass them (or simply infiltrated from the front and back through our lines.) Then they set up ambushes, snipers and artillery positions in our rear. They were extremely difficult to pinpoint.

Our artillery had their guns positioned behind us, firing in support. Every day they fired over our heads and dropped shells on the enemy just in front of us. They were easily timed, five guns firing simultaneously, a two minute wait while they reloaded, and then firing again. The Japanese in our rear waited for our artillery to fire, waited for two minutes and then fired *their* guns into *our* positions, making it appear as though our own shells were dropping short. All the guns, both ours and theirs, were firing at the same time—a clever ploy.

Our officers volunteered to send foot patrols to locate and attack these batteries to eliminate the threat. The artillery told us that they would take care of the problem. The higher-ups decided not to risk precious line outfits trying to track down and kill infiltrators. The solution, was to locate the enemy guns with observers and once discovered, turn our artillery around and destroy them. And that's exactly what they did.

Shortly thereafter, when we had moved higher into the mountains, we saw soldiers down below us, crossing a field. We immediately called the artillery and asked them if they had any people down in that area.

Negative.

But they thought that the Japanese had left their positions in our rear and were heading back north again to rejoin their units.

That was all we needed to hear.

We quickly formed a lateral firing line. Everyone took a prone or kneeling position with extra rifle clips spread out. We opened up, squeezing off rounds, exactly as we had been taught.

Aim, control your breathing, lead the target and squeeze *the trigger.*

As the Japanese jumped up from cover and ran across the open field, they were picked off, one by one.

M-1s cracked all along the line, as we fired into the running soldiers. The enemy never hesitated.

As a soldier ran from cover, his equipment bouncing, carrying his long rifle in one hand, everybody took a bead on him. Allowing him to get into the field, to the point of no return, he was riddled with bullets. Soon after he dropped, another man would try the same thing. He would run as fast as he could into the field, desperately leaping over the blood-soaked bodies of his comrades, cut down a few minutes before. Then he would be shot, dust flying from his uniform as dozens of bullets tore through his stumbling, jerking body.

It was just like being on the firing range back on Oahu only the targets were flesh and blood, not paper.

Many were shot by our snipers using specially-equipped rifles with telescopic sights. We could usually tell which had been hit by our snipers because their victims were almost always shot through the head. Dozens of Japanese littered the field until they stopped sending people through in the daytime and began trying to sneak past us under the cover of darkness.

There were always gaps where units were only loosely tied in with each other. It was a "line" in name only. There was nothing continuous about it. Sections were isolated with open flanks because of the insufficient manpower to hold the area. There were often only "hedgehogs," perimeter positions for all-around defense with distant artillery support to cover the areas left open by a lack of infantry. The whole place was basically a bowl-shaped sieve with numerous ways for the Japanese to find their way higher into the mountains.

The next night, after sunset, as we were settling in, we were hit without any warning. Before we knew what was happening, the Japanese were among us.

We were instantly overrun.

Rifles, pump shotguns and pistols cracked as each side opened fire. Japanese leaped or fell into our foxholes as the vicious fighting became hand-to-hand. Screaming, cursing men on both sides died where they fell. Our men were trained to stay in their holes and shoot the enemy as they rushed through. The Japs had run smack into our reinforced and heavily defended "hedgehog." They had evidently counted on breaking through as quickly as possible and escaping north where their comrades were fighting a series of brutal defensive actions.

Some had only knives, pistols or a grenade. Many fell into foxholes in the darkness and were strangled, beaten, knifed or hacked to death. A large number were found in the morning with their throats cut or their stomachs slashed open by machetes. A few were shot by their own comrades in their frenzied rush to get past us.

We had a much higher than normal percentage of automatic weapons in our ranks and immediately took a heavy toll of the attacking enemy. BARs and machine guns ripped into the Japs at point-blank range as they leaped over our holes. They fell all around us, spinning from the impact of the bullets, collapsing to the ground and falling in our holes.

We shot any shadow above us.

The rattle of gunfire reached a crescendo and then died off to sporadic shots as wounded Japs either killed themselves or were shot. Piles of bodies covered the area. Once again we had survived with few casualties because of our strict fire discipline and total readiness. Because everyone stayed in their holes and fought from ground level, the Japs couldn't really get at us unless they stopped and fought hand-to-hand.

When the main attack on the Pass was finally ready to go in, the line companies started down the slopes under the muzzles of the newly-emplaced anti-aircraft guns. After a solid month of fighting there had been little progress. The grizzled, weary infantry descended, holding on to trees and brush to maintain their balance on the uneven, rocky ground. The 90mm guns opened up with a stunning roar, targeting individual caves and camouflaged positions that had been previously spotted or defoliated by hundreds of air strikes.

We followed right behind the line outfits.

Everyone had more than a full complement of ammo and grenades, satchel and pole charges for blowing cave entrances and radios for communicating with the anti-aircraft gun crews.

Stumbling and sliding down the steep hillside, we finally reached the bottom and started up the next slope. The full impact of the noise from the firing rattled us. Concussion from the antiaircraft guns was tremendous, physically reverberating along the hills and echoing down the valley.

It was like being thrown into the middle of an earthquake.

Soldiers trained as cave-busters were sent up first with their heavily armed comrades providing covering fire. They began climbing, carrying long bamboo poles with blocks of dynamite taped to one end. In the meantime, there was a firestorm being unleashed on the enemy from every weapon. When our men got close to one of the caves, spotters signaled to shift fire to a different place, enabling the cave-busters to push the explosives into the mouth and then detonate them, either blowing up the enemy or sealing them inside.

There were countless spider holes (foxholes with covers) to be destroyed. The camouflage on these holes was extraordinary. Most had bushes and brush growing in the dirt on the "lids." They couldn't be seen unless they were opened from the inside to fire on us and, even then, they were usually only popped open a few inches and then quickly shut again. We could see the infantry in front of us, stop, pry up or kick open a lid and either shoot the Jap inside or drop a grenade into a small tunnel and rake it with Tommy guns or BARs.

As the attack finally groped closer to the summit, the distance between the gun positions and the target on the next slope was so close, that when they fired, the explosions washed over us before we even heard the gun's report...

WHOOOOMMP...CRRAACK!

Each cave and spider hole destroyed brought us closer to the crest. Once we gained the ridge line, Jap artillery would usually plaster the hell out of it with artillery or mortars to keep us from consolidating our positions. Therefore, everyone was ordered to stay just below the skyline.

Then it was on to the next ridge. And the next, and the next—

Over one hundred days and nights of constant fighting, broiling heat, drenching rain and deep mud, had taken its inevitable toll. The only sleep we were able to get, consisted of short cat naps haunted by horrible nightmares. Often I had trouble separating dreams from reality. We had dug so many foxholes and gun positions, our hands were always raw, cracked and bleeding. We had difficulty keeping focused on what had to be done or why it had to be accomplished. Everybody was near the end of his tether.

And that was quickly unraveling.

I received word from home that my brother, Paul, had been killed by the Germans on Christmas Eve, 1944, in Belgium. (After the war, I learned he had volunteered to escort a convoy of litter jeeps and ambulances full of wounded from behind the lines and surrendered after being surrounded by the Waffen SS. The Germans had threatened to destroy the column and the wounded if they didn't surrender. After disarming the prisoners, the Germans went to each ambulance in turn, shot all the defenseless wounded and set fire to the vehicles. Then the prisoners had their hands tied behind their backs with wire, were led into a field and murdered).

I was notified that my brother Frank had been seriously wounded fighting the Japs on the island of Ie Shima near Iwo Jima. President Roosevelt had died and there was still no end to the war in sight. As a sergeant and a squad leader, I was expected to overcome anything and everything that could possibly happen and keep going indefinitely. But I wasn't that strong.

I was starting to crack around the edges.

I had been a squad leader throughout the war, a job so demanding, heart-wrenching and horrific, that it had completely worn me down. Most of us were young on the outside but terribly old and scarred on the inside. Our basic human emotions had been ruthlessly stripped away and our minds brutalized.

Like wild animals, savage instincts of survival took over and controlled our actions. We did whatever we had to do to stay alive. There were no second thoughts. The unspeakable horrors of war had become commonplace, everyday occurrences. We were surviving from one minute to the next with no thought about tomorrow or next week or next year. We had become hardened, ruthless and merciless, in order to save ourselves and our buddies. We had a job to do before we could go home to our families. That job was to kill the enemy. I thought that it couldn't get any worse than it already was.

But I was wrong.

My outfit was in a defensive position on a ridge high up in the mountains. We were a tiny part of a line of positions that faced the Japanese on ridge lines leading up into the Pass. We had a spectacular view of the surrounding terrain and could clearly see our sister unit on a ridge below us, to our right.

It was one of the worst positions to be assigned to: an OP (Observation Post) on a ridge with very little cover. Men were tasked with occupying it for days at a time. During daylight, every man had to stay in his hole and not move. Any movement brought down sniper and mortar fire, so they stayed there with the blazing sun stewing them in their steel pots—no relief, even for a minute.

Each man lay in his hole all day, drenched in eye-blinding sweat, dizzy from the heat, insects crawling on his skin, covered with thick dust from mortar bursts. Everyone suffered from unbearable muscle cramps from being immobile in their tiny holes, more like broiling, open graves. What little water we had was hot and stagnant. It made each day a nightmare of agony.

Periodically, the Japanese would throw in a mortar barrage to keep everyone guessing when the next rounds would sail in. At night, no one could sleep for fear of being attacked and overrun. A few days of this was all anyone could take.

One morning, as I looked down past that ridge, I noticed a small cloud of dust sweeping up the steep bulldozer trail carved into the side of the mountain. I thought maybe it was suited for a mountain goat—almost straight up.

I watched in awe as a jeep with a tiny trailer loaded with supplies was dragging itself up the precarious dirt trail in broad daylight and in full view of the Japanese. The little vehicle bounced and swerved its way up towards the crest of the ridge, trailing a dirty rooster-tail of thick dust, without receiving so much as a scratch.

I grabbed our field phone, called the unit on the OP and asked, "Who is the crazy bastard driving that goddamned jeep?" He replied that it was a guy from the Red Cross bringing up hot coffee and donuts! I was stunned. Coffee and doughnuts? Was he kidding? Nope. It was true.

We all agreed that the driver must have been the bravest, craziest or luckiest guy on the island—perhaps all three. He traveled without a speck of cover the whole way up or down the slope. Under direct observation by the Japs on nearby hills, he made the same trip up and down the hill many times and was never hit.

We later learned that this man's son had been killed earlier in the war. He had tried to enlist in the service but was turned down because he was too old. Determined to do his share, he joined the Red Cross with the stipulation that he be assigned to the Pacific. Upon arriving, he volunteered to work on the front lines, helping as many men as he could. He was again told that he was too old to be in the front lines and couldn't go. With a simple reply of *"Bullshit!"* he grabbed a jeep and trailer, filled it with supplies and took off for the most forward emplacements.

Every day, he drove his jeep under fire to the forward positions he could reach and brought them hot coffee, doughnuts and words of encouragement, just to let them know they weren't forgotten. He risked his life every day to help in any way he could during some of the most hair-raising trips I'd ever witnessed.

He most certainly had one or more angels riding with him.

After being relieved from our forward positions and rejoining our unit farther down the mountain, we stayed in the rear for several days. My outfit was sent up to the front line every morning with rations, ammunition, grenades and water for the line companies. On the way back down, we carried the wounded back to the Battalion Aid Station.

There was heavy fighting as the Japanese were pressed into smaller areas in the mountains.

In early April, we moved farther into Balete Pass, suffering more casualties and receiving fewer and fewer replacements. The day-to-day grind was excruciating for everybody. When we weren't fighting, we were in support—loading up in the morning with as many supplies as we could carry and bringing them up to the lines. Unfortunately, there were always wounded to carry back down on the return trip. We traveled as quickly as possible, so that the casualties could be treated promptly.

Several teams of bearers, 8–10 men, were needed for each litter, so that one team could walk alongside and rest a little, while the other team carried the casualty. Then the teams switched back and forth until they reached the aid station. Then, it was more supplies, the long trek back to the front with more litters to carry back. Each trip took several hours. This went on from dawn to dusk.

After about a week, we were sent up to man the line again. We laboriously climbed higher into the mountains.

CHAPTER 18

Fire from the Heavens

Easter Sunday, 1945 found us thousands of feet up in the fog-shrouded mountains, waiting to kill our fellow man, just over the ridge in front of us. I opened my pack and pulled out a few sheets of crumpled, sweat-stained paper to begin a few lines to my mother and my pen pal, June. I kept the letters light and brief. All our mail was censored anyway, so I couldn't write about anything that was really happening. Besides, what good would it do to tell them? They wouldn't—couldn't—understand what it was like anyway. To keep from upsetting them unnecessarily, I made my letters as cheerful as possible.

I sat on the wet, rocky ground and scribbled with my tiny pencil stub, as the cool mist slowly swirled around me.

I had just finished writing when I looked up and saw a chaplain. He was only the second one I had seen in four years. I didn't know if his appearance was a good sign or not. I stared at him for a minute as he motioned to us to gather around him.

I thought to myself, "What the hell is he doing way up here?"

We all nervously gathered around him, holding our weapons at the ready. We never congregated in the open for fear of an incoming round nailing everybody at the same time. And we never, ever bunched up anywhere. But this was supposedly a special occasion. We all kept an eye and an ear open for any sign of an incoming shell or ground attack.

Before he could even speak to us, the thick, swirling fog that had covered us for days began to lift. As he gave his sermon, the sun came out and started to cook us, as we were all out in the open.

We knelt there on that steep, barren hillside, the stench of dead bodies and a nearby shallow latrine trench fouling the air, holding our weapons ready, watching the ridge-crest where the Japanese might storm over at any moment.

We listened as the chaplain talked about our coming salvation and our belief in Jesus Christ. He said that we would be forgiven for everything we had done, because we were on the side of righteousness.

"I sure hope he's right," I thought. It would be a tall order after everything we had seen, done and been through.

The sermon was interrupted by the sound of an aircraft flying up through the Pass behind us. Everybody jumped up, as a P-38 came screaming up between the mountains, standing vertically on one wing. He was so close that I could see the gum wrappers on the floor of his cockpit. We waved to the pilot, the same one who had been flying reconnaissance missions for days. As he passed, he waggled his wings and dropped down over the next ridge, constantly twisting his aircraft to prevent the nearby Japanese from drawing a bead on him.

As soon as he cleared the ridge, the real action began. We looked to our rear as the droning of more planes echoed off the mountains, filling the air with the unmistakable whine of fighter-aircraft engines. They were coming in below our positions to attack the enemy located about 150 yards beyond us. Sermon over. The chaplain jammed his helmet back on and took off like a flash, back down the mountain.

I dove for my foxhole.

The fighters began firing everything they had, before they even reached us. They were traveling so fast that they had to open up halfway down the mountainside and let the shells "walk" through the Japanese positions. To hit the enemy caves and trenches, pilots had to fly through ravines and up the steep side of the mountain while firing and carefully watching to be sure they didn't crash into the rock formations at the peak.

After the fighters had finished, another flight came in from the other direction and bombed and strafed caves on the ridges high above us. The planes flew past at tremendous speed and dropped their bombs right on the crest, the explosions occurring just as the tail of the plane cleared the blast zone. Then they came around again and sprayed the whole area with bullets.

The heavy rounds ricocheted off the rocks in all directions, spitting out chips of stone and jagged shrapnel. I was amazed that the aircraft could fly that low and fast without plowing right into the side of the mountain, but none did, though a few came very close.

This action achieved the same result as poking a large hornet's nest with a stick. We started receiving heavy mortar and artillery rounds from the enemy, just over the ridge. With direct observation of our positions, the Japanese dropped the explosives all over us several times in preparation for a ground assault. It seemed as though the air strikes had just mightily pissed off the Japs but hadn't done much damage. We all knew what to expect next.

At least we thought we did.

I crouched in my hole as an avalanche of hundreds of shells impacting over the area lifted me off the ground and slammed me back again. Dirt, shrapnel and chunks of splintered rock rained into my foxhole. Entire sections of our perimeter disappeared under the fierce pounding. Smoking shell holes were everywhere. I could barely breathe through the thick clouds of cordite smoke and dust blanketing the area. The noise was mind-numbing. Explosions were so close together, that it became one long, painful, roaring blast.

As soon as the shelling lifted, we readied ourselves to be hit by infantry. I shook off the dirt and stone chips that partially filled my hole and peeked over the lip. The Japanese never used that many shells unless they were going to attack. My ears were buzzing loudly, my head pounded and felt like it was jammed full of cement. Several of the men near me were bleeding profusely from their noses and ears from the concussion of the barrage. Our faces and hands were gray with dirt and rock dust. Shouts rang out along our tiny perimeter.

"Get ready!"

The Japanese came running down the side of the hill screaming and hurling grenades, some stopping to fire knee-mortars strapped to their legs. Grenades came rolling down the hill, bouncing until they exploded near our holes.

Firing broke out all along our perimeter as we frantically called for artillery support.

Our men threw grenades uphill, to try and stop the charge. To keep the grenades from rolling back to us after they were thrown, we pulled the pin, held it for a second or two (if it was a five second fuse) and then lobbed it high up the hill, giving it a two or three second "hang time." The Japs had no opportunity to pick them up and throw them back before they exploded.

The enemy started to fall under the increasing fire, but it was obvious their numbers wouldn't yield to light weapons. We needed artillery and we needed it now! The Japs had taken cover in nearby shell holes and were lobbing grenades at us. The missiles were passing each other in the air in a frenetic, deadly match. The command post down below us could see that we were in dire straits. They called us on the field phone and told us to "keep our asses down." Help was on the way.

We hadn't received any artillery support because the heavy shells couldn't be used that close to us in mountainous terrain. The artillery shells hitting the rocks increased the danger to our own men. The chances of being hit or killed by flying fragments of steel or stone multiplied many times over. For some reason, the mortars weren't ready to fire. What else did they have available?

I looked behind—over the edge of my foxhole—and almost had a heart attack.

Racing up the mountain directly toward us, just above the ground, were our aircraft, hanging napalm tanks.

"Oh, Christ! The Japs are too close to use that shit!" I yelled to my gunner.

At that moment, I knew that we were going to get wiped out by our own planes. We were surely going to die. They were simply going too fast to accurately drop their loads and we were too close to the Japanese to escape the impact of the tanks. I just ducked my head down and prayed.

This was it. No escaping this time—all over.

My internal dialogue took over. "After all the shit I've gone through, I'm going to get knocked off by our own goddamned planes!"

The first plane came in and released his napalm tanks. He was so close, I could hear the *"clinks"* as the heavy tanks dropped free. I thought, "We're going to fry, they'll never clear us!"

The plane swept by with a deafening roar directly over my hole. In slow motion, the engine, wings, fuselage and tail blotted out the sun, and he was gone.

A split-second later, the napalm tanks tumbled by just overhead, landing in a draw just beyond us. They exploded with a searing, volcanic blast of orange-red flame that exploded through the air and along the ground like a massive, boiling eruption, sucking the air out of my lungs and singeing my eyebrows and eyelashes from intense heat.

The second plane came in a little higher than the first and released his tanks. They detonated farther away from us, drenching the ground and the enemy with napalm. Thick, billowing clouds of oily black smoke mixing with the unmistakable smell of seared, burning flesh drifted over our holes. Grenades and ammunition from rifles and cartridge belts popped and crackled as they cooked off in the flames that had incinerated the attacking Japs.

The last fighter streaked by, firing his machine guns. Then it was quiet.

The only sounds were the crackling flames from burning grass and gusts of hot wind whipping the smoke into the air in rolling, twisting clouds. Everyone was stunned by the sudden, unexpected appearance of our planes and the violent, flaming impact of the napalm strikes, so close to us.

We gripped our weapons and waited for the next attempt by the enemy to throw us off our tenuous perch on the craggy hillside. I was amazed that we were still alive. I wouldn't have given a plugged nickel for our chances just a few short minutes ago. I breathed a long sigh of relief. With only a few hours of daylight left, it wouldn't be long before we could expect to be attacked again, once our planes were grounded by darkness.

The sunset that night was one of the most beautiful I had ever seen. The sky was splashed with unbelievable color as the sun quickly disappeared. Brilliant stars twinkled in a clear sky and the temperature dropped, cooling the ground, earlier baked by harsh sun and man-made fire.

As it got darker, it became chilly. I shivered because we didn't have any blankets to keep warm. Farther down the mountain, we hadn't needed them.

After dark, the Japanese tried sneaking up on us. We expected them to attack before the moon came up. We were desperately short of ammunition and grenades, but we still had a few tricks up our sleeves.

We waited while they crawled in close and started to rush us.

As the enemy jumped up and ran forward, we closed our eyes and fired flares into their faces. Then we threw magnesium and phosphorus grenades. With the enemy blinded by the flares and burning from the chemicals, we called in a pre-registered mortar barrage on the entire area.

The blasts of exploding shells tore the attackers apart as they rose from the ground to rush us. Silhouetted by the brilliant flashes of the shells impacting the area in a continuous rain of explosions, Japs caught by the barrage were thrown through our positions. The noise was terrifying as the explosions, the whine of flying shrapnel and the screams of the enemy melted into an unbearable, painful pounding. Seeming to last for hours, it was only a short, concentrated barrage. The mortars had used up all their shells in a few minutes. But they were enough; as the shelling lifted, the silence grew nerve-wracking.

The screams of wounded and dying Japanese continued for several hours, and again the battlefield fell silent. Every time a flare went off overhead, the eerie light danced over the mangled scene, outlining everything in stark definition. When caught by a breeze, the light paled and brightened as the flare twisted above us. Taut, grimy faces in the foxholes around me watched and waited for the next attack.

A dead Japanese soldier lay sprawled on the edge of a shell hole just 5 feet in front of my hole. He had been horribly mangled by mortar shells in the attack. His body was shredded and his stomach and chest cavity were laid wide open, stripped of most of his internal organs. The cruelly broken white ribs, snapped off by the force of the explosion, shone obscenely through the torn cloth of his uniform. Thick, dark ropes of intestines lay stretched out over the lip of the hole. His helmet had been blown off and his throat torn out. The dirt around him was saturated with black pools of congealing blood. The meager heat draining from around his lifeless body rose as tiny wisps into the chill night air. As flares popped overhead, I found myself staring into his glassy, sightless eyes, seemingly fixed on me in the cruel, distorted light.

I thought to myself in a haze of exhaustion, "You poor bastard. You're out of it, now."

We spent the rest of the night, shivering with cold and trying to stay awake.

In the morning, a rifle company wearily trudged up and passed through our area. They looked as badly worn out as we did. Their clothes were in tatters and their backs bent by loads of ammunition. They quickly crossed the charred, no-man's land to consolidate the line of our advancing infantry. Securing positions on the ridge above us meant we would be another 100 yards closer to Tokyo.

We packed up what remained of our equipment and staggered back down to our CP, muscles still tight and hurting from being cold and motionless in our foxholes. We were still high in the mountains, and only few hundred yards away, fierce combat still raged as the line company engaged the Japanese on the next higher ridge. We were temporarily back in reserve.

Once again, we began our drill of hauling ammunition, rations, water and empty litters up to the line infantry who fought the Japanese on the ridges high above us. As the enemy slowly pulled back deeper into the mountains, it took us more time to reach the front positions; the supply points to our rear weren't keeping pace with the advance. The roads were too far away, so more men were pulled from the support companies to speed up the advance. Stumbling up the steep rocky trails to the front, we rested for a few minutes, and then brought down the wounded and dead.

A lot of wounded soldiers knew that they weren't going to make it back. Many of them quietly asked us to put them down by the side of the trail so that they could die in peace. We just couldn't do it, and we had no way to know whether they would live or die there, and so we had to keep moving. Medics often worked miracles, but many men died as we carried them back to the rear—from shock or blood loss—often because we were too far away from the jeep roads to get them the care they needed.

One late afternoon, I was returning down the trail from the front lines. As I approached the CP area, I saw a long row of dead GI's lying there, wrapped in shelter halves. Only bare pairs of feet stuck out from under the canvas, an ID tag tied on their big toe by the medics. As I walked slowly down the long row, I was drawn to one body as if by some strange force. I stopped and looked down at the covered body for a full minute.

I slowly bent down and read the name on the tag: Lieutenant Renucci.

"My God!" I whispered. Here lay my ex-platoon sergeant who had recently received a battlefield commission to Second Lieutenant and been transferred out to a line outfit. He was with them only a few days and had been killed. I just knelt there, overcome with shock and a deep sense of sadness. Some men you thought would never be killed. They were great soldiers and seemed invincible—yet here he lay.

Several days later as we sat eating cold rations in our foxholes, we watched changing peaks of the cloud cover, far below us. The line companies up ahead of us had been taking heavy casualties attempting to knock out the extensive cave systems the Japanese had built over the last several years. Our huge field pieces were firing from far in the rear, trying to clear one of the razor-back ridges in front of us, but with little effect. The line companies were no closer than they had been before, taking more and more casualties—the Japanese positions too tough to knock out without help.

Tiny specks began appearing in the distance as we watched the artillery exploding on the ridge line. Then more of them rose up out of the clouds, gaining altitude and getting larger. We jumped up, still gawking.

A slew of B-24 bombers, more than we'd ever seen before gained altitude, quickly closing on us. I thought, "Who's going to get plastered?" They looked as if they would pass right over us. Very seldom had we been supported by heavy bombers and never in large formations. The ground began to shake from the sound of their engines.

The artillery ceased firing, and one by one we saw the bombers' bay doors open. Five hundred pound bombs began falling toward us as the planes flew over in a perfect, tight formation. We froze. Nobody tried to jump in his foxhole. Struck by everything about it, nobody could move.

The screaming of the bombs became deafening as they passed over us, curving in perfect trajectory and exploding on the ridge where Japanese were solidly dug in. The concussion was so great that we were blown off our feet and knocked to the ground, leaving us dazed and temporarily deaf.

Entire sections of the enemy-occupied ridge line disappeared in a mighty series of blasts. The ridge seemed to lift into the air as hundreds of tons of stones and dirt showered the impact area. Smoke and dust rose thousands of feet. The formations of B-24s continued on, banked to the west, southwest, and then due south, disappearing back into the clouds far below.

We had lost one man when a single bomb fell short; other than that, it had been a perfect mission. Japanese soldiers, guns, supplies and ammunition had been blown sky high from the concentrated power. The ridge had seemingly been reduced to a jagged, smoking ruin. But as much damage as the bombing caused, it hadn't destroyed all the big caves that the enemy had built on the reverse slopes or lower down on the mountain's face. No matter how many bombs were dropped or artillery shells were fired into an enemy strongpoint, the line companies still had to go in and kill the survivors before we could move on to the next ridge. There were still Japanese alive and they were ready to fight; so, as in most mountainous terrain, GI's with rifles would need to finish.

After months of combat, we were sick and tired of looking at each other. We were like a collection of ragged scarecrows. All we ever saw were filthy GI's, day and night, week after week, month after month. We smelled and our clothes were rotting and in tatters. Our shoes were falling off. Some men had tied on the soles with pieces of communications wire. We had no socks, underwear or clean uniforms. Our equipment and weapons were worn out. We began tearing pieces out of our coveralls to use as cleaning patches for our rifles.

Our lot was little better or worse than that of the civilians, who had been subjected to the terrors, brutality and privations forced upon them by the occupying Japanese for years. Their barrios, towns and cities had been looted. Family members had been arrested, imprisoned or executed as reprisals for attacks by the guerrillas. Businesses were confiscated, homes destroyed and livestock killed. Thousands of children roamed the countryside looking for food and shelter, their parents killed, murdered or missing.

The Japanese had committed atrocities against Americans and Filipinos for years. The Bataan Death March was only a preview of pathological behavior in the Philippines: civilian prisoners had been kept living in squalor and fear in the Bilibid Prison and Santo Tomas, fed just enough to keep them alive. From one day to another, they didn't know whether they'd be tortured or murdered. While we manned road block positions on Luzon, crowds of refugees, mostly women and children, tried to escape from the Japanese by running down the roads or across the adjacent paddies. The Japs fired on the civilians to make them run towards our positions, herding them like so many cattle. Then, soldiers would follow closely behind the civilians, using them as human shields to keep us from firing on them during attacks. Sometimes we discovered Japanese soldiers dressed as old men and women, moving with the crowds of refugees. We would hold our fire as long as we could to keep from killing innocent people caught in the middle, but many lost their lives.

Filipinos would walk up to our positions by the roadsides to beg for food or simply to talk to us. Most of the men wore white shirts and trousers that were visible from a long distance. The Japanese observers would watch them moving along the roads, until they saw the refugees walk over to us and stop. They knew where we were by simply watching the civilians as they unconsciously gave away our positions.

Sometimes, the enemy would wait for the refugees to leave the area before plastering us with artillery. More often than not, they would start shelling us as soon as they recognized where we were, and the unfortunate Filipinos were caught smack in the barrage with no place to hide.

I was sitting beside a steep mountain trail on the morning of May 14th, taking a short breather, when General Dalton came striding up. I hadn't talked with him since we had been in the hospital together. He greeted me warmly, and we shook hands and talked a while. He showed his usual concern for every soldier's welfare. I asked him to thank his wife for sending me another package at Christmas and wished him well as he got up to leave. We shook hands again and he disappeared up the trail.

Two days later, on May 16, 1945, he was shot and killed by a Japanese sniper, while checking a cave in the front lines—where he always was.

Shortly after his funeral, the Philippine government renamed Balete Pass in his honor. A monument and plaque were placed there to commemorate Dalton Pass.

CHAPTER 19

Last Journey

The morning of May 17th, I was called down to Company Headquarters. My platoon sergeant told me that I had been promoted to staff sergeant. There was only one hitch. I would have to stay for another three months because it put me into a different rotation schedule.

I minced no words, no feelings.

"Are you *shitting me?* You know what you can do with that stripe? I've been over here for *five goddamned years!* If I wasn't worth that stripe before, why should I get it now? I wouldn't stay over here another two hours for all of MacArthur's stars!"

That ended my promotion meeting; then and there I was dismissed. I walked back up to my squad on the ridge line. The next day, I was informed that I had been scratched from the list for staff sergeant and would be staying a buck sergeant. That was fine with me. Those stripes got heavier with each passing day.

Three days later, May 20, 1945, the company called the front and told them to send me back to the Regimental Motor Pool. My rotation had finally come through and I was going home the next day

I couldn't believe it.

I said goodbye to most of the guys the following morning; some I missed because they were at the forward OP.

I climbed on a truck with others who were going home and took a last look around the area. The officers wanted to take away our weapons before we left, but we refused. No way were we going to relinquish our weapons while we were still in a combat area. The trip back was over a hundred and fifty miles. Traveling unarmed, after surviving all this time, could have been fatal. We were all "loaded for bear" and weren't going to turn anything in. Not a single goddamned round.

The officers took one nervous look at us and wisely decided not to argue.

As we were riding back down the narrow mountain road, we approached a jeep heading in the opposite direction.

A sergeant in the front of our truck yelled to the jeep driver, "*Stop! Stop!*"

We slid to a halt, blocking the narrow dirt road as the vehicle pulled up in front of us.

There were two Japanese sitting on the front fenders of the jeep with their feet on the bumper. A third was nonchalantly sitting in the right front seat next to the driver. None of the prisoners had their hands tied. In the back of the jeep was a young lieutenant. They had no other escort. They didn't even have rifles.

We couldn't believe our eyes. It looked like they were taking the enemy out for a picnic. Several of us jumped off the truck and walked towards the jeep, our weapons trained on the Japanese.

"What the *hell* do you people think you're *doing*?" I asked incredulously.

"Well, sergeant, I captured these three soldiers down the road and I'm taking them back as my prisoners," he replied proudly, attempting to puff out his skinny chest. I couldn't help but notice that his uniform was immaculate. He was wearing bright, shiny bars on his collar and his brass glinted in the sunlight.

"Sniper bait—this kid isn't going to last two minutes." I thought. "Some goddamned sniper is going to spot him a mile off and put a bullet right through his heart."

"*Stupid bastard!*" spat a grizzled staff sergeant as he jumped down from the cab, strode over to the jeep and grabbed the nearest Jap in the front seat by his throat and roughly threw him to the ground on his face, covering him with his cocked Tommy gun. Another sergeant and I threw the other two on the road, face down, covering them with a Garand and a shotgun.

The lieutenant started screaming, "Those are *my* prisoners! Those are *my* prisoners!" as a second bearded bear of a line staff sergeant, quickly pulled an enormous, razor-sharp Bowie knife and walked over to the three, lying face down in the dirt.

All three wore G-string loin cloths. The lieutenant was screaming and yelling because he thought we were going to kill his prisoners. He had probably heard that the line companies never took prisoners.

We must have looked a desperate lot after being in combat for five months. We each had a month's growth of beard and our motley mixture of uniforms hung in tatters. Some of us wore heavy bandoleers of rifle ammunition pouches across our bare chests like Mexican bandits. We all carried pistols, grenades and at least two knives each (some strapped to our legs). Most of us had no sleeves remaining on our coveralls. They had long since been torn off to use as cleaning patches or bandages. One man had no shoes.

A corporal grabbed the blustering young officer and held him firmly by his neck.

As the G-string was cut from the first Japanese; an unarmed grenade fell out. The second Jap had a small loaded pistol, and the third was unarmed but was carrying a small bag of rice. These soldiers were probably snipers trying to get back to their lines, just waiting to use the grenade on somebody. This fuzzy-cheeked "gentleman by an act of Congress," who couldn't have been much more than nineteen had obviously never seen combat. He was taking them back to some CP, where they would have pulled the grenade and pistol and knocked out a whole tent full of Brass.

What an idiot. He hadn't even searched them. They had just climbed into the jeep and went along for the ride!

Some of the men in our truck wanted to simply kill the prisoners then and there. They were holding their weapons at the ready, fingers tightening on their triggers, arguing amongst themselves.

One of the staff sergeants angrily growled at them.

"Knock it off and wire the fucking Japs!"

The prisoners were kept naked and their hands were bound tightly behind their backs with lengths of bare wire. Then they were yanked to their feet. With Tommy guns and pump shotguns in their faces, they stood like statues. We told the apoplectic, spluttering officer, now close to tears, to make sure the prisoners walked about twenty feet in front of his jeep, where he could keep an eye on them, and take them back to his CP.

We climbed back in the truck, shaking our heads. It reinforced our conviction that we shouldn't relinquish our weapons until we got to Clark Field. After a long, dusty drive, we finally arrived there and stayed the night.

The next day we turned in our weapons. There were no shots, no bombs, no foxholes, no Japanese.

It was very strange and unsettling to be walking around without a weapon. I felt naked, nervous and defenseless.

The following morning, we were taken to a huge tent and told to get our barracks bags. They were stacked ten feet high and fifty feet across. How the hell were we going to find our bags in this mess? We'd be there for another six months. Just then a GI came in and told us that they were divided into sections and that our company's bags were way down in the other end of the tent.

An aisle on the other side of the maze had a sign that read: HEADQUARTERS: 35th INFANTRY. There was another sign: ANTI-TANK COMPANY. We found our bags, and the bags of some of our men who had been killed. We asked why the bags hadn't been sent home to the families of the men who had died. The reply was that there was a lack of manpower and the belongings would have to wait. They weren't going anywhere.

While we were waiting, we saw huge stacks of clothing, shoes, web gear, helmets and other equipment. I asked a GI what all the equipment was for.

"Oh," he said. "That's all the stuff from the guys who were killed. They launder it, patch the bullet holes and then re-distribute it. You can't throw it away."

We didn't think much of that idea.

Then we passed stacks of war materiel being stockpiled for the invasion of Japan. My God! There was everything you could possibly imagine by the thousands: row upon row of tanks, trucks, jeeps, self-propelled guns, cranes, wreckers, equipment, millions of rounds of ammunition. It was incredible.

It also made us mad as hell. While we were up at the front, we were often limited to forty rounds or less of artillery support per day! Men were dying at the front because of a lack of ammunition or armored support and here sat the largest stockpile of equipment we had—perhaps anyone—had ever seen.

The "Arsenal of Democracy" was shipping all this stuff over faster than they could stack it, and we couldn't get more than *forty goddamned rounds of artillery a day?*

Something was terribly wrong here.

I thought, "Forget about the invasion of Japan, give this stuff to the poor guys that need it up at the front, *right now*. We have to take *these* islands first. Use everything we have and save as many American lives as we can. Defeat the Japs on *Luzon* before we worry about moving on to the next place. If we have it, use it now." My internal dialogue went unnoticed, probably to my benefit. It all left a bad taste in my mouth.

The morning we were to leave for Leyte, we were given a physical examination. Anyone having a venereal disease was scratched from the list and had to stay behind for treatment. How would we get venereal disease, fighting way the hell up in the mountains? Usually, the only guys who had venereal diseases were the rear echelon people. We were too busy trying to stay alive.

We moved on to the next station where we traded our worn-out and heavily-patched coveralls for new suntans and shoes. The clerks immediately tossed our disgusting clothes and stinking, slimy shoes in a barrel and burned everything. It was just so much putrid, unusable scrap. Then we were sent to the barber shop for haircuts. Most of us looked like mountain men from the Old West with dirty, matted beards and long hair.

After being spruced up, everyone went back to the aid station to have their wounds and injuries patched up. I was very nearly scratched from the list, because men with infected wounds were required to report to the main hospital for evaluation. My knee was still infected and raw, even though five months had passed since the injury. As we all headed out of the Administration Building, I suspected that they would try and keep me from leaving because of my leg.

Instead of heading to the hospital, I simply moved into the line going to the airfield. While I was in line, I removed the medical sticker from the front of the jacket containing my records and shoved it in my pocket. Nothing was going to keep me from taking the freedom bird, the first step on the way home after five years.

Nobody asked and I didn't tell.

We climbed onto several smoking, dusty trucks, real oil-burning clunkers, and proceeded to the airfield. Once on the runway, we tossed our duffel bags into a battered old Douglas DC-3, (it looked like a junk pile with engines) and climbed in after them. Taking our seats amid all the cargo, the pilot fired up the leaking engines and we taxied out for take-off. With the rickety old cargo plane shaking and straining, we lifted off and banking slightly, set a course for Leyte.

Sitting there, looking down on the South China Sea below, I was lost in thought. It seemed a lifetime ago, when our vast armada of warships and transports fought their way through the brutal *kamikaze* attacks and then the sheer hell of the fighting—wondering if we would ever get home. Now, it seemed as if that dream was finally going to come true.

Just then, the plane lurched sickeningly to one side and banked sharply. My heart felt as if it had stopped. I knew that the finger of Fate wasn't going to overlook me after all. That cruel, bony finger was going to point me out after all I had been through. Wasn't this a macabre joke? Surviving all that combat to die in a rust bucket with wings—this couldn't be happening.

We leveled off and the cockpit cabin door opened. A sergeant stepped through and told us not to sweat it; we had developed a problem with the starboard engine and were returning to the field to get another plane.

My mind raced: Don't sweat it? *Don't sweat it?* There were only *two* engines and *one* was on its last legs, puking oil! What happens if the other engine conks out? *Where the hell were the parachutes?*

Our approach was smooth enough and we touched down to the immense relief of all concerned. To the crew it was just another flight: business as usual. As we reached the end of the runway and turned toward the revetments, the starboard engine gave up the ghost and seized up with a loud, spluttering, sickly screech, coughing smoke and pissing hot oil all over the sun-baked tarmac.

We weren't too enthusiastic about boarding another flying bucket of bolts, but we weren't going to be able to voice our sentiments. After nervously climbing into the "new" plane, we took off and flew to Leyte without incident.

Trucks took us from the runway to a "holding facility" constructed to house men who were on their way home. It was nothing to brag about, but it was a giant step in the right direction. After sleeping in slimy, water-filled holes in the ground like wild animals for five months, anything with a wall or even a hint of a roof was an oft-dreamed-about luxury.

Every day, names were posted of the men who would leave on the next ship, most of them small Liberty ships built for carrying cargo. They had "bare bones" accommodations for passengers and crew, but we didn't mind. The ships had been jerry-rigged to hold about 75 troops for the long voyage home. All we cared about was whether it was heading in the right direction.

After waiting for a ship, pulling every little rotten duty they could find for us (like digging new latrines for the WACs, all of whom were in better physical condition than we were), I received my orders to go home. I was assigned to a ship, and on the 24th of May 1945, we sailed into the South China Sea on the next leg of our journey. Our ship had only two cooks, so we took turns volunteering to work in the galley to help out. It was going to be a long, boring trip. Time would pass more quickly if we kept busy. Plus, we would have real food.

The cargo ship was as slow as a hobbled snail, bobbing and rolling like a damp cork. Many of the troops were seasick for the first few days until they got their sea legs.

Finally, we had fresh and refrigerated food, after eating canned rations for months, was a dream come true: fresh fruit, vegetables, meat, milk and even fresh coffee. The unpredictable rolling of the ship, however, meant that quite a lot of the food went "over the side" to feed the fish.

We began to think that maybe it was going to be a nice cruise home after all. Slowly heading south, it seemed strange to be passing a steady stream of warships and troop transports headed toward Luzon. It was a stark reminder that there were more battles to be fought, more killing and more unimaginable suffering before servicemen could return home.

Sailing from the South China Sea into the Celebes Sea, we passed hundreds of small islands called the Philippine Archipelago. We thanked our lucky stars that we hadn't had to fight on every one of them. It would have taken several more years and thousands of lives to clear every island of the enemy. It was better to let some "wither on the vine."

Entering the Caroline Basin, everyone worried about Japanese submarines. We didn't have to worry about enemy planes, but their subs could be anywhere in the area, ready to stick a torpedo in us at any time without warning. At the same time, we thought about all who had given their lives to get us this close to victory.

Days sailed by under blue sky. But the ship was so slow that when we watched over the side, the water barely slid past the rust-blistered hull as though we were still anchored. Most days, the ocean was calm and as smooth as glass. And we cruised: a rusted ship on a painted sea.

At sunset, towering clouds on the horizon hung low over the water, and a magnificent red-orange sun appeared to sink into a flame-tinged ocean. Instead of mortar fire, blasts and blood, we saw nature's intense color reflected in a silver sea, like molten metal. Multi-hued rays shone from the clouds, so bright it hurt our eyes. We were transfixed—and temporarily transformed.

On other days, we encountered severe storms that scared the "bejeezus" out of us. We thought our ship would sink; we donned life jackets as enormous waves engulfed the ship, its creaking, protesting hull popping rivets under the strain. We rolled heavily almost to the point of no return and rolled back in the opposite direction, back and forth, back and forth, each time praying she would survive the punishment. She always rolled back again.

During the last storm, something broke loose inside the hold, threatening to smash through the hull. There was no way to check it out until the seas subsided and someone could safely climb down there to see what could be done. We rode out the storm hoping that the creaking old tub would hold together.

The storms finally blew themselves out and the ocean calmed down. I felt like I had aged fifty years. My mind was weary and my cruelly-emptied stomach was sore and tender. The fear and stress had completely worn us all out. I thanked God that I hadn't been in the merchant marine. How could anybody put up with this all the time? The crew finally opened up the rear hatch cover to check on the loose cargo and re-secured it. We stopped at a small island only long enough to refuel, (I can't remember which one—since by now they all looked the same) and resumed our voyage.

We reached Honolulu on June 7, 1945. I had returned to where it had all started. I was the only person on board the ship who had been involved in the December 7th attack. It made me feel very sad, lonesome and even morose. A wave of despair washed over me, thinking of all my friends who had been with me in Hawaii when the war started.

I was the only one left. I went to a deserted part of the ship and wept.

I became frightened because I couldn't stop. I thought I was cracking up. All my emotions were draining out of me. I don't know how long I sat there, but then I felt a hand on my shoulder and a calm, firm voice said "It's OK, Don, it's OK." As I stood up and turned around, there was no one visible, just the feeling of a hand on my shoulder. I knew then that everything was going to be all right.

There wasn't any shore leave for any of us, and I wouldn't have gone anyway. I just wanted to be on my way as soon as they patched up our bobbing bucket of rivets. As soon as the storm damage was fixed, we sailed for the *Golden Gate Bridge*, hopefully just seven days away.

It was smooth sailing the whole way to the States. As we approached the West Coast we encountered what are known as "rollers," huge waves caused by the Continental Shelf on the sea bed. This caused the ship to rise sharply, bow first. As we got to first the rolling wave, we slammed down into the trough between waves, and large chunks of the cement bottom of the ship broke off. We had been told that steel was at a premium so reinforced concrete was used in the bottoms of many cargo vessels. It was extremely disconcerting to be out in the open ocean with no land in sight, and to hear parts of the ship unceremoniously departing for the deep.

After two days of impenetrable fog and pounding seas, we saw that our dream had come true—the *Golden Gate Bridge!* The only thing that didn't measure up to our expectations was the horn on our ship which sounded exactly like the Tooterville Trolley. But who the hell cared about that after being gone for so long? I loved the homely little sucker. My ship had literally come in.

We tied up to the dock on June 16, 1945. An Army band from the Presidio Army Post and a Red Cross reception committee welcomed us home and served us hot coffee and fresh donuts. We were then herded onto a small ferry carrying people who worked on Alcatraz, out in the Bay. We dropped them off on our way to Angel Island. Looking up at the sheer rock walls, it really looked foreboding.

It had been over five years since I had last been to Angel Island. The only difference now was that all the KP duties were handled by German POWs. We were assigned to squad rooms in a barracks and sent to the mess hall for supper. What a meal!

There were actual tablecloths, real china dinner plates, silverware and cloth napkins. It was a little hard to get used to after eating out of tiny ration cans for years. Usually we were lucky just to have—a spoon. We ate fresh fruit and our choice of three kinds of meat. There were three different desserts after the meal to choose from. It was like going to Valhalla, I thought.

That night, the fog horn started bellowing, but despite the noise, I slept like a baby. It was my first night back in my country's embrace, a very comforting feeling; we were safe.

No planes overhead to drop bombs on us, no Japanese soldiers out in the darkness trying to slit our throats, no enemy submarines to sink our ship in the desolate, watery wastes. It was the first sound sleep that I had experienced in many years.

The following morning we luxuriated in long, hot showers with fresh water and then on to that miracle of miracles, breakfast: my first bowl of cereal in two and a half years with fresh milk and real sugar. Then there were fresh eggs, bacon, toast, juice, real coffee and pastry. We all latched on to extra pastry just to carry around as spares.

After stuffing ourselves to bursting points, we formed up and our duffels were checked for contraband. The MPs "confiscated" whatever they wanted. Then we were sent to get full medical check-ups. I finally had to report to the station hospital and have my injuries checked. They suggested I stay and receive more treatment, but I talked them out of it.

Consequently, I landed in the Newport (RI) Naval Hospital a few months after I was discharged. I had begun to lose weight and became very sick, diagnosed with intestinal parasites from drinking polluted water on Luzon. I also suffered from recurring fevers from my encounters with malaria, hepatitis and yellow jaundice.

The doctors allowed me to rejoin the men I came in with, and we took another ferry to San Francisco. Once there, we boarded a train headed east, a combination civilian and troop train. There were about twenty Pullman sleepers, a dining car and lounge car on the civilian section. We were hooked onto the very end of the train with ten "cattle" cars for the enlisted men and Pullman sleeping coaches for the Brass.

One of the Army colonels "chaperoning" us came into our section and gave us a speech. He knew how rowdy enlisted men were and we had a reputation to live down. This colonel had never seen combat and hadn't even been overseas during the entire war. He wasn't wearing a Combat Infantry Badge or a single campaign ribbon. Needless to say, his pompous attitude signaled the start of a rocky relationship for the rest of his time with us.

It took two days just to get to Nevada. The train kept getting sidetracked because of all the trains heading west carrying troops and equipment for the Pacific, Tokyo bound. We decided to visit the club car on the civilian section. All we wanted was a beer or a drink. We moseyed in, sat down at a table and struck up a conversation with some of the passengers.

"Where are you guys coming from?" asked one of the civilians.

"We just got back from the Pacific," I answered.

"Oh, really? I didn't know the Army was in the Pacific. I thought it was only Marines doing all the fighting."

We looked at each other, shaking our heads.

The porter came in with drinks for the civilian passengers, so we asked him for drinks and he left. Soon, a conductor came in and told us that we didn't belong in that car and to get lost. We were beginning to get a jaundiced view of civilians. At the same time, our colonel made his entrance and proceeded to give us the same message.

The following day we pulled into Denver, Colorado. The station platform was crowded with men in blue denim work clothes with PW on the back in large white letters. MPs were standing around the edge of the platform, near the train, holding rifles with fixed bayonets. We wanted to get off and buy some candy and cigarettes but the MPs wouldn't let us off the train. We opened the windows and talked to them.

"What the hell kind of homecoming is this?"

"Why can't we get off the train and buy some cigarettes?"

"Hey, give us a *break,* for Christ's sake!"

"Yeah! We've been off fightin' the fuckin' Japs while you guys were sittin' on your fat asses, babysittin' these goddamned prisoners!"

The MPs didn't want to hear it. They had their orders. They weren't there to guard the German prisoners. They were there to keep us from getting off the train—unbelievable. The only good thing about the stop was that we got rid of our pompous Army colonel. In his place, an Air

Corps colonel took over and came in to our car. He laid out the situation in plain language.

"Boys, we've been getting screwed long enough. At the next station, our engineer says that they will have to stop to refuel and take on water. He is going to take a long time to finish so we can have time to stretch our legs and pick up a few things in the shops. What do you think?"

Needless to say, we liked him from that moment on.

We sat as the train refueled and then slowly pulled out of the station.

During the trip, everyone grumbled about our treatment at the hands of the civilians, the Brass and the MPs. What bullshit. Was this how we were going to be treated after fighting for our country? What the hell was going on?

When we pulled into the next station, the same thing happened. Armed MPs were ringing the platform to keep us from leaving the train. The situation was rapidly approaching boiling point. We were all mad as hell and weren't going to take this abuse much longer. The German POWs weren't the prisoners, we were! We were supposed to get off and take a break from our enforced confinement.

Shortly after the train stopped, a squad of armed MPs boarded the train and entered our car. The officer in charge, a captain, looked at us with disdain, as if we were prison convicts on the way to the "big house." He stood there in his immaculate, heavily starched uniform, brightly polished captain's "railroad tracks" gleaming, legs spread and hands on hips.

"Well, well! What do we have here? What a sorry looking lot! It stinks in here. Okay, men. We're going to search this car for contraband. You there, step back! You, too!" He pointed to several sergeants nearest to him and motioned for them to move out of the way. Everyone stepped back a few paces and stood there, incredulous. What did they think they were going to find—a dismantled howitzer? We knew that the MPs had already stolen, rather, "confiscated" most of our belongings that we had captured from the Japanese in combat and brought home. Japanese money, battle flags and such had been taken away from us in San Francisco. Neither had the items been sent back to Headquarters.

Our bunks were "flip-down" arrangements that served as a bunk at night. In the morning, it was filled with our meager possessions and strapped back up against the car's side with leather straps to keep everything neat and secure. As the MPs began to spread out into the car, instead of asking us to lower our bunks their captain shouted, "Cut those straps and search those bunks!" The MPs took out their bayonets and sliced the straps holding up our bunks, spilling everything we owned onto the dirty floor. They began ransacking the place, tearing apart the few uniforms we had, picking through our belongings and stuffing their pockets with whatever they wanted.

It was the final insult.

A scuffle ensued between a corporal and one of the MPs. The MP hit him on the head and knocked him down. This spark had struck a powder keg. A wild melee began within seconds as soldiers surrounded the MPs, grabbed their rifles and bayonets and threw them out the windows onto the platform. Standing no chance against seasoned combat veterans, the MPs and their captain were quickly "subdued" and unceremoniously tossed from the train. But not before soldiers reclaimed their stolen possessions.

Having seen the weapons and their comrades flying out through the windows and doors of the train, fresh MPs began blowing their whistles and calling for reinforcements. The Air Corps colonel in charge of the train ran forward to the engineer and told him to get it moving. The engineer, a wounded veteran of the fighting in Europe, fired up the engine and pulled out from the station. MPs were running down the platform blowing their whistles and yelling for the engineer to stop. As the train moved away, faster and faster, the furious MPs fell farther behind.

But it wasn't over yet, because we knew the MPs would call ahead to the next station. We spent our time cleaning the mess left from the "search" of our bunks. The car was ankle deep in uniforms, letters, shaving gear and broken glass.

When the train approached the next station, the engineer never even slowed down. He blew the whistle and roared right through the rail yard. Screaming MPs were waving and yelling at the cars as we flashed by—waving and yelling back at them. The train's whistle blast and the clatter of the wheels completed the racket. We continued homeward. The excursion would bring me many laughs even years later.

We arrived in Pennsylvania, where our colonel allowed us to leave the train for the afternoon. He didn't try to threaten us with dire warnings or harsh measures for "conduct unbecoming." He simply told us to have a good time and be back at a certain time so we wouldn't miss the train when it left. He reminded us that anyone arrested would have to wait a lot longer to get out of the Army and go home—their choice. They would have plenty of time to celebrate after they were discharged. Every single man was back on the train when it left that afternoon.

No fights, no arrests—no problems.

Most of us simply went to restaurants to get a decent meal or walked around taking in the sights.

As we pulled into a terminal in New York, the same colonel invited all of us to a great little lounge and restaurant nearby where we spent the afternoon. It was his home town, and the owners of the restaurant wouldn't take any money from us. They treated us with respect and gratitude for what we had done overseas. We thanked the colonel and the owners of the restaurant profusely and wished them all the best. What a tremendous lift they had given us after such a negative start.

The train whizzed through New York, Connecticut and my home state of Rhode Island. But we shot right through into Massachusetts. I was only 70 miles from home, but I wasn't free yet. I had to stay at Fort Devens, Massachusetts for a week for processing, but it seemed forever. We had to fill out stacks of paperwork and pass a complete medical exam. The end was in sight.

CHAPTER 20

New Beginning

Finally turned loose, I was free as a bird. I arrived back in Rhode Island the next morning and began my big day. My mother didn't know that I had returned from the war yet and nearly fainted when I walked up the path to our house. As I hugged her tightly, she sobbed uncontrollably. My poor mother had gotten so many telegrams during the war that she was emotionally worn out.

Three of her children had been in combat overseas. I had been at Pearl Harbor on December 7 and then shipped out to Guadalcanal. My brother Paul had been severely wounded on D-Day 1944. He was sent back to England to recuperate. After several months, he volunteered to return to his outfit and the heavy fighting in Europe. My brother Frank, with the 77th Division, fought his way through the Pacific on Leyte, Saipan and Ie Shima, a small island near Iwo Jima. Then she received word that Paul was reported "Missing in Action" during the fighting in Belgium, the Battle of the Bulge. In February 1945, she received a telegram informing her that I had been wounded. She was visited by two Army officers in March 1945, who told her that Paul had been killed.

My mother received another telegram that Frank had been seriously wounded on Ie Shima by mortar fire. He was hit at the same time Ernie Pyle was killed by a sniper a few hundred yards away. Several weeks later, she received yet another telegram that I had been wounded twice more on Luzon. Then, my sister Mary became deathly ill and needed constant care. It made me so sad to see how she had suffered.

I had only one more mission to take care of. I wanted to meet my pen pal, June. She kept up my spirits when things seemed so hopeless while fighting through the worst of the combat on Luzon. Without her letters and cheerful support, I wouldn't have made it back. I had seen it happen so many times overseas. Guys could take just so much punishment and then either lost hope or cracked up. Not many of them ever made it home.

I headed over to her house, which was only a few houses down the road. I knocked on the door and held my breath. This was just like waiting to go ashore before a landing! My palms were sweating and I felt nervous and unsure of myself. After all, she had never sent me a photo of herself so I had no idea *what* she looked like. How would I recognize her? What would I say?

Her mother opened the door. I explained who I was, and she invited me in. She told me that June was visiting her girlfriend in another city and wouldn't be home for another three days. That was when I saw my first picture of her on the mantle. I asked if that was a photo of June, and her father, who was sitting in his easy chair said, "Yes, that's the pest."

I thought to myself, "Boy, some pest!"

She was absolutely beautiful.

I had a long talk with her father, who had been in the cavalry. He fought in Cuba with Teddy Roosevelt and the Rough Riders and then in the Philippines against the Spanish over the exact trails and mountains that I had fought the Japanese. Two of June's brothers were still in the Army. Buddy was in the infantry in the Aleutians, and Jimmy was in an armored division in Austria.

I really sweated out the next three days, wondering what I was going to say to June when I finally met her. My backbone was turning to jelly and my stomach was tied in knots. I hadn't felt this nervous since climbing down the landing net at Luzon.

On the fourth day, I headed back over to her house.

As I approached, I couldn't shake the feeling that the girl bending over fussing with her bicycle chain by the front fence knew exactly who I was and what I was up to.

I walked up and she demurely stood up and said, "Hi, Don!"

My legs felt like rubber, my pulse raced and my heart fell in love.

I thought to myself; "Jesus, this had better be June, because she is definitely the girl I am going to marry!"

She raised her hand to shake mine. Instead, I gave her a long bear hug. As I held her in my arms, I felt her warm tears on my face as she gently kissed me. Then, I couldn't see through my own tears. At long last, after all those horrible days and nights, months and years of death and fear, I was lifted up from the dark past of terror and loneliness, into a future of new hope and happiness.

EPILOGUE

Many years after the war was over, I met a man at work, who, as it turned out, flew transports for the Army Air Corps in the Pacific. As we talked, I discovered that he had flown in the same campaigns that we had fought on the ground. The more we discussed the subject, the more amazing the story became. I described to him how transports had saved us up in the mountains on Luzon by flying through the mountain passes, standing on one wing, while the crews kicked the supplies out to us.

He looked at me with astonishment and told me that he was piloting the first plane that came over us with the supplies without the parachutes so that the ammo wouldn't drift into the Japanese positions on the other side of the ridge. The Brass figured that we would be low on ammo and that would be needed first. We could go without food and fuel for our vehicles; they weren't necessary at the moment. But we wouldn't stand a snowball's chance in hell without ammunition.

The second plane had been deliberately loaded with ration cases attached to parachutes. That pilot was told to drop part of his load a little late to allow it to drift into the enemy positions. Reasoning that the enemy was low on food, the planes could delay an assault on us by allowing the Japanese to scavenge some of our food drop while we readied our weapons. It turned out to be a good plan.

He told me that as they flew over us at low level, we looked like drowned rats coming up out of our water-filled holes in the ground, waving to him as he passed by. He told his co-pilot that he was damned glad that he wasn't in the infantry.

After all those years, I finally learned what really happened that day in the mountains of Luzon. The pilot and his crew knew we were in a tough spot and had volunteered to make the dangerous flight to keep us from getting overrun. I shook that ex-pilot's hand and thanked him for saving my life. He just smiled and said, "You're welcome!"

Donald E. Anderson signed on with the 243rd Coast Artillery, Rhode Island National Guard in 1939 at the age of seventeen. Joining the Regular Army in 1940, he chose overseas duty in Hawaii because of its exotic appeal. As a member of the 35th "Cactus" Infantry Regiment, 25th "Tropic Lightning" Division, he was stationed at Schofield Barracks, Oahu, Hawaii when the Japanese attacked on the morning of December 7, 1941. He saw combat as an infantryman on Guadalcanal in the Solomon Islands and as an infantry and anti-tank squad leader on Luzon, Philippine Islands, where he earned three Purple Hearts. After serving for five years in the Pacific, he returned to his home in Rhode Island in July 1945.

D. E. Anderson Jr. lives with his wife, Christine, in Connecticut.